Grammar Sense 3B

SECOND EDITION

SERIES DIRECTOR
and AUTHOR
Susan Kesner Bland

OXFORD

UNIVERSITY PRESS

OXFORD
UNIVERSITY PRESS

198 Madison Avenue
New York, NY 10016 USA

Great Clarendon Street, Oxford, OX2 6DP, United Kingdom

Oxford University Press is a department of the University of Oxford.
It furthers the University's objective of excellence in research, scholarship,
and education by publishing worldwide. Oxford is a registered trade
mark of Oxford University Press in the UK and in certain other countries

First published in 2012

2016 2015 2014

10 9 8 7 6 5 4 3

General Manager, American ELT: Laura Pearson
Publisher: Stephanie Karras
Associate Publishing Manager: Sharon Sargent
Managing Editor: Alex Ragan
Director, ADP: Susan Sanguily
Executive Design Manager: Maj-Britt Hagsted
Electronic Production Manager: Julie Armstrong
Senior Designer: Yin Ling Wong
Image Manager: Trisha Masterson

Publishing and Editorial Management: hyphen S.A.

ISBN: 978 0 19 448918 8 Student Book 3B with Online Practice pack
ISBN: 978 0 19 448908 9 Student Book 3B as pack component
ISBN: 978 0 19 448928 7 Online Practice as pack component

Printed in China

This book is printed on paper from certified and well-managed sources

ACKNOWLEDGEMENTS

*Although every effort has been made to trace and contact copyright holders before
publication, this has not been possible in some cases. We apologize for any apparent
infringement of copyright and if notified, the publisher will be pleased to rectify any
errors or omissions at the earliest opportunity.*

*The authors and publisher are grateful to those who have given permission to
reproduce the following extracts and adaptations of copyright material:*
pp. 192–193. From ESSENTIALS OF PSYCHOLOGY, 5/E 5th Edition by
RATHUS. © 1997. Reprinted with permission of Wadsworth, a division of
Thomson Learning: www.thomsonrights.com. Fax 800 730-2215;
pp. 230–231. From *Don't Sweat the Small Stuff … and It's All Small Stuff,*
by Richard Carlson, Ph.D. Copyright © 1997, Richard Carlson, Ph.D.
Reprinted by permission of Hyperion; pp. 256–257. Pages 336–339
[adapted] from *Food: Your Miracle Medicine* by Jean Carper. Copyright © 1993
by Jean Carper. Reprinted by permission of HarperCollins Publishers, Inc;
pp. 302–303. "The new face of a role model." Copyright 1999, *USA Today.*
Reprinted with permission; pp. 352–353. "Ifs: Destiny and the Archduke's
Chauffeur" by Hans Koning. Copyright © 1988 by *Harper's Magazine.*
All rights reserved. Reproduced from the May 1998 issue by special
permission; pp. 372–373. "Career Currents," by Margaret Steen, Infoworld.
com, July 19, 1999, vol. 21, issue 28. Reprinted by permission; p. 387
"Work and Family Pressures Undercutting Widespread Job Statisfaction,
'Work Trends' Survey Finds," adapted from U.S. Newswire, 3/18/99.
Copyright 1999, All rights reserved.

Illustrations by: Thanos Tsilis (hyphen): 14, 37, 55, 73, 111, 133, 179, 290,
292; Alexandros Tzimeros / SmartMagna (hyphen): 11, 12, 22, 42, 44, 57,
84, 91, 108, 129, 135, 175, 224, 231, 256, 285, 334, 337, 349, 357.

*We would also like to thank the following for permission to reproduce the following
photographs:* Devation - Edwin Verbruggen / www.shutterstock.com,
Andreas Gradin / shutterstock.com, homydesign / www.shutterstock.com,
marekuliasz / www.shutterstock.com, Travel Ink / Getty Images, Cover l to
r and interior; Marcin Krygier / iStockphoto, Front matter and back cover
(laptop); Freitag / Corbis, pg. 4; GoGo Images Corporation / Alamy, pg. 8;
Rune Hellestad / Corbis, pg. 23; Tanya Constantine / Blend Images / Corbis,
pg. 25; Ralph White / Corbis, pg. 28; Deborah Feingold / Corbis, pg. 50;
David Matthew Walters / Gerald Celente, pg. 51; Corel / OUPpicturebank,
pg. 78; Paul Fleet / OUPpicturebank, pg. 99; Geray Sweeney / Corbis,
pg. 102; Photodisc / OUPpicturebank, pg. 119; Anthony West / Corbis,
pg. 122; New York Times Co. / Contributor / Getty, pg. 126;
Phase4Photography / Shutterstock, pg. 146; AF Archive / Alamy, pg. 150;
Tom & Dee Ann McCarthy / Corbis, pg. 157 (outdoor event); Serge Kozak
/ Corbis, pg. 157 (people throwing papers); Sally A. Morgan / Ecoscene
/ Corbis, pg. 168; Jonathan Blair / Corbis, pg. 172; Chris Howes / Wild
Places Photography / Alamy, pg. 177; Corbis / OUPpicturebank, pg. 192
(happiness); UpperCut / OUPpicturebank, pg. 192 (anger); Chris Carroll /
Corbis, pg. 192 (surprise); Eugene Duran / Corbis, pg. 192 (fear); Charles
O'Rear / Corbis, pg. 196; galvezrc / Demotix / Corbis, pg. 204; Anna Clopet
/ Corbis, pg. 209; Comstock / OUPpicturebank, pg. 212; JGI / Tom Grill
/ Blend Images / Corbis, pg. 220; Photodisc / OUPpicturebank, pg. 241;
Corbis/OUPpicturebank, pg. 251; Blaine Harrington III / Corbis, pg. 260;
Glowimages / Corbis, pg. 273 (spatula); StudioSource / Alamy, pg. 273
(crib); Bill Ross / Corbis, pg. 273 (iris); Bialy / Dorota i Bogdan / the food
passionates / Corbis, pg. 273 (octopus); Ned Therrien / Visuals Unlimited
/ Corbis, pg. 273 (elm); Ingram / OUPpicturebank, pg. 273 (calculator);
Photodisc / OUPpicturebank, pg. 273 (pineapple); OUP / OUPpicturebank,
pg. 273 (screwdriver); Ambrophoto / Shutterstock, pg. 280; Jonathan
Larsen / Diadem Images / Alamy, pg. 302; Anthony J. Causi / Icon SMI
/ Corbis, pg. 321; Bettmann / Corbis, pg. 352; Corbis / Corbis, pg. 353
(van Gogh); Sandro Vannini / Corbis, pg. 353 (Cleopatra); Renphoto /
iStockphoto, pg. 372; Photodisc / OUPpicturebank, pg. 389; Steve Prezant /
Corbis, pg. 392; Asia Images RF / OUPpicturebank, pg. 398; Kevin Peterson /
OUPpicturebank, pg. 405 (woman); Kevin Peterson / OUPpicturebank,
pg. 405 (man); Kevin Peterson / OUPpicturebank, pg. 406 (older
woman); Naho Yoshizawa / Aflo / Corbis, pg. 406 (man); Kevin Peterson /
OUPpicturebank, pg. 406 (woman).

Reviewers

We would like to acknowledge the following individuals for their input during the development of the series:

Marcia Adato, Delaware Technical and Community College, DE
Donette Artenie, Georgetown University, DC
Alexander Astor, Hostos Community College/CUNY, Bronx, NY
Nathalie Bailey, Lehman College, CUNY, NY
Jamie Beaton, Boston University, MA
Michael Berman, Montgomery College, MD
Linda Best, Kean University, NJ
Marcel Bolintiam, Kings Colleges, Los Angeles, CA
Houda Bouslama, Virtual University Tunis, Tunis, Tunisia
Nancy Boyer, Golden West College, Huntington Beach, CA
Glenda Bro, Mount San Antonio Community College, CA
Shannonine Caruana, Kean University, NJ
Sharon Cavusgil, Georgia State University, GA
Robin Rosen Chang, Kean University, NJ
Jorge Cordon, Colegio Internacional Montessori, Guatemala
Magali Duignan, Augusta State University, GA
Anne Ediger, Hunter College, CUNY, NY
Begoña Escourdio, Colegio Miraflores, Naucalpan, Mexico
Marcella Farina, University of Central Florida, FL
Carol Fox, Oakton Community College, Niles, IL
Glenn S. Gardner, Glendale Community College, Glendale, CA
Ruth Griffith, Kean University, NJ
Evalyn Hansen, Rogue Community College, Medford, OR
Liz Hardy, Rogue Community College, Medford, OR
Habiba Hassina, Virtual University Tunis, Tunis, Tunisia
Virginia Heringer, Pasadena City College, CA
Rocia Hernandez, Mexico City, Mexico
Kieran Hilu, Virginia Tech, VA
Rosemary Hiruma, California State University, Long Beach, CA
Linda Holden, College of Lake County, Grayslake, IL
Elke Holtz, Escuela Sierra Nevada Interlomas, Mexico City, Mexico
Kate de Jong, University of California, San Diego, CA
Gail Kellersberger, University of Houston-Downtown, ELI, Houston, TX

Pamela Kennedy, Holyoke Community College, MA
Elis Lee, Glendale Community College, Glendale, CA
Patricia Lowy, State University of New York-New Paltz, NY
Jean McConochie, Pace University, NY
Karen McRobie, Golden Gate University, CA
Hafid Mekaoui, Al Akhawayn University, Ifrane, Morocco
Elizabeth Neblett, Union County College, NJ
Patricia Palermo, Kean University, NJ
Maria E. Palma, Colegio Lationamericano Bilingue, Chihuahua, Mexico
Mary Peacock, Richland College, Dallas, TX
Dian Perkins, Wheeling High School, IL
Nancy Herzfeld-Pipkin, Grossmont College, El Cajon, CA
Kent Richmond, California State University, Long Beach, CA
Ellen Rosen, Fullerton College, CA
Jessica Saigh, University of Missouri-St. Louis, St. Louis, MO
Boutheina Lassadi-Sayadi, The Faculty of Humanities and Social Sciences of Tunis, Tunis, Tunisia
Anne-Marie Schlender, Austin Community College-Rio Grande, Austin, TX
Shira Seaman, Global English Academy, NY
Katharine Sherak, San Francisco State University, CA
Maxine Steinhaus, New York University, NY
Andrea Stewart, Houston Community College-Gulfton, Houston, TX
Nancy Storer, University of Denver, CO
Veronica Struck, Sussex Community College, Newton, NJ
Frank Tang, New York University, NY
Claude Taylor, Baruch College, NY
Marshall Thomas, California State University, Long Beach, CA
Christine Tierney, Houston Community College, Houston, TX
Anthea Tillyer, Hunter College, CUNY, NY
Julie Un, Massasoit Community College, MA
Marvaette Washington, Houston Community College, Houston, TX
Cheryl Wecksler, California State University, San Marcos, CA
Teresa Wise, Associated Colleges of the South, GA

Contents

Welcome to Grammar Sense

A Sensible Solution to Learning Grammar

Grammar Sense Second Edition gives learners a true understanding of how grammar is used in authentic contexts.

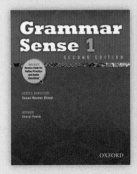 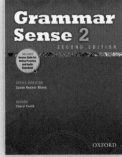 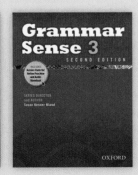 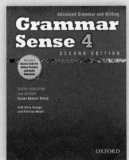

With Grammar Sense Online Practice

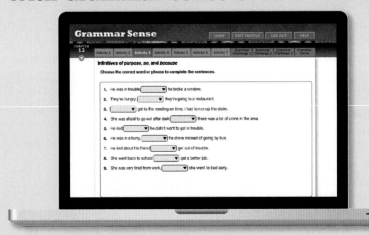

- **Student Solutions:** a **focus on Critical Thinking** for improved application of grammatical knowledge.

- **Writing Solutions:** a **Writing section in every chapter** encourages students to see the relevance of grammar in their writing.

- **Technology Solutions:** *Grammar Sense Online Practice* provides additional practice in an easy-to-use **online workbook**.

- **Assessment Solutions:** the Part Tests at the end of every section and the Grammar Sense Test Generators allow **ongoing assessment**.

Each chapter in *Grammar Sense Second Edition* **follows** this format.

The Grammar in Discourse section introduces the target grammar in its natural context via high-interest readings.

A GRAMMAR IN DISCOURSE

You Snooze, You Win at Today's Workplace

A1 Before You Read

Discuss these questions.
How much sleep do you get each night? Do you usually get enough sleep?
Why or why not? Do you ever take naps?

A2 Read
 CD1 T2 Read this magazine article to find out how some businesses are helping their
tired employees.

You Snooze, You Win at Today's Workplace

It's early afternoon and lunch is over. You're <u>sitting</u> at your desk and plowing through paperwork. Suddenly you're fighting to keep your eyes open. The
5 words on your computer are zooming in and out of focus, and your head is beginning to bob in all directions. A nap <u>sounds</u> good right about now—so does a couch or reclining armchair.

10 Well, a growing number of companies are beginning to accept the idea of sleeping on the job. No, it's not a dream. Employees are increasingly sleeping less and working longer
15 hours at the office. Some employers, therefore, are warming up to the idea that a midday nap helps increase productivity, creativity, and safety.

Some companies are now providing
20 tents in quiet areas of their offices. Each one contains a sleeping bag, a foam pad, an MP3 player, eye shades, and yes, an alarm clock. In Japan, some firms have "nightingale rooms"
25 where employees are encouraged to take "power naps," and nap salons are springing up around the globe in cities like London, Amsterdam, Tokyo, and New York.

fact, it sometimes leads
till, that doesn't stop
, according to Professor
und that "they're
r cars, in the bathroom,
oms. Others are trying to
in their cubicles.
the phone to their ear,
o write or read

> Exposure to **authentic readings** encourages awareness of the grammar in daily life: in textbooks, magazines, newspapers, websites, and so on.

Adapted from *The Christian Science Monitor*

bob: to move repeatedly up and down
cubicle: a small enclosed area
dismissal: telling an employee that he or she is fired
plow through: to force one's way through

productivity: the amount of work you can do in a certain time
snooze: to nap
warm up to: to begin to like

> Pre- and post-reading tasks help students understand the text.

A3 After You Read

Write *T* for true or *F* for false for each statement.

___T__ **1.** Tired workers produce fewer products.

_____ **2.** Some employers provide special napping areas.

_____ **3.** People need to sleep a total of five hundred hours a year.

_____ **4.** One study shows that most adults get eight hours of sleep per night.

_____ **5.** Most companies do not encourage napping.

_____ **6.** Employees only nap at the office.

The Form section(s) provides clear presentation of the target grammar, detailed notes, and thorough practice exercises.

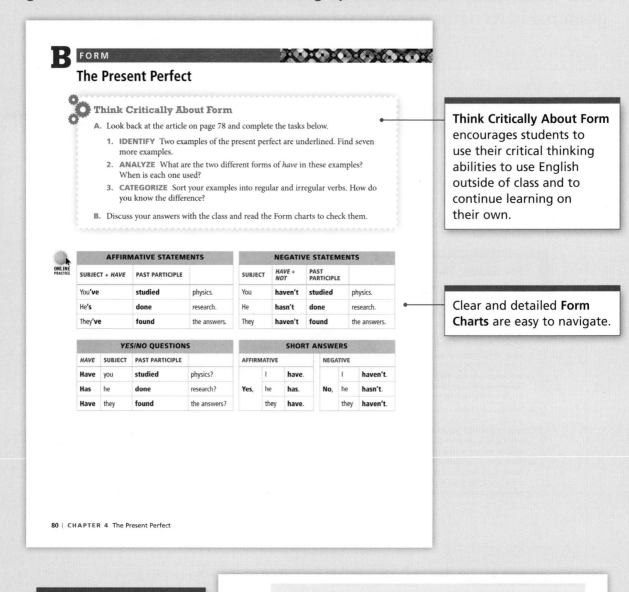

B FORM
The Present Perfect

Think Critically About Form

A. Look back at the article on page 78 and complete the tasks below.

1. **IDENTIFY** Two examples of the present perfect are underlined. Find seven more examples.
2. **ANALYZE** What are the two different forms of *have* in these examples? When is each one used?
3. **CATEGORIZE** Sort your examples into regular and irregular verbs. How do you know the difference?

B. Discuss your answers with the class and read the Form charts to check them.

Think Critically About Form encourages students to use their critical thinking abilities to use English outside of class and to continue learning on their own.

ONLINE PRACTICE

AFFIRMATIVE STATEMENTS		
SUBJECT + *HAVE*	PAST PARTICIPLE	
You**'ve**	**studied**	physics.
He**'s**	**done**	research.
They**'ve**	**found**	the answers.

NEGATIVE STATEMENTS		
SUBJECT	*HAVE* + NOT	PAST PARTICIPLE	
You	**haven't**	**studied**	physics.
He	**hasn't**	**done**	research.
They	**haven't**	**found**	the answers.

YES/NO QUESTIONS		
HAVE	SUBJECT	PAST PARTICIPLE	
Have	you	**studied**	physics?
Has	he	**done**	research?
Have	they	**found**	the answers?

SHORT ANSWERS				
AFFIRMATIVE			NEGATIVE	
	I	**have.**		I	**haven't.**
Yes,	he	**has.**	No,	he	**hasn't.**
	they	**have.**		they	**haven't.**

Clear and detailed **Form Charts** are easy to navigate.

Form notes offer clear and concise explanations students can understand.

- The past participle of regular verbs is the same as the simple past form (verb + *-ed*). See Appendices 4 and 5 for spelling and pronunciation rules for verbs ending in *-ed*.
- Irregular verbs have special past participle forms. See Appendix 6 for irregular verbs and their past participles.
- See Appendix 14 for contractions with *have*.

Common error tips help students avoid mistakes.

Do not confuse the contraction of *is* with the contraction of *has* in the present perfect.

He's **doing** research. = He **is doing** research. (He's currently doing research.)

He's **done** research. = He **has done** research. (He did research at some time in the past.)

Do not repeat *have/has* when present perfect verb phrases are connected by *and* or *or*.

He **has washed** his face and **brushed** his teeth.

The Meaning and Use section(s) offers clear and comprehensive explanations of how the target structure is used, and exercises to practice using it appropriately.

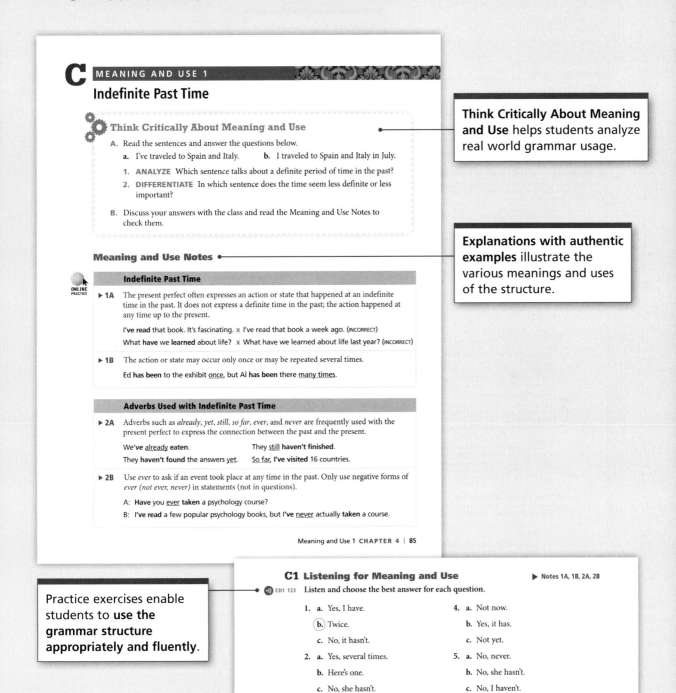

C MEANING AND USE 1

Indefinite Past Time

Think Critically About Meaning and Use

A. Read the sentences and answer the questions below.

   a. I've traveled to Spain and Italy.   **b.** I traveled to Spain and Italy in July.

   1. ANALYZE Which sentence talks about a definite period of time in the past?

   2. DIFFERENTIATE In which sentence does the time seem less definite or less important?

B. Discuss your answers with the class and read the Meaning and Use Notes to check them.

Think Critically About Meaning and Use helps students analyze real world grammar usage.

Meaning and Use Notes

Indefinite Past Time

ONLINE PRACTICE

▶ **1A** The present perfect often expresses an action or state that happened at an indefinite time in the past. It does not express a definite time in the past; the action happened at any time up to the present.

   I've read that book. It's fascinating. ✗ I've read that book a week ago. (INCORRECT)

   What have we learned about life? ✗ What have we learned about life last year? (INCORRECT)

▶ **1B** The action or state may occur only once or may be repeated several times.

   Ed has been to the exhibit once, but Al has been there many times.

Adverbs Used with Indefinite Past Time

▶ **2A** Adverbs such as *already, yet, still, so far, ever,* and *never* are frequently used with the present perfect to express the connection between the past and the present.

   We've already eaten.   They still haven't finished.

   They haven't found the answers yet.   So far, I've visited 16 countries.

▶ **2B** Use *ever* to ask if an event took place at any time in the past. Only use negative forms of *ever (not ever, never)* in statements (not in questions).

   A: Have you ever taken a psychology course?

   B: I've read a few popular psychology books, but I've never actually taken a course.

Explanations with authentic examples illustrate the various meanings and uses of the structure.

Meaning and Use 1 CHAPTER 4 | 85

C1 Listening for Meaning and Use
▶ Notes 1A, 1B, 2A, 2B

CD1 T23 Listen and choose the best answer for each question.

Practice exercises enable students to **use the grammar structure appropriately and fluently.**

1. **a.** Yes, I have.   4. **a.** Not now.
   b. Twice.   **b.** Yes, it has.
   c. No, it hasn't.   **c.** Not yet.

2. **a.** Yes, several times.   5. **a.** No, never.
   b. Here's one.   **b.** No, she hasn't.
   c. No, she hasn't.   **c.** No, I haven't.

3. **a.** No, I haven't.   6. **a.** No, not yet.
   b. She's coming soon.   **b.** Everything, except the laundry.
   c. Yes, it has.   **c.** I've already done it.

Special sections appear throughout the chapters with clear explanations, authentic examples, and follow-up exercises.

Beyond the Sentence demonstrates how structures function differently in extended discourses.

Beyond the Sentence

Introducing a Topic with the Simple Present

The simple present is often used in the first sentence of a paragraph to express a general statement about a topic. The sentences that follow offer more specific details and may be in the simple present or other tenses. For example:

Many people **suffer** from a condition called insomnia. In fact, insomnia **is becoming** the most common sleep disorder in the United States. People with insomnia **are** unable to fall asleep easily, and they **wake up** many times during the night. As a result, they always **feel** tired during the day. Their constant fatigue **can affect** their work and all aspects of their lives.

C6 Introducing a Topic with the Simple Present

A. Write five or six general statements about people in the country or city you are living in. Write about children, adults, college students, teenagers, men, women, senior citizens, and so on.

College students don't get enough sleep.
In the United States, not many people retire before they're 60.

B. Choose one of your general statements as the topic sentence of a paragraph. Write a paragraph that explains the statement in more detail.

College students don't get enough sleep. They often stay up very late. Then they sleep for only four or five hours and drag themselves to morning classes…

Informally Speaking clarifies the differences between written and spoken language.

Informally Speaking

Omitting Auxiliaries and *You*

CD1 T4 Look at the cartoon and listen to the conversation. How is each underlined form in the cartoon different from what you hear?

Are you feeling OK?

No. I have a headache. Do you have any aspirin?

Simple Present Questions In informal speech, *do* is often omitted from *Yes/No* questions with *you. You* is omitted only if the question is easy to understand without it.

Standard Form	What You Might Hear
Do you take the subway to work?	"You take the subway to work?"
Do you want some help?	"(You) want some help?"

Present Continuous Questions In informal speech, *are* is often omitted from *Yes/No* questions with *you. You* may also be omitted.

Standard Form	What You Might Hear
Are you having a good time?	"(You) having a good time?"
Are you feeling OK?	"(You) feeling OK?"

B5 Understanding Informal Speech

CD1 T5 Listen to the advertisements and write the standard form of the words you hear.

1. _Are you feeling_ tired in the morning?
2. _____ a vacation?
3. _____ car problems again?
4. _____ it yourself?
5. _____ any old clothes in your closets?
6. _____ to shop late?
7. _____ too hard?
8. _____ a house sitter?

Vocabulary Notes

Habitual Past with *Used To* and *Would*

Used To *Used to* is a special simple past tense verb. *Used to* suggests a comparison between the past and the present. It suggests that a repeated action or state was true in the past, but is not true now, even if the present is not mentioned.

We **used to** go skating a lot. Now we go skiing.
We **didn't use to** play cards.

Used To and Would In affirmative statements, *would* can sometimes replace *used to* without changing the meaning. *Would* generally combines only with verbs that express actions.

When I was young, we **would** go skating a lot.
✗ We would live in China. (INCORRECT)

In a description about the past, *used to* can appear once or twice at the beginning of a paragraph, but *would* is used to provide the details in the rest of the story.

In the 1980s, I **used to** work for a big company that was far from my home. Every morning I **would** get up at 6:00 A.M. to get ready for work. I **would** leave the house by 7:00 A.M. Sometimes I **would** carpool with a neighbor…

C5 Describing the Habitual Past

Work with a partner. Put these sentences in order to form a meaningful paragraph. Discuss the use of the simple past, *used to*, and *would*.

_____ That all changed a few summers ago after we finished college and got our first jobs.

_____ In the mornings, my twin brother and I would get up early and go for hikes in the woods.

__1__ My family and I used to spend all our summers at a cottage on a lake.

_____ We didn't have a TV at the cottage, so we would spend our evenings talking and reading.

_____ We miss the lake and all the wonderful times we used to have there.

_____ Our cottage there was like our home away from home, and we loved our life there.

_____ In the afternoons, we'd meet our friends and go swimming at the lake.

_____ Every June we would leave our apartment in New York City and head for the lake.

Vocabulary Notes highlight the connection between the key vocabulary and grammatical structures.

The Writing section guides students through the process of applying grammatical knowledge to compositions.

WRITING — Write an Article for Your School's Online Newspaper

 Think Critically About Meaning and Use

A. Work with a partner. Read each situation. Choose the sentence that is the most certain.

1. The key is missing.
   a. It may be on the table.
   b. It must be on the table.
   c. It ought to be on the table.

2. A letter has just arrived.
   a. It can't be from Mary.
   b. It must not be from Mary.
   c. It might not be from Mary.

3. Thomas is doing his homework.
   a. He might finish by four o'clock.
   b. He could finish by four o'clock.
   c. He won't finish by four o'clock.

4. The answer is 25.
   a. That may not be right.
   b. That couldn't be right.
   c. That might not be right.

5. The doorbell is ringing.
   a. It has to be the mail carrier.
   b. It should be the mail carrier.
   c. It ought to be the mail carrier.

6. My car is at the service station.
   a. It won't be ready soon.
   b. It will probably be ready soon.
   c. It ought to be ready soon.

B. Discuss these questions in small groups.

1. **GENERATE** Look at sentence 1. Imagine you know for sure that the key is <u>not</u> on the table. What two modal forms could you use to replace *must be*?

2. **PREDICT** Look at sentence 6a. What might the speaker say next to support the idea?

> Integrating grammar into the writing process helps students **see the relevance of grammar to their own writing.**

Edit

Find the errors in this paragraph and corre

A migraine is a severe headache that can

sufferers often experience symptoms such as

vision. However, there are other symptoms th

coming. You maybe sensitive to light, sound,

The good news is that treatment must often

> Editing exercises focus students on **identifying and correcting problems** in sentence structure and usage.

Write

Imagine that you are the health editor of your school's online newspaper. Write an article discussing ways that students might stay fit while they are studying at your school. Use modals and phrasal modals of present and future possibility.

1. **BRAINSTORM** Think about all the problems that students face and the solutions that you might include. Use these categories to help you organize your ideas into three or four paragraphs.
   - **Problems:** Why might students find it difficult to stay fit while they are studying (e.g., sitting for too many hours, study/sleep habits, food)?
   - **Solutions/Advice:** What are some of the things that students might do to stay fit (e.g., exercise, eat properly, get enough sleep)?
   - **Conclusion:** What may happen if they don't follow your advice? What benefits might they experience if they follow your suggestions?

2. **WRITE A FIRST DRAFT** Before you write your first draft, read the checklist below and look at the examples on pages 146–147. Write your draft using modals of possibility.

3. **EDIT** Read your work and check it against the checklist below. Circle grammar, spelling, and punctuation errors.

DO I ...	YES
give my article a title?	
organize my ideas into paragraphs?	
use a variety of modals of possibility to speculate about the problems students may be facing now and the solutions they might consider in the near future?	
use adverbs such as *maybe*, *perhaps*, and *probably* to soften my ideas?	

4. **PEER REVIEW** Work with a partner to help you decide how to fix your errors and improve the content. Use the checklist above.

> Collaborating with classmates in **peer review** helps students improve their own grammar skills.

Assessment

Choose the correct word or words to complete each sentence.

1. What _____ at his corporate job?
   a. your father does   c. does your father do
   b. do your father   d. does your father

2. Passengers used to wait on long lines before the airlines _____ electronic check-in machines.
   a. introduce   c. introduced
   b. used to introduce   d. introducing

3. In what city _____ going to be?
   a. the next Olympic games will   c. will the next Olympic games
   b. are the next Olympic games   d. the next Olympic games are

What is expressed in each sentence? Choose the correct answer.

4. I'm living with John this semester.

> **Part Tests** allow ongoing assessment and evaluate the students' mastery of the grammar.

Teacher's Resources

Teacher's Book

- Creative techniques for presenting the grammar, along with troubleshooting tips, and suggestions for additional activities

- Answer key and audio scripts

- Includes a *Grammar Sense Online Practice* Teacher Access Code

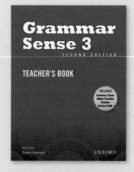

Class Audio

- Audio CDs feature exercises for discriminating form, understanding meaning and use, and interpreting non-standard forms

Test Generator CD-ROM

- Over 3,000 items available!

- Test-generating software allows you to customize tests for all levels of Grammar Sense

- Includes a bank of ready-made tests

Oxford **Teachers' Club**

Grammar Sense Teachers' Club site contains additional teaching resources at www.oup.com/elt/teacher/grammarsense

ONLINE PRACTICE

Grammar Sense Online Practice is an online program with all new content. It correlates with the *Grammar Sense* student books and provides additional practice.

FOR THE STUDENT

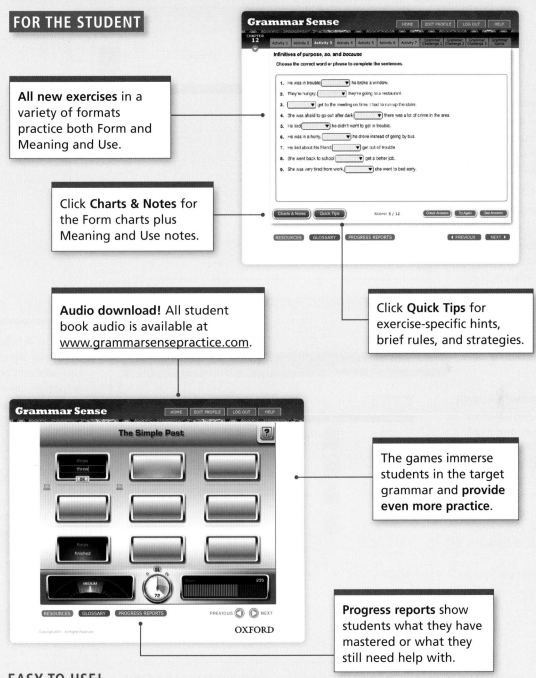

All new exercises in a variety of formats practice both Form and Meaning and Use.

Click **Charts & Notes** for the Form charts plus Meaning and Use notes.

Audio download! All student book audio is available at www.grammarsensepractice.com.

Click **Quick Tips** for exercise-specific hints, brief rules, and strategies.

The games immerse students in the target grammar and **provide even more practice**.

Progress reports show students what they have mastered or what they still need help with.

EASY TO USE!

Use the access code printed on the inside back cover of this book to register at www.grammarsensepractice.com. See the last page of the book for registration instructions.

Flexible enough for use in the classroom or easily assigned as homework.

Grammar Sense Online Practice automatically **grades** student exercises and tracks progress.

The easy-to-use online management system allows you to **review**, **print, or export** the reports you need.

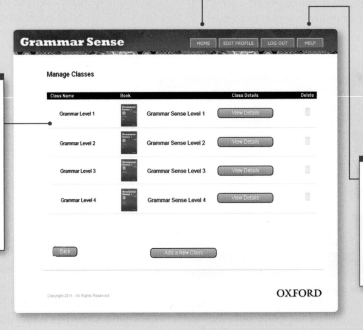

You can **access all** *Grammar Sense Online Practice* **activities**, download the student book audio, and utilize the additional student resources.

The **straightforward online management system** allows you to add or delete classes, manage your classes, plus view, print, or export all class and individual student reports.

Click Help for simple, step-by-step support that is **available in six languages**: English, Spanish, Korean, Arabic, Chinese, and Japanese.

FOR ADDITIONAL SUPPORT
Email our customer support team at grammarsensesupport@oup.com and you will receive a response within 24 hours.

FOR ADMINISTRATOR CODES
Please contact your sales representative for an Administrator Access Code. A Teacher Access Code comes with every Teacher's Book.

CHAPTER

9

Passive Sentences (Part 1)

The Expression of Emotions

A1 Before You Read

 Discuss these questions.

Look at the photographs below. Discuss what emotion you think each person is expressing. Do you agree with your classmates?

A2 Read

 CD2 T2 **Read this excerpt from a psychology textbook to find out if the expression of emotions is universal.**

The
Expression
of Emotions

The four basic emotions

Joy and sadness <u>are found</u> in diverse cultures around the world, but how can we tell when other people are happy or despondent? It turns out that
5 the expression of many emotions may be universal (Rinn 1991). Smiling is apparently a universal sign of friendliness and approval. Baring the teeth (was noted) by Charles Darwin
10 (1872) as a possible universal sign of anger. Darwin believed that the universal recognition of facial expressions would have survival value. For example, facial expressions could
15 signal the approach of enemies (or friends) in the absence of language.

Most investigators (e.g., Brown 1991, Buss 1992, etc.) agree that certain facial expressions suggest the
20 same emotions in all people. Moreover, people in diverse cultures recognize the emotions that are signaled by the facial

expressions. In classic research, Paul Ekman (1980) took photographs of
25 people exhibiting the emotions of anger, disgust, fear, happiness, sadness, and surprise. He then asked people around the world to indicate what emotions were being shown in the
30 photos. Ekman's results suggested that the expression of several basic emotions such as happiness, anger, surprise, and fear is universally recognized. The subjects of the study ranged from
35 European college students to members of the Fore, a New Guinea highlands tribe that had had almost no contact with Western culture. It was found that all groups, including the Fore,
40 agreed on the emotions the pictures expressed.

Ekman and his colleagues obtained similar results in a study of ten different cultures. In this study, the

45 participants were permitted to report whether they thought that more than one emotion was shown by a facial expression. The participants generally agreed on which two emotions were
50 being expressed and which emotion was the most intense.

Emotions are also being studied from other perspectives. For example, although it is generally recognized that
55 facial expressions reflect emotional states, it is not unreasonable to ask whether feelings must always come before facial expressions. Are positive feelings ever produced by smiling? Is

60 anger ever produced by frowning? Psychological research has shown in experiments that when participants are induced to smile first, they rate cartoons as funnier. When they are
65 induced to frown first, they rate cartoons as more aggressive. Psychologists have a number of complicated explanations for these results, but not surprisingly, they have
70 also concluded that none of the theories of emotion apply to all people in all situations. Our emotions are not quite as easily understood as some theories have suggested.

Adapted from *Essentials of Psychology*

baring the teeth: showing the teeth by moving one's lips
despondent: sad and without hope

diverse: different from each other
induce: to make someone do something
perspective: view; a way of judging something

A3 After You Read

Choose the answer that best completes each sentence.

1. The expression of many of our emotions appears to be _____.

   a. universal *boks lika*

   b. limited by culture

2. Psychologists would be surprised to find a culture with people who _____.

   a. never smile

   b. frown

3. Darwin was interested in emotions and their relationship to _____.

   a. love

   b. survival

4. Ekman showed _____ to people around the world.

   a. photos

   b. reports

5. The reactions of the Fore are important because _____.

   a. they show Western influence

   b. they suggest similarity across cultures

6. Other research has shown that _____ may produce _____.

   a. facial expressions; emotions

   b. emotions; facial expressions

B FORM

The Present and Past Passive

 Think Critically About Form

A. Look back at the excerpt on page 192 and complete the tasks below.

1. **CATEGORIZE** An example of the simple present passive is underlined. Find three more examples. Sort them into singular and plural.

2. **CATEGORIZE** An example of the simple past passive is circled. Find three more examples. Sort them into singular and plural.

3. **APPLY** Look at the examples of the present continuous and past continuous passives below. Find one example of each of these forms in the text.
   a. A great deal of research **is being done**.
   b. A great deal of research **was being done**.

B. Discuss your answers with the class and read the Form charts to check them.

▶ **The Present Passive**

▶ **The Past Passive**

ONLINE
PRACTICE

SIMPLE PRESENT PASSIVE
AM / IS / ARE + PAST PARTICIPLE (+ *BY* + NOUN)
The directions **are explained (by the teacher)**.
The answer **isn't explained**.
Is the study **published** yet?   **Yes**, it **is**. / **No**, it **isn't**.
When are the results **announced**?

SIMPLE PAST PASSIVE
WAS / WERE + PAST PARTICIPLE (+ *BY* + NOUN)
The directions **were explained (by the teacher)**.
The answer **wasn't explained**.
Was the study **published**?   **Yes**, it **was**. / **No**, it **wasn't**.
Where were the results **announced**?

▶ The Present Passive

PRESENT CONTINUOUS PASSIVE
AM / IS / ARE + *BEING* + PAST PARTICIPLE (+ *BY* + NOUN)
The directions **are being explained (by the teacher)**.   The answer **isn't being explained**.   **Is** the study **being published**?   **Yes**, it **is**. / **No**, it **isn't**.   **How are** the results **being announced**?

▶ The Past Passive

PAST CONTINUOUS PASSIVE
WAS / WERE + *BEING* + PAST PARTICIPLE (+ *BY* + NOUN)
The directions **were being explained (by the teacher)**.   The answer **wasn't being explained**.   **Was** the study **being published**?   **Yes**, it **was**. / **No**, it **wasn't**.   **Why were** the results **being announced**?

- Only transitive verbs can be in the passive. A transitive verb is a verb that is followed by an object. For example: **give** <u>an exam</u>, **throw** <u>a baseball</u>, **cook** <u>a meal</u>.
- *By* + a noun phrase is optional at the end of passive sentences.

    The directions **were explained (by the teacher)**.

    The study **is being published (by *Psychology Today*)**.

- See Appendices 4 and 5 for spelling and pronunciation rules for verbs ending in -*ed*.
- See Appendix 6 for irregular verbs and their past participles.

B1 Listening for Form

CD2 T3   Listen to this information about facial expressions and write the passive forms you hear.

1. Last year some research _____was being done_____ on smiling across cultures.

2. I _____ to join the study after it began.

3. A number of questions _____ at the same time.

4. For example, _____ the general meaning of a smile always _____?

5. Why _____ the mouth _____ in some cultures?

6. Is it true that smiles _____ for friends and family in some cultures?

7. The results of this research _____ at a psychology conference.

8. The results _____ also _____ in a popular psychology magazine.

B2 Asking and Answering Questions with Simple Present Passives

Work with a partner. Complete this conversation with the words in parentheses and the simple present passive. Then practice the conversation.

A: When ___is the trash collected___ (the trash/collect) in your neighborhood?
1

B: It ___is picked up___ (pick up) on Mondays, but we don't have much
2

trash anymore. Almost everything we use ___is recycled___
3

(recycle).

A: And _____ (the recycled items/collect) too?
4

B: Some of them _____ (collect). Newspapers, glass, and
5

cans _____ (take away) by a private recycling company.
6

A: And then what _____ (do) with all of that stuff?
7

B: It _____ (sell) to other companies for further recycling.
8

B3 Working on Simple Past Passives

Work with a partner. Complete this paragraph about how glass was made in the picture. Use the words in parentheses and the simple past passive.

When the glass ___was made___ (make),
1

certain materials _____ (melt)
2

together and then they _____ (cool).
3

The materials _____ (heat) in large
4

furnaces that _____ (build) of ceramic
5

blocks. When the bubbles _____
6

(remove) from the hot mixture, the hot liquid

_____ (pour) into molds, and it
7

_____ (form) into different shapes.
8

B4 Working on Present and Past Continuous Passives

A. Complete this paragraph with the words in parentheses and the present continuous passive.

The building where I work _____is being renovated_____ (renovate) right
                                        1

now, and a number of changes _____ (make). For
                                        2

example, all of the offices _____ (paint), and the
                                        3

carpeting _____ (replace). New shelves _____
                       4

_____ (build), and the computer system _____
     5   6

(upgrade). Finally, a new kitchen _____ (add) for the
                                              7

staff. A refrigerator, microwave, and sink _____ (install)
                                                        8

in the new kitchen.

B. Now rewrite the paragraph in the past continuous passive.

The building where I work was being renovated last month, and a number
of changes…

B5 Working on Passive Questions

A. Imagine you are interviewing the director of the computer lab at your school about changes that are taking place. For items 1–4 write information questions with the present continuous passive. For items 5–8 write *Yes/No* questions with the present continuous passive.

1. what kind of computers/buy

   What kind of computers are being bought?

2. how many computers/not replace

3. which software program/install

4. how much money/spend

5. more employees/hire

6. new furniture/purchase

7. the old equipment/throw away

8. the hours of operation/expand

B. Change questions 1–4 to the past continuous passive.

What kind of computers were being bought?

C. Change questions 5–8 to the simple past passive. End each question with *last semester.*

Were more employees hired last semester?

Changing Focus from Active to Passive

 Think Critically About Meaning and Use

A. Read the sentences and answer the questions below.

1a. High winds damaged the bridge.
1b. The bridge was damaged by high winds.
2a. The state inspects the bridge once a year.
2b. The bridge is inspected by the state once a year.

1. **EVALUATE** Do the sentences in each pair have about the same meaning or different meanings?

2. **ANALYZE** Which sentences focus more on a noun that is performing an action or causing something to happen?

3. **ANALYZE** Which sentences focus more on a noun that receives an action?

B. Discuss your answers with the class and read the Meaning and Use Notes to check them.

Meaning and Use Notes

ONLINE
PRACTICE

Contrasting Active and Passive Sentences

▶ **1A** The passive form changes the usual order of the subject and object of an active sentence. The object of an active sentence becomes the subject of a passive sentence.

Active Sentence: Jonah **sent** the letter.

Passive Sentence: The letter **was sent by** Jonah.

▶ **1B** In active sentences, the agent (the noun that is performing the action) is in subject position. In passive sentences, the receiver (the noun that receives or is the result of an action) is in the subject position. Passive sentences often do not mention the agent.

	Agent		**Receiver**
Active Sentence:	Jonah	**sent**	the letter.

	Receiver		**Agent**
Passive Sentence:	The letter	**was sent**	by Jonah.
	The letter	**was sent.**	

▶ 2   Choosing the active or the passive form of a sentence does not change the meaning, but it does affect the way you think about the information in the sentence. Use an active sentence to focus on who or what performs the action. Use a passive sentence to focus on the receiver or the result of an action.

Active Sentence

<u>We</u> **tried** to get help during the storm, but <u>we</u> **couldn't get through** on the phone, so <u>we</u> **waited** until the next morning.
(The focus is on us—the speakers—and what <u>we did</u> during the storm.)

Passive Sentence

The next morning, <u>our roof</u> **was damaged** and <u>the basement</u> **was flooded**. Next door, <u>the porch</u> **was ruined** and <u>several windows</u> **were broken**.
(The focus is on the <u>results</u> of the storm. The sentences describe the damage caused by the storm.)

C1 Listening for Meaning and Use

▶ Notes 1A, 1B

CD2 T4   Listen to this description of a research study. Check (✓) whether each sentence is active or passive.

	ACTIVE	PASSIVE
1.		✓
2.		
3.		
4.		
5.		
6.		
7.		
8.		

C2 Using Agents and Receivers

▶ Notes 1A, 1B

Create meaningful active or passive sentences in the simple past. Use the words given. The first words in each item must be the subject of your sentence.

1. the medicine/take/the patient <u>The medicine was taken by the patient.</u>

2. the patient/take/the medicine <u>The patient took the medicine.</u>

3. the window/break/the child _____

4. the concert/attend/many people _____

5. she/make/the cake _____

6. we/cancel/the appointment _____

7. the car/repair/two mechanics _____

C3 Focusing on Receivers

▶ Note 2

Work with a partner. Use the words in parentheses and the past continuous passive to tell what was happening. Then add another idea of your own.

1. Your friend's wedding reception started at 2:00 P.M. When you arrived at 2:15,

   a. (the guests/greet) <u>the guests were being greeted.</u>

   b. (the bride and groom/photograph) _____

   c. (appetizers/serve) _____

   d. _____

2. When your dinner guests arrived, you were still getting ready and

   a. (the roast beef/slice) _____

   b. (the salad/make) _____

   c. (the table/set) _____

   d. _____

3. When you arrived at the scene of the accident,

   a. (one person/lift into an ambulance) _____

   b. (a man/give oxygen) _____

   c. (two witnesses/question) _____

   d. _____

Vocabulary Notes

Verbs with No Passive Forms

Intransitive Verbs Verbs that cannot be followed by objects are called intransitive verbs. They have no passive forms. Here are some common intransitive verbs:

appear	come	die	go	look	rain	stay
arrive	cry	emerge	happen	occur	sleep	walk

See Appendix 7 for a list of more intransitive verbs.

Transitive Nonpassive Verbs Verbs that can be followed by objects are called transitive verbs. Most transitive verbs have passive forms, but some do not. Notice how the passive form of *fit* does not make sense in English.

Active	**Passive**
The dress fits Valerie.	x Valerie is fit by the dress. (INCORRECT)

Here are some more transitive verbs that have no passive forms:

Ben **has** a CD player.   Jenny **resembles** her father.   She **became** a doctor.

We **lack** funds.   The test **consists of** two parts.   The book **costs** ten dollars.

The dress **suits** her.   Ten pounds **equal** 4.5 kilos.   He **weighs** 150 pounds.

Verbs That Are Intransitive or Transitive Some verbs can be transitive or intransitive. When they are intransitive they do not have passive forms. Here are some examples:

begin	break	close	end	freeze	open	start	stop

C4 Choosing Verbs with Active or Passive Forms

Change these active sentences to passive sentences if possible. Some of the sentences cannot be changed. Explain why some of the sentences have no passive form.

1. A graduate student is gathering data for a study on emotions.

   Data is being gathered by a graduate student for a study on emotions.

2. A psychologist proposed a new theory about facial expressions.

3. Some interesting results are emerging from cross-cultural data.

4. The research team was considering the new theory.

5. They already have 75 participants for the study.

6. The psychology department is paying each participant.

7. Some new equipment for the project arrived yesterday.

8. The researchers still need more equipment for data analysis.

D | MEANING AND USE 2

Reasons for Using the Passive

Think Critically About Meaning and Use

A. Read the sentences and answer the questions below.

A radio broadcast
1a. A former employee robbed the C&R bank at about 8:00 P.M. last night.
1b. The C&R bank was robbed at about 8:00 P.M. last night.

A sign in a doctor's office
2a. Patients are requested to pay before leaving.
2b. Dr. Lewis requests that patients pay before leaving.

1. **ANALYZE** In which sentence is the agent probably unknown?

2. **EVALUATE** In sentences 2a and 2b, which sign is more impersonal and indirect?

B. Discuss your answers with the class and read the Meaning and Use Notes to check them.

Meaning and Use Notes

ONLINE PRACTICE

| **Focus on Results or Processes** |

▶ **1**   Use the passive when the receiver or result of an action is more important than the agent. The passive is often used in descriptions of results or processes involving things rather than people.

Many homes **were damaged** by the flood. (The result is more important than the agent.)

The mixture **is boiled** before it **is poured** into the bowl. (The focus is on the process.)

| **Omitting the Agent** |

▶ **2A**   Passive sentences that do not mention the agent are called agentless passives. They are used when the agent is unimportant, unknown, or obvious.

Unimportant Agent

Supercomputers **were developed** to solve complex problems.

Unknown Agent

This package **was left** on my desk. Do you know who left it?

Obvious Agent

The mail **is delivered** at noon. (It is obvious that a mail carrier delivers the mail.)

▶ **2B** The agentless passive is used to avoid very general subjects such as *people, someone, we, one,* and impersonal *you* and *they*. The passive often sounds more indirect or impersonal.

Agentless Passive	**Active**
ID photos **are being taken** today.	<u>They</u> are taking ID photos today.
Calcium **is needed** for strong bones.	<u>People</u> need calcium for strong bones.
Reservations **are required**.	<u>We</u> require reservations.
Parsley is an herb that **is used** as a garnish.	Parsley is an herb that <u>one</u> uses as a garnish.

▶ **2C** Sometimes the agentless passive is used to avoid taking responsibility for an action or to avoid blaming another person.

A Boss Speaking to His Employees

A serious error **was made** in the payroll.
(The boss deliberately doesn't say who made the error.)

D1 Listening for Meaning and Use ▶ Notes 1, 2A, 2B

CD2 T5 **Listen to each situation. Check (✓) the sentence that has approximately the same meaning as the passive sentence you hear.**

1. _____ **a.** You can park in front of the building.

   _✓_ **b.** We ask visitors not to park in front of the building.

2. _____ **a.** They speak French in Quebec.

   _____ **b.** Nobody speaks French in Quebec.

3. _____ **a.** We permitted Julie to speak.

   _____ **b.** They permitted Julie to speak.

4. _____ **a.** A falling tree injured several people.

   _____ **b.** Several people injured a tree.

5. _____ **a.** The author wrote the book in 1966.

   _____ **b.** My friend wrote the book in 1966.

6. _____ **a.** You appreciate our assistance.

   _____ **b.** We appreciate your assistance.

D2 Describing Results

▶ Notes 1, 2A,

Work with a partner. Describe the results of the situations below by completing each sentence with the simple past passive. Try to use a different verb in each sentence.

1. An earthquake rocked a small town in southern Chile last night.

   a. No major power lines _were knocked down._

   b. One major road _____

   c. Twelve people _were killed_

   d. A person _was falled down_

   e. One building _was shaked_

   f. Many windows _were broken_

2. A serious flu epidemic spread through the area last month.

   a. One school _was closed_

   b. A basketball tournament _was stopped canceled delaied_

   c. Many flu shots _were given by dictor_

   d. Dozens of people _were effected_

3. John was surprised to see that his roommate had cleaned their apartment.

   a. The dishes _were not washed_

   b. The carpets _were swept vacuum_

   c. The furniture _was set ed dusty_

   d. The windows _were opened wipped_

   e. The kitchen floor _wwa was mopped_

D3 Omitting Agents

▶ Notes 2A–2C

Work with a partner. Change each sentence to the agentless passive. Choose a reason for omitting the agent. Is it (a) unknown, (b) unimportant or obvious, (c) a general subject, or (d) not used to avoid blame?

1. Some painters were painting the office yesterday.

   The office was being painted yesterday. (b)

2. The vendors are always reducing the prices at the farmer's market.

3. They're accepting applications for summer employment at the supermarket.

4. When a pipe burst in our house, the water ruined our new carpet.

5. I lost the report sometime during the week.

6. At that moment, somebody was unlocking the door.

7. Attention, please. We are now selling tickets for the 5:00 P.M. show.

8. Authors are writing many books about health and nutrition.

9. Last year, the university required undergraduates to take a minimum of four courses per semester.

10. In Brazil people speak Portuguese and a number of other languages.

D4 Writing Definitions

▶ Notes 2A, 2B

A. Work with a partner. Use the words in parentheses and your own words to write definitions for these terms. Use the passive in your definition.

1. Caffeine (stimulant/find) _Caffeine is a stimulant that is found in coffee._

2. Soccer (sport/play) _Soccer is a sport that is played with feet._

3. The tuxedo (garment/wear) _The tuxedo is a garment that is worn by man_

4. Farsi (language/speak) _Farsi is a language that is spoken by Iran people_

5. The Great Sphinx of Giza (statue/build) _The Great Sphinx of Giza is a statue that was built in Egypt_

6. Rice (food/eat) _Rice is a food that is eaten by_

B. Now make a list of six nouns. Exchange papers with your partner and write definitions like those above for any three nouns on the list your partner gives you.

Beyond the Sentence

Keeping the Focus

You can choose between an active or passive sentence in order to keep the focus on a noun that was mentioned in a previous sentence. To keep the focus, make the noun the subject of the next sentence. Sometimes you will need an active sentence to do this; sometimes you will need a passive sentence. It is easier to follow ideas from sentence to sentence when the focus is understood.

Active Sentence Followed by Passive Sentence

Yesterday, the old man lost <u>his wallet</u>. Fortunately, <u>it</u> **was found** by a police officer a few hours later.

Active Sentence Followed by Active Sentence

Yesterday, the old man lost his <u>wallet</u>. Fortunately, <u>it</u> **had** no money inside.

D5 Keeping the Focus

A. Choose the active or passive sentence that best completes each item. Your answer will depend on the underlined focus.

1. <u>Charlotte</u> opened the door to her house,

   a. and she was greeted by an unknown child.

   b. and an unknown child greeted her.

2. When <u>we</u> lived in that house,

   a. a garden was never planted.

   b. we never planted a garden.

3. <u>Golf</u> is one of the most popular sports in the United States.

   a. It is played by people of all ages.

   b. People of all ages play it.

4. My uncle got <u>a new car</u>.

   a. It was purchased in New Jersey.

   b. He bought it in New Jersey.

5. In 1994, <u>she</u> wrote a best-selling novel.

   a. After that, many offers were received to write more fiction.

   b. After that, she received many offers to write more fiction.

6. Bhutan and Nepal have many <u>mountains</u>.

   a. In those countries, transportation is difficult.

   b. They make transportation difficult in those countries.

7. <u>The Great Lakes</u> are the largest group of freshwater lakes in the world.

   a. They were formed by glaciers about 250,000 years ago.

   b. Glaciers formed them about 250,000 years ago.

8. As soon as <u>the robber</u> tried to leave the bank,

   a. he was arrested by a detective waiting outside.

   b. a detective waiting outside arrested him.

B. Each of these sentences has an underlined noun indicating the focus. For each noun, write an appropriate active or passive sentence that gives additional information about the focus. Use nouns or pronouns.

1. <u>Sushi</u> is a rice delicacy in Japan. *It is often filled or topped with raw fish.*

   Sushi is a rice <u>delicacy</u> in Japan. *Another popular delicacy is sashimi.*

2. <u>Antibiotics</u> kill certain bacteria. _____

   Antibiotics kill <u>certain bacteria</u>. _____

3. <u>French</u> is a Romance language. _____

   French is a <u>Romance language</u>. _____

4. <u>Music</u> used to be recorded on cassettes. _____

   Music used to be recorded on <u>cassettes</u>. _____

5. <u>Psychologists</u> are interested in facial expressions. _____

   Psychologists are interested in <u>facial expressions</u>. _____

6. <u>Rice</u> is a staple in many countries around the world. _____

   Rice is a <u>staple</u> in many countries around the world. _____

C. Choose one of the sentences from part B and expand it into a short paragraph of four or five sentences. Work on maintaining the focus between sentence pairs. Use active or passive sentences where appropriate.

Sushi is a rice delicacy in Japan. Another popular delicacy is sashimi. While both delicacies are made from very thinly sliced raw fish, sushi is served with…

Think Critically About Meaning and Use

A. Read each sentence and the statements that follow. Choose the statement that best explains the meaning of the sentence.

1. Students are required to take the final exam.
   a. The students require the final exam.
   (b.) The professor requires the final exam.

2. Student photos are being taken in the gym.
   a. Students are taking pictures.
   b. Students are being photographed.

3. He has been called a liar by the manager.
   a. The manager has called him a liar.
   b. He has called the mayor a liar.

4. Laser beams are used in surgery.
   a. Laser beams use surgery.
   b. Surgeons use laser beams.

5. He was asked to resign by the board of directors.
   a. He asked the board of directors to resign.
   b. The board of directors asked him to resign.

6. It is believed that she will run for president.
   a. It is certain that she will run for president.
   b. People think that she will run for president.

7. The letter was sent to all patients by the doctor.
   a. The patients sent the letter.
   b. The doctor sent the letter.

8. He is not being hired for the job.
   a. He is not going to get the job.
   b. He is not hiring us for the job.

B. Discuss these questions in small groups.

   1. **EVALUATE** Why is it important to include the agent in sentences 3 and 5?

   2. **COMPARE AND CONTRAST** Look at sentences 2 and 6. In which is the agent obvious? In which is the agent unimportant?

Edit

Find the errors in these paragraphs and correct them.

It is ~~claiming~~ *claimed* by psychologists that everyone lies at some time or other. Moreover, many people can lie without showing it in their facial expressions or body language. For this reason, lie detector tests are frequently use in police investigations. The use of such tests to detect lies is many hundreds of years old.

For example, it is believe that in China suspected liars were forced to chew rice powder and then spit it out. If the powder was dry, the suspect is considered guilty. In Spain, another variation for lie detection used. The suspect was being required to swallow a slice of bread and cheese. It was believed that if the bread stuck inside the suspect's mouth, then he or she was lying. Psychologists report that these strange methods actually show a basic principle that is know about lying: Anxiety that is related to lying is linked to lack of saliva, or dry mouth.

Modern lie detectors, which are calling polygraphs, are used to indicate changes in heart rate, blood pressure, breathing rate, and perspiration while a person is be examined. Questions about the validity of the polygraph, however, are frequently raising. Consequently, results from polygraphs are often thrown out in legal cases.

Write

Imagine you and two of your classmates are doing a lab project for a science course. Write an email informing your professor of your progress. Use present and past passives.

1. **BRAINSTORM** Decide on the project you will describe. Make a list of what you have already done and what you are currently working on. Use these categories to help you organize your ideas into paragraphs:

   • **Opening:** Say why you're writing (e.g., to update your professor on your progress).
   • **Stage 1:** What things were done? What problems were encountered? What solutions were found?
   • **Stage 2:** What things are being done now? How are problems being dealt with?
   • **Closing:** Assure the instructor that everything is going. If desired, suggest a meeting to discuss your progress.

2. **WRITE A FIRST DRAFT** Before you write your first draft, read the checklist below and look at the sentences you wrote for D2 and D3 on pages 204–205. Write your draft using present and past passives.

3. **EDIT** Read your work and check it against the checklist below. Circle grammar, spelling, and punctuation errors.

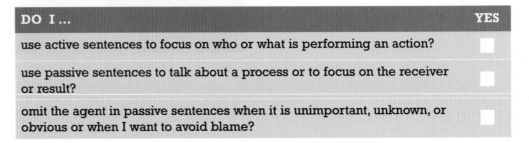

DO I ...	YES
use active sentences to focus on who or what is performing an action?	☐
use passive sentences to talk about a process or to focus on the receiver or result?	☐
omit the agent in passive sentences when it is unimportant, unknown, or obvious or when I want to avoid blame?	☐

4. **PEER REVIEW** Work with a partner to help you decide how to fix your errors and improve the content. Use the checklist above.

5. **REWRITE YOUR DRAFT** Using the comments from your partner, write a final draft.

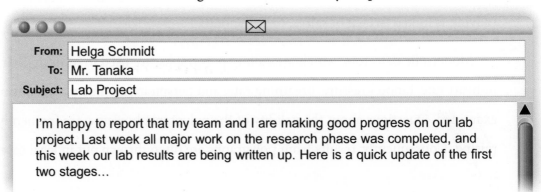

From: Helga Schmidt
To: Mr. Tanaka
Subject: Lab Project

I'm happy to report that my team and I are making good progress on our lab project. Last week all major work on the research phase was completed, and this week our lab results are being written up. Here is a quick update of the first two stages...

CHAPTER

10

Passive Sentences
(Part 2)

At-Risk Students Can Be Helped, But Not by Budget Cuts...

A1 Before You Read

Discuss these questions.

What are some reasons why students drop out of high school in your country? What do you think could be done to stop students from dropping out of school?

A2 Read

CD2 T6 Read this letter to the editor to find out what one student thinks must be done to help at-risk students stay in school and finish their high-school education.

LETTER TO THE EDITOR

At-Risk Students Can Be Helped, but Not by Budget Cuts...

Dear Editor:

I'm writing to congratulate you on your excellent article about the rise in high school dropout rates. This issue

5 has been ignored for far too long, and I'm glad that the silence has finally been broken. If enough people speak out, perhaps the message will be heard. Over a third of all high school students

10 drop out before graduation, and the situation simply cannot be allowed to continue.

I consider myself lucky, and I hope others can be helped by my story. I

15 grew up in a "bad" neighborhood. Most of the adults around me were high school dropouts, and education wasn't important to them. Nobody took time to read stories to me or help me with

20 my homework, and my elementary school teachers weren't much help

either. By the time I was ten, I could barely read and I hated school. Luckily, a caring middle-school teacher took an

25 interest in me and got me into an after-school tutoring program and a free summer reading camp. Within a year, I was making great progress and, to the amazement of family and friends, I

30 have just been given a full scholarship to a local college. Sadly, however, many of my classmates have not had the same good fortune.

I have recently been told that due 35 to budget cuts, a certain caring middle school teacher has been forced into early retirement, and a certain after-school tutorial program will be canceled. In addition, our school's 40 work-study program will be shut down and a new community job center won't be built. Why? Because the government says that teaching staff and special programs must be cut back until the

45 economy improves.

How many more teachers will be fired? How many more job-skills programs will be closed? How many more students are going to be forced to 50 lead a life of poverty because the system has failed them?

I'm living proof that at-risk students can be helped. That's why I feel strongly that ways must be found 55 to protect the people and programs that have been designed to help them.

Sincerely,
Tony Diaz

---

at-risk student: a student in danger of dropping out or having other problems at school

be condemned to: be forced to experience something difficult or unpleasant

budget cut: decrease or reduction in the amount of money that a government or other organization plans to spend

caring: kind and understanding

ignore: not pay attention to

poverty: the state of being poor

scholarship: money given by a school or organization to help a student pay for his or her education

tutoring program: program that gives extra, usually one-on-one, help to students who are not doing well in one or more school subjects

A3 After You Read

Choose the answer that best completes each sentence.

1. At the beginning of his letter, Tony mentions an article about _____.

   a. budget cuts   **b.** student ignorance   **c.** the high dropout rate

2. According to Tony, _____ saved him from dropping out of high school.

   a. a journalist   **b.** a middle school teacher   **c.** his family

3. Tony is concerned that budget cuts will negatively affect the future of _____.

   a. at-risk students   **b.** the economy   **c.** high-school dropouts

4. The main point of Tony's letter is that at-risk students _____.

   a. are going to fail   **b.** come from poor families   **c.** ought to be helped

The Future, Present Perfect, and Modal Passive

 Think Critically About Form

A. Look back at the article on page 212 and complete the tasks below.

1. **IDENTIFY** An example of the present perfect passive has been underlined. Find five more examples. What are the three parts of the present perfect passive?

2. **IDENTIFY** An example of the future passive with *will* is circled. Find three more examples. What are the three parts of the future passive with *will*? Can you think of another way to form the future passive?

3. **ANALYZE** Look at this example sentence. What are the three parts of the modal passive?

   "The situation simply cannot be allowed to continue."

B. Discuss your answers with the class and read the Form charts to check them.

▶ The Future Passive

ONLINE PRACTICE

FUTURE PASSIVE WITH *WILL*
WILL + *BE* + PAST PARTICIPLE (+ *BY* + NOUN)
The teacher **will be fired**.
The job center **won't be built**.
Will the programs **be cut**?   **Yes**, they **will**. / **No**, they **won't**.
Why will the teachers **be fired**?

FUTURE PASSIVE WITH *BE GOING TO*
BE GOING TO + *BE* + PAST PARTICIPLE (+ *BY* + NOUN)
The teacher **is going to be fired**.
The job center **isn't going to be built**.
Are the programs **going to be cut**?   **Yes**, they **are**. / **No**, they **aren't**.
Why are the teachers **going to be fired**?

▶ The Present Perfect Passive

PRESENT PERFECT PASSIVE
HAS / HAVE + *BEEN* + PAST PARTICIPLE (+ *BY* + NOUN)
The teacher **has been fired**.
The job center **hasn't been built**.
Have the programs **been cut**?   **Yes**, they **have**. / **No**, they **haven't**.
Why have the teachers **been fired**?

▶ The Modal Passive

MODAL PASSIVE
MODAL + *BE* + PAST PARTICIPLE (+ *BY* + NOUN)
The teacher **must be fired**.
The job center **should not be built**.
Could the programs **be cut**?   **Yes**, they **could be**. / **No**, they **couldn't be**.
Why should the teachers be **fired**?

PHRASAL MODAL PASSIVE
MODAL + *BE* + PAST PARTICIPLE (+ *BY* + NOUN)
The teacher **has (got) to be fired**.
The job center **ought to be built**.
Do the programs **have to be cut**?   **Yes**, they do. / **No**, they don't.
Why do the teachers **have to be fired**?

Future, Present Perfect, and Modal Passive

- In passives with more than one auxiliary verb (*will be built, is going to be built, has been built, should be built*), only the first auxiliary changes position or combines with *not* in questions and negative sentences.

    Isn't it going to be built?

    It **isn't** going to be built.

Phrasal Modal Passive

- The negative and question forms of *have to* and *need to* use *do*.

    It **doesn't** have to be built.

    Does it have to be built?

- *Have got to* is not used with negatives or questions.

B1 Listening for Form

CD2 T7   Listen to each sentence. Is it active or passive? Check (✓) the correct column.

	ACTIVE	PASSIVE
1.		✓
2.		
3.		
4.		
5.		
6.		
7.		
8.		

B2 Working on Future and Modal Passives

A. Complete these sentences with the words in parentheses and the future passive with *will*.

Community Center Policies

1. New courses ___will be offered___ (offer) every six weeks.

2. Instructor schedules ___will be posted___ (post) at the front desk.

3. Schedule changes ___won't be announced___ (not/announce) until the first day of classes.

4. Classes with fewer than five participants ___will be canceled___ (cancel).

Online Shopping

1. Your order ___will be shipped___ (ship) within 48 hours.

2. Shipping and handling ___will added___ (add) to all orders.

3. Refunds for credit card purchases ___will be credited___ (credit) to your account.

4. Refunds ___won't be made___ (not/made) for goods that are returned after 30 days of receipt.

B. Complete these sentences with the words in parentheses and a modal passive.

Product Instructions

1. This product ___should be refrigerated___ (should/refrigerate) after opening.

2. This prescription ___can't be refilled___ (can/not/refill).

3. This product ___should be kept___ (should/keep) out of the reach of children.

4. After opening, this product ___may be stored___ (may/store) for up to three months in a cool, dry place.

Online Returns Policy Information

1. Your package ___need to insured___ (need to/insure) before mailing.

2. Any damage ___have to be reported___ (have to/report) within two weeks.

3. Each return ___must be accompanied___ (must/accompany) by the return form.

4. Returns ___should be ~~be~~ sent___ (should/send) to the address below.

B3 Working on Present Perfect Passives

Complete each sentence with the words in parentheses and the present perfect passive.

1. The exam ___has been canceled by the teacher.___
   (cancel/the teacher)

2. These products _____
   (manufacture/the company/for three years)

3. This book _____
   (translate/into many languages)

4. The furniture _____
   (move/to the new house)

5. The recipes _____
   (create/a famous chef)

6. A new prescription _____
   (recommend/the doctor)

B4 Asking and Answering Passive Questions

A. **Work in small groups. Take turns asking and answering questions using the words below and the modal *should*. Then make up two more questions to ask the class.**

1. cars/permit/town center

   A: *Should cars be permitted in the town center?*
   B: *Yes, they should.* OR *No, they shouldn't.*

2. bicyclists/allow/on busy streets ___Should bicyclists be allowed on busy street?___

3. violent films/ban/from television ___Should violent films be banned from television?___

4. a new community center/build/downtown? ___Should a new community center be built in downtown?___

5. men/give/parental leave for childcare ___Should men be given parental leave for childcare?___

6. women/pay/the same wages as men ___Should women be paid the same wages as men?___

7. children/punish/for coming home late ___Should children be punished for coming late home?___

8. animals/use/for medical research ___Should animals be used for medical research.___

B. **Which issues did your group agree on? Which ones didn't you agree on?**

The Role of the Agent

 Think Critically About Meaning and Use

A. Read the sentences and complete the tasks below.

1a. The course will be given by the instructor on Mondays.
1b. The course will be given by a team of experts via satellite on Mondays.
2a. The article was written by Gregory Marks in one day.
2b. The article was written by the author in one day.

1. IDENTIFY Underline the agent in each sentence.

2. ANALYZE Which agents give important or unexpected information? Which ones seem unnecessary?

B. Discuss your answers with the class and read the Meaning and Use Notes to check them.

Meaning and Use Notes

ONLINE PRACTICE

Including the Agent

▶ **1A** Passives are often used without agents if the agent is unimportant, unknown, or obvious. However, the agent is necessary when it is surprising or unexpected.

Agentless Passive	**Passive with an Agent**
The mail **has been delivered**.	The mail **has been delivered** <u>by an experimental robot</u>. (The agent is surprising.)
We **were given** six pages of homework.	We **were given** six pages of homework <u>by a substitute teacher</u>. (The agent is unexpected.)

▶ **1B** An agent is used to provide additional or new information.

Agentless Passive	**Passive with an Agent**
You **will be notified** about the exam date.	You **will be notified** about the exam date <u>by email</u>.

▶ **1C** An agent is used to complete the meaning of the sentence or to add important information—especially a proper noun, such as the name of an author, artist, composer, inventor, or designer.

Agentless Passive	**Passive with an Agent**
Washington, D.C. **was designed**.	Washington, D.C. **was designed** <u>by Pierre L'Enfant</u>.

C1 Listening for Meaning and Use

▶ Notes 1A–1C

CD2 T8 Listen to each sentence. Does the agent complete the meaning and/or provide necessary information? Check (✓) whether the agent is necessary or unnecessary.

	NECESSARY AGENT	UNNECESSARY AGENT
1.		✓
2.		
3.		
4.		
5.		
6.		
7.		
8.		

C2 Including or Omitting Agents

▶ Notes 1A–1C

Work with a partner. Change each sentence to the passive. Decide whether to keep or omit the agent. Be prepared to explain your decision.

1. Next week a painter will paint our house.

   Next week our house will be painted.
   (The agent is omitted because it is obvious.)

2. Pablo Picasso painted *The Three Musicians*.

   The Three Musicians *was painted by Pablo Picasso. (The agent is included because it adds important information.)*

3. Teenage drivers have caused many car accidents in this community.

4. Parents shouldn't allow children to watch too much television.

5. Lawmakers will pass new tax law soon.

6. Winston Churchill led the British government during World War II.

7. Will the city council pass stronger environmental laws this year?

8. A young child has written this incredible story.

C3 Including or Omitting Agents

▶ Notes 1A–1C

Rewrite these active descriptions using the future passive. Then work in small groups and discuss whether or not you needed to use the agent in any of your sentences. What is the difference between the active and passive descriptions?

At the Hospital

1. When Derek arrives at the emergency room, they are going to examine his arm.

   When Derek arrives at the emergency room, his arm is going to be examined.

2. Then they will send him for an X-ray.

   Then he'll be sent for an X-ray.

3. They will tell him whether it is broken.

4. If his arm is broken, they will send him back to the emergency room.

5. First they will put his arm in the proper position.

6. Then they will put a cotton sleeve over his arm, and they will wrap it with wet bandages.

7. After it sets, they will tell him how to care for the cast.

At School

1. Please listen carefully. The teacher is going to read the instructions only once.

2. He will give each student a test booklet and a pencil.

3. He will ask the students to turn to the first page.

4. Then he will show them a set of pictures.

5. He will tell them to check the correct answer in the booklet.

6. After the last picture, he will collect the booklets.

7. Finally, he will dismiss the students.

MEANING AND USE 2

The Passive in Academic and Public Discourse

Think Critically About Meaning and Use

A. Read the sentences and complete the tasks below.

    a. Sulfur dioxide is used to produce sulfuric acid.
    b. As a special benefit to online customers, orders will be shipped free of charge.
    c. Your vehicle must be insured. Proof of insurance must be presented.

    1. GENERATE Change each sentence to an active sentence.

    2. EVALUATE Think about the differences between the active and passive sentences. Which type of sentence sounds more formal and impersonal? Why?

    3. PREDICT In what context would you expect to find each of the passive sentences?

B. Discuss your answers with the class and read the Meaning and Use Notes to check them.

Meaning and Use Notes

ONLINE PRACTICE

| **Common Uses of the Passive in Academic Discourse** |

▶ **1** Academic discourse, such as textbooks and other factual materials, tends to focus on objects, processes, and results. Such materials try to present an objective and impersonal perspective to convey a sense of authority. To express this tone, writers often use passive expressions with *it*-subjects (e.g., *It is expected that*) as well as other passive constructions.

Psychology Text

It **is** generally **agreed** that people can learn something much more rapidly the second time.

Encyclopedia

Dams **may be built** on main streams or their branches. They **are** usually **built** at a spot where the river becomes narrow.

Computer Programming Book

Subprograms **are defined** between SUB and END SUB statements.

(Continued on page 222)

Common Uses of the Passive in Public Discourse

▶ 2   In public discourse, such as newspaper headlines, public announcements, and signs, the passive is used to convey an objective or impersonal tone. The passive often sounds more formal, factual, or authoritative. Note that newspaper headlines and signs often omit forms of *be*.

Newspaper Headlines

Over 100 People **Injured** by Aftershocks

News Report

More than a hundred people **have been injured** by the aftershocks.

Sign

No Pets **Allowed**

Telephone Recording

Please continue to hold. Your call **will be answered** by the next available agent.

Rules at a Health Club

Handball courts **may be reserved** one week in advance.

Announcement on an Airplane

Passengers **are requested** to remain seated.

D1 Listening for Meaning and Use

▶ Notes 1, 2

CD2 T9   **A.** Listen to each example. Is it from academic discourse (e.g., college lectures), public discourse (e.g., ads, announcements, TV broadcasts), or personal discourse (e.g., conversations between friends)? Check (✓) the correct column.

	ACADEMIC DISCOURSE	PUBLIC DISCOURSE	PERSONAL DISCOURSE
1.		✓	
2.			
3.			
4.			
5.			
6.			
7.			
8.			

 B. Work in groups. Listen to each example again. Discuss what specific features of each announcement influenced your choice.

D2 Understanding News Headlines

► Note 2

A. Change each news headline into two full sentences, one using the present perfect passive and one using the simple past passive. If necessary, add articles and other missing words.

> ### Two Children Injured in Train Accident

1. Two children have been injured in a train accident. OR Two children were injured in a train accident.

> ### New Cancer Treatment Discovered

2. A New Cancer Treatement have been discovered. or A New Cancer Treatment was discovered.

> ### President's Trip Delayed by Weather

3. Presidents's Trip was delayed by weather.

> ### Site Selected for Recycling Plant

4. A site was selected for recycling Plant.

> ### Restaurant Closed by Health Department

5. A restaurant was cloused by health department.

> ### Golfer Struck by Lightning

6. A Golfer was struck by lightnig.

B. Think about the active forms of each of the headlines. Why do you think the passive was used instead? Why was the agent used in certain headlines?

Informally Speaking

CD2 T10

Using Passives with *Get*

Look at the cartoon and listen to the conversation. How is the underlined form in the cartoon different from what you hear?

> Guess what? I'm going to <u>be promoted</u> to district manager.

> Congratulations!

Get commonly replaces *be* in informal conversation. *Get* passives are often more dynamic and emotional than *be* passives. Sentences with *get* passives are usually about people rather than objects and especially about situations people can't control.

STANDARD FORM	WHAT YOU MIGHT HEAR
Tran **was accepted** by several colleges, but his best friend **was rejected** by the same ones.	"Tran got accepted by several colleges, but his best friend got rejected by the same ones."

D3 Understanding Informal Speech

CD2 T11 Listen and write the standard form of the words you hear.

1. Do you think you <u>'ll be sent</u> to the convention in Hawaii?

2. I _____ soon.

3. John _____ to the Boston office.

4. He _____ by Harvard Business School.

5. The manager _____ breaking the rules.

6. He _____.

7. Steve finally _____ for all of his extra work.

8. He _____ for a special award yesterday.

D4 Writing Rules

A. Change the rules on the first sign to a more formal, impersonal style by using passive instead of active sentences. Write your rules on the second sign.

SWIMMING POOL RULES

1   Members must show their membership passes at the gate.
2   Members can purchase guest passes at the main office.
3   We may limit the number of guests on weekends.
4   We do not admit children under 12 unless an adult accompanies them.
5   You must supervise small children at all times.
6   You must take a shower before entering the pool.
7   You must obey the lifeguard at all times.
8   We permit diving in designated areas only.
9   We prohibit eating, gum chewing, and glass bottles in the pool area.
10 You may eat food in the picnic area only.

SWIMMING POOL RULES

1   _Membership passes must be shown at the gate._
2   _____
3   _____
4   _____
5   _____
6   _____
7   _____
8   _____
9   _____
10 _____

B. Now write a set of rules for one of these topics or a topic of your choice: (a) course requirements at your school, (b) rules for using books and other materials at the library, (c) rules for living in an apartment building, or (d) rules for members of a health club. Use the passive to give your rules a more formal, impersonal tone.

 Think Critically About Meaning and Use

A. Read each sentence. Check (✓) the sentences that have approximately the same meaning.

1. Your application should be sent to us by email.

   ___✓___ **a.** You should email us your application.

   _____ **b.** We will email an application to you.

2. The problem could be solved.

   _____ **a.** The problem will be solved.

   _____ **b.** Someone might solve the problem.

3. He got robbed twice last year.

   _____ **a.** He has robbed two people.

   _____ **b.** On two different occasions, someone robbed him.

4. All reservations must be accompanied by a 25 percent deposit.

   _____ **a.** Deposit some money in the bank in order to make a reservation.

   _____ **b.** Customers need to pay a 25 percent deposit when they make a reservation.

5. No one will be hired by the company.

   _____ **a.** No one will get fired by the company.

   _____ **b.** The company won't be hiring anyone.

6. Your prescription can be refilled three times.

   _____ **a.** You will be able to get three refills.

   _____ **b.** You must get three refills.

7. Passengers have been requested to check in at the gate.

    ____ **a.** Passengers have requested to check in at the gate.

    ____ **b.** We have requested that passengers check in at the gate.

8. Several factors need to be considered by the judge.

    ____ **a.** The judge needs to consider several factors.

    ____ **b.** We need to consider several factors.

B. Discuss these questions in small groups.

1. **PREDICT** Which sentence would most likely be heard over a loudspeaker system? Why?

2. **PREDICT** Which sentence would most likely be heard in a conversation between two friends? Why?

Edit

Find the errors in these sentences and correct them.

1. These pills should be ~~take~~ ^{taken} every four hours.

2. The letter ought to delivered in the afternoon.

3. The bell will be rang several times.

4. A young man has seriously injured in a car accident. That's terrible!

5. The mail has sent to the wrong address.

6. Will a new road build soon, or will the old one be repaired?

7. It will be not needed any longer.

8. All online orders must get paid by credit card.

Write

Write a letter to the editor of a national newspaper proposing steps that should be taken to improve education. Use future, present perfect, modal, and other passive forms where appropriate.

1. **BRAINSTORM** Makes notes about (a) improvements that have been made in education in recent years and (b) problems that still need to be solved. Use these categories and questions to help you organize your ideas into paragraphs:
   - **Opening:** What improvements have been made in recent years? What areas have been ignored and still need improvement?
   - **Body:** What problems need to be solved? What steps should be taken?
   - **Closing:** How urgent is the situation? What will happen if improvements aren't made? What actions should be taken?

2. **WRITE A FIRST DRAFT** Before you write your first draft, read the checklist below and look at the example on pages 212–213. Write your draft using passive forms.

3. **EDIT** Read your work and check it against the checklist below. Circle grammar, spelling, and punctuation errors.

DO I ...	YES
use a range of present perfect, future, and modal passives to make my writing sound more formal and objective?	☐
use active forms, where appropriate, to keep the focus on an agent?	☐
use at least one example of a passive expression with an *it-subject* (e.g., *It is expected/generally agreed that...*)?	☐
use or omit agents as appropriate?	☐

4. **PEER REVIEW** Work with a partner to help you decide how to fix your errors and improve the content. Use the checklist above.

5. **REWRITE YOUR DRAFT** Using the comments from your partner, write a final draft.

> Dear Editor,
>
> I'm proud to say that education in our country has improved greatly in recent years. Hundreds of new schools have been built in rural areas, and many more students are being given the opportunity to complete high school and college...

C H A P T E R

11

Contrasting Gerunds and Infinitives

Become a Less Aggressive Driver

A1 Before You Read

Discuss these questions.

Driving aggressively means driving in an unsafe and angry manner. How safe do you feel on the road? Do you ever see angry drivers? What do you do?

A2 Read

CD2 T12 **Read this book excerpt to find out what psychologist Richard Carlson has suggested for aggressive drivers.**

Become a Less Aggressive Driver

Where do you get the most uptight? If you're like most people, (driving in traffic) is probably high on your list. Most major highways these 5 days are more like racetracks than like roadways.

There are three major reasons for becoming a less aggressive driver. First, when you are aggressive, you put 10 yourself and everyone around you in extreme danger. Second, driving aggressively is extremely stressful. Your blood pressure goes up, your grip on the wheel tightens, your eyes are 15 strained, and your thoughts are spinning out of control. Finally, you end up saving no time at all.

Recently, I was driving south from Oakland to San Jose. Traffic was 20 heavy, but it was moving. I noticed an extremely aggressive and angry driver who kept weaving in and out of his lane. He was constantly speeding up and slowing down. Clearly, he was in 25 a hurry. For the most part, I remained in the same lane for the entire 40-mile journey. I was listening to a new audio tape and daydreaming along the way. I enjoyed the trip a great deal because 30 driving gives me a chance to be alone. As I was exiting off the highway, the aggressive driver came up behind me and raced on by. His weaving, rapid acceleration, and putting families at 35 risk had earned him nothing except perhaps some high blood pressure. On average, he and I had driven at the same speed.

The same principle applies when you see drivers who are speeding past you in order to beat you to the next stoplight. It simply doesn't pay to speed.

When you make the conscious decision to become a less aggressive driver, you begin using your time in the car to loosen up. Instead of tensing your muscles, try to relax them. I even have a few audio tapes that are specifically for muscular relaxation. Sometimes I put one in and listen. By the time I reach my destination, I feel more relaxed than I did before getting into the car. During the course of your lifetime, you'll probably spend a great deal of time driving. You can spend those moments being frustrated, or you can use them wisely. If you do the latter, you'll be a more relaxed person.

Adapted from *Don't Sweat the Small Stuff ... And It's All Small Stuff*

---

grip: a strong hold or grasp
it doesn't pay: it's not worth doing
latter: the second of two things just mentioned
sweat: (informal) to worry about something

uptight: (informal) tense
weave: to move around things and change directions quickly

A3 After You Read

Write *T* for true and *F* for false for each statement about the author.

__F__ **1.** He is always in a hurry.

_____ **2.** He gets angry at other drivers when they pass him.

_____ **3.** He sees a direct relationship between stress and driving.

_____ **4.** He tries to find ways to relax in the car.

_____ **5.** He probably follows and honks at aggressive drivers.

_____ **6.** He probably allows himself extra time in order to get to places on time.

B FORM 1

Gerunds and Infinitives

 Think Critically About Form

A. Look back at the excerpt on page 230 and complete the tasks below.

1. **IDENTIFY** A gerund can act as the subject of a sentence. An example is circled. Find another example.

2. **IDENTIFY** A gerund can directly follow a verb. An example is underlined. Find another example.

3. **RECOGNIZE** Look in the last paragraph. Find an infinitive that directly follows a verb.

4. **EVALUATE** Look at the example sentence below. The infinitive appears at the end of the sentence. What word is in the subject position?

   "It simply doesn't pay to speed."

B. Discuss your answers with the class and read the Form charts to check them.

▶ Overview

ONLINE PRACTICE

AFFIRMATIVE AND NEGATIVE GERUNDS	
	GERUND
I hate	**driving**. **driving slowly**. **driving in traffic**. **driving a big car**.
I prefer	**not driving**.

AFFIRMATIVE AND NEGATIVE INFINITIVES	
	INFINITIVE
I hate	**to drive**. **to drive slowly**. **to drive in traffic**. **to drive a big car**.
I prefer	**not to drive**.

▶ Gerunds

GERUNDS AS SUBJECTS	
GERUND	VERB PHRASE
Owning a car	costs a lot. is expensive.

GERUNDS AFTER VERBS		
SUBJECT	VERB	GERUND
Drivers	should consider	**slowing down**.
Experts	suggest	**driving slowly**.

▶ Infinitives

IT SUBJECT... + INFINITIVE		
IT	VERB + NOUN	INFINITIVE
It	costs a lot	**to own a car**.

IT	VERB + ADJECTIVE	INFINITIVE
It	is expensive	**to own a car**.

INFINITIVES AFTER VERBS		
	VERB	INFINITIVE
Drivers	agree	**to slow down**.

	VERB	OBJECT	INFINITIVE
Experts	warn	people	**to drive slowly**.

	VERB	(OBJECT)	INFINITIVE
I	want		**to drive carefully**.
I	want	him	**to drive carefully**.

Overview
- All verbs, except modal auxiliaries, have gerund and infinitive forms.
- A gerund can be one word (*driving*) or part of a longer phrase, with an adverb (*driving slowly*), a prepositional phrase (*driving in traffic*), or an object (*driving a big car*).
- All verbs, except modal auxiliaries, have infinitive forms.
- An infinitive can be two words (*to drive*) or part of a longer phrase with an adverb (*to drive slowly*), a prepositional phrase (*to drive in traffic*), or an object (*to drive a big car*).

Gerunds as Subjects
- A gerund can function as the subject of a sentence. Gerunds function as singular nouns and take singular verbs. A gerund can be replaced by the pronoun *it*.

    Owning a car costs a lot.   (**It** costs a lot.)

Gerunds After Verbs
- Here are some examples of verbs followed by gerunds (see Appendix 8 for a list of more verbs):

advise	consider	deny	enjoy	go	miss	practice	suggest
avoid	delay	dislike	finish	mind	postpone	recommend	

It Subject ... + Infinitive
- Although an infinitive can function as the subject of a sentence (*To own a car is expensive*), this is not common. Instead, the pronoun *it* begins the sentence. It has the same meaning as the infinitive it replaces.

    It costs a lot **to own a car**. (It = to own a car)

- *It* is followed by be or one of a limited group of verbs. For example:

appear	be	cost	look	pay	seem	take

(Continued on page 234)

Infinitives After Verbs

- Infinitives after verbs appear in one of three patterns:

Verb + Infinitive

agree	decide	learn	plan	refuse
appear	hope	offer	seem	wait

Verb + Object + Infinitive

advise	force	invite	remind	teach	urge
cause	get	order	require	tell	warn

Verb + (Object) + Infinitive

(These verbs can be followed by the infinitive with or without an object.)

ask	expect	need	promise	wish
choose	help	pay	want	would like

- See Appendix 9 for a list of more verbs followed by infinitives.

B1 Listening for Form

CD2 T13 Listen to each sentence. Do you hear an infinitive or a gerund? Check (✓) the correct column.

	GERUND	INFINITIVE
1.		✓
2.		
3.		
4.		
5.		
6.		

B2 Rephrasing Subject Gerunds as *It* ... + Infinitive

Rewrite each of these opinions. Change the subject to *It* and the gerund to an infinitive. Remember to put the infinitive at the end of the sentence.

1. Raising children is not easy.   It's not easy to raise children.

2. Studying all night is not a good idea.   It's a good idea to study all night.

3. Walking to work takes too much time.   It takes too much time to walk to work

4. Getting exercise is important. _It's important to get exercise._

5. Owning a house costs a lot of money. _It costs a lot of money to own a house_

6. Knowing a foreign language can be useful. _It can be useful to Knowing a foreign language_

B3 Working on Subject Gerunds and *It* ... + Infinitive

 A. Work with a partner. Choose one of the topics below and make a list of five common problems related to that topic. Use affirmative and negative gerunds.

Living in a big city   Owning a car

Learning a language   Living in a foreign country

Problems with living in a big city: parking, making friends, not having a garden,...

B. Write two sentences about each of the problems you listed, one with a subject gerund and one with *it* + an infinitive.

Parking is difficult in a big city.
It is difficult to park in a big city.

B4 Building Sentences with Gerunds and Infinitives

Build as many meaningful sentences as possible. Use an item from each column, or from the first and third columns only. Punctuate your sentences correctly.

He told me to go more slowly.

he told she expects he learned they advised don't delay	me	to go more slowly to speak Spanish leaving taking a driving class

B5 Distinguishing Gerunds and Infinitives After Verbs

Imagine that some people are discussing a controversial new movie. Complete each sentence with *seeing it* or *to see it*.

1. I'm planning _to see it._

2. Do you recommend _seeing it_

3. You should consider _seeing it_

4. I've decided _to see it_

5. I suggest _seeing it_

6. Don't expect me _to see it_

7. He refuses _to see it_

8. I warn you not _to seeing it_

9. You should avoid _to see it_ _seeing_

10. I urge you _to see it._

Vocabulary Notes

Short Answers to Questions with Infinitives

Short answers in response to questions with infinitives can contain the main verb + *to*.

> Do you plan to take a vacation soon? Yes, **I plan to**. / No, **I don't expect to**.

If you begin a short answer with an infinitive, *to* is omitted.

> What do you want to do later? **Take a walk**.

When you join two or more infinitives with *and* or *or*, *to* appears only with the first infinitive.

> Do you want **to eat out** or **make dinner at home**?

B6 Using Short Answers to Questions with Infinitives

Take turns asking and answering questions. Use the verbs in parentheses to form affirmative or negative short answers with infinitives.

1. **A:** Are you going to graduate in June?

   B: Yes, _____I hope to_____. (hope)

2. **A:** Are your parents taking a vacation this summer?

   B: No, they __don't expect to__. (expect)

3. **A:** Do you think you'll go to the wedding?

   B: Yes, we __would like to__. (would like)

4. **A:** Is she interested in going with us?

   B: No. She __doesn't want to__. (want)

5. **A:** Are you going to buy a house?

   B: Yes, we __plan to__ soon. (plan)

6. **A:** Please ask him not to leave so early.

   B: I'm sorry, but he really __needs to__. (need)

B7 Asking Information Questions with Gerunds and Infinitives

 A. Work with a partner. Ask questions using *What* and these words and phrases + the verb *do* as a gerund or an infinitive. Answer the questions and then ask *What about you?*

1. expect/this weekend

    A: *What do you expect to do this weekend?*

    B: *Sleep late. What about you?*

    A: *I expect to study most of the time.*

2. enjoy/in your free time *What do you enjoy doing in your free time* ,

3. suggest/after dinner *doing*

4. would like/on your birthday *to do*

5. want/during your vacation *to do*

6. avoid/on the weekend *doing*

7. hope/next summer *to do*

8. dislike/in the morning *doing*

B. Now write three sentences that compare your partner's answers with yours. Use the appropriate verbs or phrases with gerunds or infinitives.

Anna expects to sleep late this weekend, but I expect to study most of the time.

B8 Asking *Yes/No* Questions with Gerunds and Infinitives

 Work with a partner. Take turns asking and answering questions with gerunds or infinitives.

1. expect/travel/stay home/next summer

    A: *Do you expect to travel or stay home next summer?*

    B: *Stay home.*

2. suggest/stay home/see a movie/tonight

3. hope/live in a big city/a small town

4. need/study a lot/a little

5. recommend/eat breakfast/skip breakfast

6. want/stay in your apartment/find a new apartment

Verbs Used with Gerunds and Infinitives

Think Critically About Meaning and Use

A. Read the sentences and answer the questions below.

1a. I stopped to shop at London's Bakery. It's so inexpensive.
1b. I stopped shopping at London's Bakery. It's so expensive.
2a. He started to talk as soon as he saw me. He's not shy.
2b. He started talking as soon as he saw me. He's very friendly.

EVALUATE Which pair has the same meaning? Which pair has a different meaning?

B. Discuss your answers with the class and read the Meaning and Use Notes to check them.

Meaning and Use Notes

ONLINE
PRACTICE

Same Meanings with *Begin*, *Start*, and *Continue*
Some verbs are used with both infinitives and gerunds. See Appendix 10 for a list of these verbs.

▶ **1** After *begin*, *start*, and *continue*, the infinitive and the gerund have the same meaning. If the main verb is in the continuous, use the infinitive, not the gerund.

Infinitive	**Gerund**
He <u>started</u> **to laugh**.	He <u>started</u> **laughing**.
We <u>**continued**</u> **to read**.	We <u>**continued**</u> **reading**.
It <u>began</u> **to snow**.	It <u>began</u> **snowing**.
It <u>was beginning</u> **to snow**.	x It was beginning snowing. (INCORRECT)

Similar Meanings with *Like, Love, Hate,* and *Prefer*

▶ **2**   After *like*, *love*, *hate*, and *prefer*, the infinitive and the gerund are similar in meaning. However, sometimes it is more common to use an infinitive to talk about an activity at a specific time, and a gerund to talk about an activity in general.

Infinitive	Gerund
I <u>like</u> **to swim** early in the morning.	I <u>like</u> **swimming** and **boating**.
Would you <u>prefer</u> **to play tennis** or **swim** today?	Do you <u>prefer</u> **playing tennis** or **swimming**?

Different and Similar Meanings with *Try*

▶ **3A**   After *try*, the infinitive and the gerund are similar in meaning.

Infinitive	Gerund
<u>Try</u> **to relax** more.	<u>Try</u> **relaxing** more.

▶ **3B**   When *try* is in the past, the infinitive often implies that an action did not occur. The gerund implies that an action occurred but may or may not have been successful.

Infinitive (Didn't Occur)	Gerund (Did Occur)
I <u>tried</u> **to take some aspirin** for the pain, but I couldn't open the bottle. (I didn't take any aspirin.)	I <u>tried</u> **taking some aspirin** for the pain, but it didn't help. (I took some aspirin.)

Different Meanings with *Remember, Stop, Forget,* and *Regret*

▶ **4A**   After *remember*, *stop*, *forget*, and *regret*, the infinitive refers to an action that happens after the action of the main verb. The gerund refers to an action that happened before the action of the main verb.

Infinitive Action Happens After Verb	Gerund Action Happened Before Verb
I <u>remembered</u> **to mail the letter**. (I remembered the letter. Then I mailed it.)	I <u>remembered</u> **mailing the letter**. (I mailed the letter. Later I remembered doing it.)
I <u>stopped</u> **to listen** to him. (I stopped what I was doing. Then I listened to him.)	I <u>stopped</u> **listening** to him. (I was listening to him. Then I stopped listening.)

(Continued on page 240)

> **▶ 4B**   *Forget* is more commonly used with an infinitive. With a gerund, it occurs mostly in sentences with *will never*.

Infinitive Action Happens After Verb	**Gerund Action Happened Before Verb**
I <u>forgot</u> **to pay my telephone bill**. (I forgot, so then I didn't pay the bill.)	I <u>will never forget</u> **living in Ecuador**. (I lived there. Now I'll never forget it.)

> **▶ 4C**   *Regret* can take either an infinitive or a gerund with verbs such as *inform*, *tell*, *say*, and *announce*. With all other verbs, *regret* takes a gerund.

Infinitive Action Happens After Verb	**Gerund Action Happened Before Verb**
I <u>regret</u> **to inform you** that I'm leaving. (I feel regret. Then I inform you.)	I <u>regret</u> **informing you** that I'm leaving. (I informed you. Now I regret it.)
✗ I regret to leave. (INCORRECT)	I <u>regret</u> **leaving**.

C1 Listening for Meaning and Use

▶ Notes 3A, 3B, 4A, 4B

 CD2 T14   **Listen to each situation. Choose the sentence that is more likely to follow it.**

1. **a.** He was rude to me.
   b. He was so grateful to me.

2. **a.** It's a good thing I did, though.
   b. That was a terrible mistake.

3. **a.** But I couldn't stand the smell.
   b. It really helped me feel better.

4. **a.** But I had no choice.
   b. But I have no choice.

5. **a.** I like the editorials.
   b. It's not well written.

6. **a.** It's on my calendar for tomorrow.
   b. It was so exciting.

C2 Rephrasing Gerunds and Infinitives

▶ Notes 1, 2

Work with a partner. Change each gerund to an infinitive, and each infinitive to a gerund. Then practice the conversations.

1. **A:** I love skiing. What about you?

   B: I like skiing, but I prefer staying indoors in the winter.

   A: I love to ski. What about you?

   B: I like to ski, but I prefer to stay indoors in the winter.

2. **A:** I hate to drive in traffic.

   B: Then you should continue to take the bus home.

A: _____

B: _____

3. **A:** It started to rain a few minutes ago.

   B: Then let's wait here for a while. I don't like to walk in the rain.

   A: _____

   B: _____

4. **A:** I hate waiting in line.

   B: So do I. That's why I prefer to shop late at night.

   A: _____

   B: _____

C3 Making Suggestions

▶ **Notes 3A, 4A, 4B**

Work in small groups. Choose one of the topics below. Make suggestions by completing each sentence with a gerund or infinitive. Then read your suggestions to the class without mentioning your topic. The class guesses what topic the advice is for.

Reducing stress

Cleaning your apartment

Studying for a test

Finding a job

Improving your English

Making more friends

Suggestions for reducing stress

1. Try _to get more sleep._

2. Consider _taking a yoga class._

3. Avoid _____

4. Don't forget _____

5. Plan _____

6. Don't delay _____

7. Aim _____

8. Volunteer _____

C4 Expressing Feelings and Preferences ▶ Notes 1, 2, 3A, 4A

 A. Work with a partner. Jay is visiting his cousin Joe in Chicago. Complete these conversations with the words in parentheses and gerunds or infinitives. In some cases, you may use either one.

1. **Joe:** Another beautiful day! I love ___getting up/to get up___ (get up) in
   the morning.

   Jay: You're kidding! I really dislike _____ (get up) in the
   morning. I immediately start _____ (worry) about
   all of the things I need _____ (do).

2. **Joe:** Let's go _____ (shop). I like _____
   (watch) the crowds, and I'd like _____ (buy)
   some gifts.

   Jay: Do we have to? I don't like _____ (fight) my way
   through crowds.

   Joe: Well, would you like _____ (go) to the top of the Sears
   Tower? The view is great. You can see the lake from there.

   Jay: I remember _____ (go) up there once. It was terrible.
   I prefer _____ (have) both of my feet on the ground.

3. **Joe:** I'm beginning _____ (feel) hungry. Let's try
   _____ (find) a good restaurant.

   Jay: I try _____ (avoid) eating out. You wouldn't mind
   _____ (cook) something at home, would you?

B. Now work on your own and write a paragraph about a person that you know. Use gerunds and infinitives to discuss the person's feelings and likes or dislikes.

My friend Alex is hoping to be a food critic someday, so he loves to eat at new restaurants. He prefers going to five-star French restaurants. That's fine, except that he always wants me to go with him, and he refuses to listen to my objections. He considers...

D FORM 2

More About Gerunds and Infinitives

Think Critically About Form

A. Read the sentences and complete the tasks below.

- **a.** Instead of <u>tensing your muscles</u>, try to relax them.
- **b.** During your lifetime, you'll probably spend a lot of time <u>driving on the highway</u>.
- **c.** You end up <u>saving no time at all</u>.
- **d.** Some drivers are too anxious <u>to reach their destinations</u>.

1. ANALYZE Write the letter of the sentence that contains one of these forms before a gerund:

_____ a verb phrase ending in a noun   _____ a phrasal verb (verb + particle)
_____ a preposition or prepositional phrase

2. DIFFERENTIATE Which sentence has a phrase containing an infinitive? What part of speech does it follow?

B. Discuss your answers with the class and read the Meaning and Use Notes to check them.

▶ Gerunds

ONLINE PRACTICE

VERB PHRASE + GERUND		
	VERB PHRASE	**GERUND**
She	is busy	**talking**.
He	spent some time	**relaxing**.

PREPOSITION + GERUND		
PREPOSITION	**GERUND**	
Without	**realizing it**,	drivers speed.
In addition to	**swimming**,	we played tennis.

		PREPOSITION	**GERUND**
Drivers speed		without	**realizing it**.

VERB + PREPOSITION + GERUND	
VERB + PREPOSITION	**GERUND**
Think about	**slowing down**.

	PHRASAL VERB	**GERUND**
We	ended up	**waiting an hour**.

BE + ADJECTIVE + PREPOSITION + GERUND		
	***BE* + ADJECTIVE + PREPOSITION**	**GERUND**
We	were afraid of	**driving in the snow**.

(Continued on page 244)

- Some common verb phrases that end in adjectives or nouns can be followed by gerunds:

be busy	have a good time	it's no use	spend an hour	waste time
have fun	have trouble	it's (not) worth	spend time	

- Examples of one-word prepositions and longer phrases followed by gerunds:

after	besides	in	instead of	
before	by	in addition to	without	

- Examples of verb + preposition combinations followed by gerunds:

approve of	depend on	insist on	talk about	work on
believe in	disapprove of	look forward to	think about	worry about

- Examples of *be* + adjective + preposition combinations followed by gerunds:

be accustomed to	be good at	be surprised at	be used to
be afraid of	be interested in	be tired of	be worried about

- Phrasal verbs (*end up*, *call off*) can be followed by gerunds.
- See Appendix 8 for a list of more combinations with prepositions followed by gerunds.
- See Appendix 15 for a list of common phrasal verbs.

▶ Infinitives

ADJECTIVE + INFINITIVE			
	VERB	ADJECTIVE	INFINITIVE
She	was	ready	**to talk**.

IN ORDER + INFINITIVE	
	(*IN ORDER* +) INFINITIVE
Put on some music	(in order) **to relax**.

(*IN ORDER* + *NOT*) INFINITIVE	
In order not **to panic**,	take a deep breath.

- Many adjectives can be followed by infinitives.

afraid	eager	excited	hesitant	sorry
determined	embarrassed	happy	ready	surprised

- See Appendix 9 for a list of more adjectives followed by infinitives.
- Infinitives do not directly follow prepositions.
- Infinitives may follow the expression *in order*. They are called purpose infinitives.

- In affirmative purpose infinitives, *in order* may be omitted. In negative purpose infinitives, *in order* is necessary.

 Do not confuse expressions ending in the preposition *to* followed by gerunds with verbs followed directly by the infinitive.

I <u>look forward to</u> **leaving** soon.　　I <u>expect</u> **to leave** soon.

D1 Listening for Form

CD2 T15　**Listen to this conversation. Write the gerunds or infinitives you hear.**

A: You should consider ___taking___ a vacation. You could spend some time

　　　　_____.
　　　　　2

B: I can't. I'm busy _____ on a project that's due soon. My boss has told me
　　　　　　　　　　　　3

　　　_____ it as quickly as possible.
　　　　　4

A: I know. That's the point. Aren't you sick of _____?
　　　　　　　　　　　　　　　　　　　　5

B: Well, instead of _____ a long vacation, I might be interested in
　　　　　　　　　　6

　　　_____ away for a weekend. But I'd have trouble _____ before noon
　　　　　7　　　　　　　　　　　　　　　　　　　　　　　　8

　　　on Saturday. I save Saturday morning for _____ on my office email.
　　　　　　　　　　　　　　　　　　　　　9

A: Didn't you promise _____ more?
　　　　　　　　　　　10

D2 Using Gerunds After Prepositions

Follow each preposition with the gerund form of the expressions below. Then complete each sentence.

clean your apartment	do the laundry	look for an apartment	take a trip
cook dinner	find a job	reduce stress	use a computer

1. Before _taking a trip, check your car carefully._ _____

2. After _____

3. Instead of _____

4. Besides _____

5. By _____

6. In addition to _____

7. Before _____

8. After _____

D3 Choosing Between Gerunds and Infinitives

 A. Work with a partner. Switch roles for each question.

Student A: Ask a *What* question using the phrase and the verb *do* as a gerund or an infinitive.

Student B: Answer and then ask *What about you?*

1. be hesitant

   A: What are you hesitant to do?

   B: I'm hesitant to take too many classes. What about you?

   A: I'm hesitant to look for a part-time job.

2. be good at

3. be eager

4. be afraid of

5. be ready/right now

6. be accustomed to

7. be determined/before you are 50

8. look forward to/next year

 B. Report three of your partner's answers to the class using full sentences with gerunds or infinitives.

Leroy is hesitant to take too many classes.

D4 Working on Purpose Infinitives

A. Complete these sentences about errands with affirmative purpose infinitives. Use your own ideas. You can omit *in order*.

1. First I went to the bank *to get some money.* _____

2. Then I stopped at the dry cleaners _____

3. Next I went to the drugstore near my home _____

4. After that I stopped by the library _____

5. On the way home, I stopped at the gas station _____

 B. Work with a partner. Choose two items from the suggested topics below and write simple instructions for each. Use affirmative and negative purpose infinitives.

how to open a jar of jelly, a can of beans, a box of crackers, or a carton of juice
how to operate your DVD player or computer
how to start your car, drive safely in traffic, fix a flat tire, or fill your car with gas

To open a jar of jelly, grip the jar tightly and twist the lid.
In order to loosen the top, run it under hot water.

Interpreting Gerunds and Infinitives

Think Critically About Meaning and Use

A. Read the sentences and answer the questions below.

1a. Tom worries about Jane's driving at night.
1b. Tom worries about driving at night.
2a. Susan wants Sam to come early.
2b. Susan wants to come early.

1. **ANALYZE** Compare 1a and 1b. In each sentence, who is driving?

2. **ANALYZE** Compare 2a and 2b. In each sentence, who might come early?

B. Discuss your answers with the class and read the Meaning and Use Notes to check them.

Meaning and Use Notes

ONLINE PRACTICE

The Performer of Gerund Actions

▶ **1A** Like other actions, the actions expressed by gerunds are performed by someone. Sometimes the performer of the gerund action is the sentence subject. Sometimes the performer of the gerund action is not the subject. In these cases, a possessive adjective is used to indicate the performer.

Gerund Only	**Possessive Adjective + Gerund**
We were surprised at **passing the exam**. (We passed the exam.)	We were surprised at <u>Tim's/his</u> **passing the exam.** (Tim passed the exam.)

▶ **1B** When a gerund occurs after a verb, an object pronoun can replace the possessive adjective. Sentences with object pronouns convey a less formal tone than those with possessive adjectives.

Verb + Object Pronoun + Gerund

We were surprised at <u>him</u> **passing the exam.**

(Continued on page 248)

The Performer of Infinitive Actions

▶ **2A** Like other actions, the actions expressed by infinitives are performed by someone. When an infinitive directly follows a verb, the performer of the infinitive action is the sentence subject. When an infinitive follows an object, the performer of the infinitive action is the object.

Verb + Infinitive Only	**Verb + Object + Infinitive**
I <u>want</u> **to take a different route**.	I <u>want</u> him **to take a different route**.
(I may take a different route.)	(He may take a different route.)

▶ **2B** *Help* + object can be followed by an infinitive or a base form with no change in meaning. The verbs *make*, *have*, and *let* + object are followed by the base form of a verb, but not the infinitive. Like all objects before infinitives, the objects of these verbs perform the action expressed by the base form.

Verb + Object + Base Form of Verb	**Verb + Object + Infinitive**
He <u>helped me</u> **get** there safely.	He <u>helped me</u> **to get** there safely.
He <u>made me</u> **get** some rest.	
He <u>had me</u> **call** the doctor.	
He <u>let me</u> **call** the hospital.	

E1 Listening for Meaning and Use

▶ Notes 1A, 1B, 2B

◗)) CD2 T16 **Listen to each situation and choose the statement that is true.**

1. **a.** My friend shouldn't work so hard.

   b. The doctor shouldn't work so hard.

2. **a.** I recommended some exercises.

   b. The doctor recommended some exercises.

3. **a.** She called a health club.

   b. We called a health club.

4. **a.** We called in the evening.

   b. They called us in the evening.

5. **a.** We made arrangements.

   b. The manager made arrangements.

6. **a.** We invited him.

   b. He invited us.

7. **a.** He drove in the rain.

   b. I drove in the rain.

8. **a.** The manager left a deposit.

   b. We left a deposit.

E2 Expressing Intentions and Desires

▶ Notes 1A, 1B, 2A

Choose either Situation A or B and complete the sentences that you might say.
Use sentences with appropriate infinitives or gerunds. Add an object before infinitives
or a possessive adjective before gerunds, if possible.

Situation A: You are going to run for president.

Situation B: You are going to resign from your position because of a scandal.

1. I have decided _to run for president._

2. I appreciate _your encouraging me so much._

3. I expect _____

4. I invite _____

5. I'm concerned about _____

6. I urge _____

7. I want _____

8. I don't mind _____

E3 Talking About Teaching

▶ Notes 2A, 2B

A. In small groups, discuss the best way to teach someone to do something. Choose
    one of the suggested topics below. Use the verbs *make*, *let*, *help*, and *have* followed
    by an infinitive or base form where possible.

    teaching a foreign friend how to speak your language
    teaching a friend how to drive
    teaching a child how to cook

    A: To teach a foreign friend your language, you need to be very patient.

    B: It is important to practice as much as possible.

    C: Yes. Also, let him make mistakes. That's how you help him make progress.

B. Write a summary of your discussion and read it to the class. Find out whether the
    class agrees with your methods.

Think Critically About Meaning and Use

A. Read each sentence and the statement that follows. Write *T* if the statement is true and *F* if it is false.

1. I forgot to mail the letter.

___F___ I mailed the letter.

2. I didn't remember to take out the garbage.

___F___ I took out the garbage.

3. I'll never forget opening that letter.

___T___ I opened the letter.

4. I always avoid eating sweets.

___F___ I eat sweets.

5. They permitted me to leave.

___T___ I left.

6. She stopped to eat lunch.

___F___ She didn't eat lunch.

7. I tried soaking my ankle, but it still hurts.

___T___ I soaked my ankle.

8. I heard about his winning the race.

___T___ He won the race.

9. He was surprised at my failing the exam.

___T___ I failed the exam.

10. I had him complain to the manager.

___F___ I complained to the manager.

B. Discuss these questions in small groups.

1. PREDICT Look at sentence 2. How would the meaning change if the speaker had said, "I didn't remember taking out the garbage"?

2. PREDICT Look at sentence 6. How would the meaning change if the speaker had said, "She stopped eating lunch."

Edit

Find the errors in these paragraphs and correct them.

Unfortunately, it is very common ^to encounter aggressive drivers every day. They are usually trying to getting [get] somewhere in a hurry. Them [Their] speeding can cause them ^to follow too closely or ^to change lanes frequently without signaling.

In order ^to avoid becoming an aggressive driver, there are a number of rules following [to follow]. First, allow enough time to reaching [reach] your destination. Second, change your schedule to keep from drive [driving] during rush hours. Third, call ahead for [to] explain if you are going to be late. Then you can relax.

If you see an aggressive driver, try [trying to] get out of the way safely. Never challenge an aggressive driver by speed [speeding] up or attempting [attempt] to hold your position in your lane. Don't let others make you driving [drive] dangerously. You need ^to be in control at all times.

Write

Write a persuasive essay advising readers how to manage the stress in their lives. Use gerunds and infinitives.

1. **BRAINSTORM** Research your topic on the Internet or at the library. Make a list of all the different ways to manage stress (e.g., using relaxation techniques, doing leisure-time activities, and so on.) Use these categories to help you organize your ideas into paragraphs.

   - **Introduction:** What role does stress play in our lives? Why is it important that people learn how to manage stress?
   - **Analysis/Advice:** Choose 2–3 methods and devote a paragraph to each. What is the method? Why do you think it is effective? Why should readers try it?
   - **Conclusion:** What "call to action" can you give readers to persuade them to take your ideas seriously?

2. **WRITE A FIRST DRAFT** Before you write your first draft, read the checklist below and look at the examples in A2 on pages 230–231 and C3 on page 241. Write your draft using gerunds and infinitives.

3. **EDIT** Read your work and check it against the checklist below. Circle grammar, spelling, and punctuation errors.

DO I...	YES
use gerunds and gerund phrases as subjects and objects, and after prepositions or common verb phrases?	☐
use the correct gerund or infinitive form after specific verbs?	☐
use at least one example of a sentence with *It...* + infinitive?	☐
make suggestions with imperatives + appropriate gerunds or infinitives?	☐

4. **PEER REVIEW** Work with a partner to help you decide how to fix your errors and improve the content. Use the checklist above.

5. **REWRITE YOUR DRAFT** Using the comments from your partner, write a final draft.

Dealing with stress is a fact of living in the modern world. Our lives are all about keeping the bills paid, juggling career and family, and generally never having enough hours in the day. The bad news is that living with a high level of stress can lead to...

Choose the correct word or words to complete each sentence.

1. _____C_____ repairing a twenty-five year old television set.

   a. I decided   **c.** It's not worth

   b. We refused   **d.** They asked me

2. Would you mind _____d_____ me the time, please?

   a. tell   **c.** told

   b. to tell   **d.** telling

3. Why _____a_____ believed that infants should be read aloud to often?

   a. is it   **c.** do we

   b. there is   **d.** should it

4. When _____b_____ substituted for gasoline in automobiles?

   a. other fuels are going to be   **c.** are other fuels going

   b. are other fuels going to be   **d.** other fuels are going

5. Typewriters _____a_____ in offices any longer.

   a. not used   **c.** are being used

   b. are used   **d.** are not being used

Choose the best answer to complete each conversation.

6. **A:** I stopped to listen to his advice.
   B: Oh, I'm glad you did. _____b_____

     a. He has bad ideas.   **c.** What did you recommend?

     b. He has good ideas.   **d.** He's a good listener.

7. **A:** The doctor permitted Tanya to fly to New York.
   B: Really? _____d_____

     a. Has she considered coming by train?   **c.** What flight did the doctor take?

     b. It pays to be cautious sometimes.   **d.** What flight did she take?

8. **A:** I avoid cooking with butter.
   B: Me, too. _____c_____

     a. I love using it.   **c.** I've stopped using it.

     b. Unfortunately, I've run out.   **d.** I used to hate it.

Choose the most likely source of each item.

9. Karl Marx was born in Germany on May 5, 1818.
   - **a.** encyclopedia
   - **b.** public notice
   - **c.** formal letter
   - **d.** newspaper headline

10. Congratulations. You have been accepted to City College.
    - **a.** sign
    - **b.** formal letter
    - **c.** recorded announcement
    - **d.** textbook

11. Credit Cards Not Accepted
    - **a.** rule book
    - **b.** formal letter
    - **c.** newspaper
    - **d.** sign

Complete each sentence with the correct form of the word or words in parentheses.

12. I'm on vacation next week. I'm planning ___not to do___ (not/do) any work.

13. He isn't accustomed ___to eating___ (eat) spicy food.

14. The children had fun ___to ride riding___ (ride) on the roller coaster.

Match each sentence ending to the correct beginning.

___a___ 15. We're interested
___d___ 16. He insists
___g___ 17. She's not used

- **a.** in buying a hybrid car.
- **b.** of driving on icy roads.
- **c.** obeying speed limits.
- **d.** about selling his car.
- **e.** parking such a big car.
- **f.** on being a back-seat driver.
- **g.** to driving in bad weather.
- **h.** at backing up.

Change each sentence from active to passive. Use the agent only if needed.

18. If it snows, the coach will cancel the game.
    ___If it snows, the game will be canceled by the coach___

19. Someone has seen the mayor at that restaurant.
    ___The mayor has been seen at that restaurant.___

20. Pablo Picasso painted *The Three Musicians*.
    ___The Three Musicians was painted by Pablo Picasso___

PART 5

Modifying Nouns

CHAPTER 12

Indefinite and Definite Articles; Review of Nouns

Chicken Soup, Always Chicken Soup

A1 Before You Read

 Discuss these questions.

What do you do when you have a cold? Do you take medicine? vitamins? herbs? What special treatments are used in your family? Do they work?

A2 Read

 CD2 T17 **Read this book excerpt to find out about the special medicinal properties of old-fashioned chicken soup.**

Chicken Soup,
Always Chicken Soup

Have you ever wondered why chicken soup is such a popular remedy for the common cold? The first authority to recommend chicken soup
5 was the distinguished twelfth-century physician Moses Maimonides. According to the story, when Sultan Saladin, a powerful Muslim military leader, begged Maimonides for a cure
10 for his son's asthma, Maimonides prescribed chicken soup. The prescription was probably effective because chicken soup is now known to have medicinal properties.
15   Scientific research has begun to explain why age-old food remedies, passed down for centuries by medical sages and grandmothers, have been effective against respiratory problems
20 such as colds and the flu. The doctor who knows most about this is Irwin Ziment, M.D., a lung specialist at the University of California at Los Angeles. Dr. Ziment has concluded
25 from a study of early medical literature that foods used to fight diseases for centuries are very similar to many of the drugs we now use. Chicken, for example, contains a
30 certain chemical which is released when you make the soup. This substance is remarkably similar to a common drug for bronchitis and respiratory infections. In fact, the
35 drug was originally made from chicken feathers and skin. The substance in chicken soup has been shown to help clear the lungs of

congestion in much the same way as
40 certain drugs.

Marvin Sackner, M.D., a lung
specialist at Mount Sinai Medical
Center in Miami Beach, agrees.
"There's an aromatic substance in
45 chicken soup... that helps clear your
airways." Dr. Sackner is the author of
the famous chicken soup study,
published in 1978. Dr. Sackner did
not believe that chicken soup, often
50 called "grandma's penicillin," fought
cold symptoms any better than hot
water. In his study, 15 healthy men
and women sipped hot chicken soup,
hot water, or cold water. Five minutes
55 and 30 minutes later, he measured the
rate at which substances passed
through the subjects' nasal passages.

To Dr. Sackner's surprise, chicken
soup was better at fighting congestion
60 than hot or cold water. Furthermore,

even the chicken soup vapors were
superior to those of hot water. Dr.
Sackner even thinks that cold chicken
soup "will help clear the 'cold in your
65 nose,' and if the chicken soup is hot
and steamy, it will work even faster
and more efficiently."

And for a super-congestion-
fighting dose of grandma's penicillin,
70 Dr. Ziment advises adding lots of
garlic, onions, pepper, and hot spices
like curry or hot chillies. He calls such
soup "the best cold remedy there is."
To avoid or fight colds and the flu, a
75 bowl of spicy chicken soup every day
is Dr. Ziment's prescription. One last
thing: It's better to sip chicken soup
slowly rather than drink it, in order to
get the maximum therapeutic effect.
80 So sit back, relax, and enjoy your
chicken soup. Grandma was right
after all!

Adapted from *Food—Your Miracle Medicine*

---

aromatic: having a pleasant smell
congestion: blockage
medicinal: having the curing properties of medicine
remedy: something that helps an illness; a cure

respiratory: related to breathing
sage: a very wise person, usually old and
highly respected
therapeutic: able to heal or cure

A3 After You Read

Write *T* for true or *F* for false for each statement. Change the false statements to
true ones.

___T___ **1.** Chicken soup has been used for centuries as a cold remedy.

___F___ **2.** Chicken soup makes you feel better emotionally, but not physically.

___T___ **3.** There is a chemical in chicken that fights colds.

___F___ **4.** Dr. Sackner showed that hot water was most effective.

___F___ **5.** Chicken soup is good for colds, but when ill you should avoid spices.

___T___ **6.** For maximum health benefit, you shouldn't eat chicken soup too fast.

Indefinite and Definite Articles; Review of Nouns

Think Critically About Form

A. Look back at the book excerpt on page 256 and complete the tasks below.

1. **IDENTIFY** Look at the third, fourth, and fifth sentences in the second paragraph (lines 24–34). Then find these common nouns:

literature	drugs	chemical	drug
centuries	chicken	soup	

2. **RECOGNIZE** Which nouns have adjectives before them? Which have articles? Which have both adjectives and articles? What are those adjectives and articles?

3. **RECOGNIZE** Which nouns do not have adjectives or articles before them?

4. **LABEL** Which nouns are singular? Which are plural?

B. Discuss your answers with the class and read the Form charts to check them.

▶ Nouns

ONLINE
PRACTICE

COUNT NOUNS		NONCOUNT NOUNS
SINGULAR	**PLURAL**	**SINGULAR**
(one) **banana** (one) **physician**	(two) **bananas** (two) **physicians**	**soup** **research**

▶ Indefinite Articles

SINGULAR COUNT NOUNS
A / AN + SINGULAR COUNT NOUN
I ate **a banana**.
Did you eat **an apple**?

PLURAL COUNT NOUNS
Ø + PLURAL COUNT NOUN
I ate **Ø bananas**.
Did you eat **Ø apples**?

NONCOUNT NOUNS
Ø + NONCOUNT NOUN
I didn't eat **Ø fruit**.
Did you eat **Ø fruit**?

SOME / ANY + PLURAL COUNT NOUN
I ate **some bananas**.
Did you eat **any apples**?

SOME / ANY + NONCOUNT NOUN
I didn't eat **any fruit**.
Did you eat **some fruit**?

▶ Definite Articles

SINGULAR COUNT NOUNS	PLURAL COUNT NOUNS	NONCOUNT NOUNS
THE + SINGULAR COUNT NOUN	*THE* + PLURAL COUNT NOUN	*THE* + NONCOUNT NOUN
I ate **the banana**.	I ate **the bananas**.	I didn't eat **the fruit**.
Did you eat **the apple**?	Did you eat **the apples**?	Did you eat **the fruit**?

Nouns
- Common nouns can be count or noncount.
- Count nouns can be used with numbers. They have both singular and plural forms.
- Noncount nouns cannot be used with numbers. They do not have plural forms.
- Common nouns that occur with an indefinite article or no article (Ø) are indefinite nouns.
- Common nouns that occur with a definite article are definite nouns.

Indefinite Articles with Singular Count Nouns
- Indefinite articles can occur before a singular count noun (*an apple*) or before an adjective + singular count noun (*a green apple*).
- Use *an* before words that begin with a vowel sound; use *a* before all others.

  If a noun begins with the letter *h*, use *an* if the *h* is not pronounced. Use *a* if the *h* is pronounced.

  > **an** hour   **an** honor   **a** house   **a** human

- If a noun begins with the letter *u*, use *an* if the *u* is a short vowel. Use *a* if the *u* is pronounced like the *y* in yellow.

  > **an** umbrella   **an** understanding   **a** unit   **a** utensil

Indefinite Articles with Plural Count and Noncount Nouns
- Do not use indefinite articles before plural count nouns or noncount nouns.
- *Some* and *any* often act like indefinite articles with plural count nouns or noncount nouns. We often use *some* in affirmative sentences and questions and *any* in negative sentences and questions.
- Indefinite articles, *some*, and *any* do not have to be repeated when nouns are combined with *and*.

  > **a** banana and **(an)** apple   **some** fruit and **(some)** cereal

Definite Articles with Count and Noncount Nouns
- The definite article *the* can be used before all common nouns—singular and plural count nouns and noncount nouns.

(Continued on page 260)

- Definite articles can occur before a noun (*the apple*) or before an adjective + noun (*the green apple*).
- Definite articles do not have to be repeated when nouns are combined with *and*.

    the bananas and (**the**) apples

B1 Listening for Form

CD2 T18 Listen to these facts about the common cold. Write the articles you hear. Write Ø if there is no article. After you finish, check the capitalization.

Although ___the___ common cold is generally not serious, it causes ___Ø___
          1   2
people to be absent from ___Ø___ work and go to ___the___ doctor more often than
                          3   4
___Ø the___ other illnesses. ___The___ majority of colds come from ___Ø___ contact
   5   6   7
with ___Ø___ surfaces that ___Ø___ people touch frequently. People transmit
     8   9
___the___ cold viruses on these surfaces to their eyes, noses, and mouths. Once
   10
___the___ symptoms appear, there are many treatments for relieving ___the___
   11   12
discomfort. Whatever ___a___ person does, unfortunately, ___a___ cold will
                      13   14
probably still last from six to ten days.

B2 Identifying Indefinite and Definite Articles

Read the passage and underline all the common nouns, along with their articles and adjectives. Then write *D* for definite or *I* for indefinite to indicate whether the noun is used definitely or indefinitely in its context.

Have you ever eaten <u>coconut</u>? You probably have, but you may not be very familiar with <u>coco palms</u>. <u>Coconuts</u> come from <u>coco palms</u>, which are <u>trees</u> that grow in <u>tropical regions</u>. Coco <u>palms</u> are very unusual because all of the <u>parts</u> of the <u>tree</u> have a commercial <u>value</u>. For example, <u>coconuts</u> are an important <u>food</u> in <u>tropical regions</u>, and <u>coconut milk</u>, which comes from inside the <u>coconut</u>, is a nutritious <u>drink</u>. <u>Coconut oil</u>, the most valuable <u>product</u> of all,

also comes from coconuts. Some of the other parts of the tree that are eaten include the buds and young stems. Besides food, the tree is also used for manufacturing commercial products. The leaves are used for making fans and baskets, and the fibers from the husks and trunks are made into mats, cord, and rope. Even the hard shells and the husks are used to make fuel, and the trunks are used for timber.

B3 Building Sentences with Indefinite and Definite Articles

Build as many meaningful sentences as possible. Use an item from each column. Punctuate your sentences correctly.

I ate some rice.

I ate they had	a an some Ø the	pencil rice fun vegetables idea

B4 Transforming Sentences

A. **Change the underlined singular nouns to plural nouns, and the underlined plural nouns to singular nouns. You may also need to change pronouns and verbs.**

1. I took <u>a book</u> and <u>a pen</u> with me.

   I took books and pens with me. OR
   I took some books and pens with me.

2. Take a <u>peach</u>. *Take peaches.*

3. Those are <u>herbs</u>. *That is a herbs.*

4. <u>Children</u> get more colds than <u>adults</u>. *A child get a cold more than an adult.*

5. We need <u>some magazines</u> with more information.

6. I watched <u>a movie</u> last night.

B. **Change the underlined definite articles to indefinite articles, and the indefinite articles to definite articles.**

1. I went to <u>a</u> bank and took out <u>some</u> money.

   I went to the bank and took out the money.

2. Take <u>the</u> sheet of paper and <u>the</u> pen.

   Take a sheet of paper and a pen

3. Did you eat <u>some</u> cookies or <u>Ø</u> cake? *Did you eat the cookies or cake?*

4. I'm taking <u>the</u> medication and eating <u>the</u> yogurt twice a day. *some*

5. Did you see <u>a</u> movie last week? *the*

6. I went to <u>a</u> store yesterday. *the*

C MEANING AND USE 1

The Indefinite Article

Think Critically About Meaning and Use

A. Read the sentences and answer the questions below.

1a. My friend wants to marry <u>a millionaire</u>. She met him last year.
1b. My friend wants to marry <u>a millionaire</u>. She hasn't found one yet.
2a. <u>Bananas</u> are tropical fruits.
2b. Please buy <u>some bananas</u> on your way home.

1. **ANALYZE** Compare the meanings of 1a and 1b. In which sentence does the speaker have a specific mental picture of the underlined noun?

2. **DIFFERENTIATE** Compare the meanings of 2a and 2b. Which sentence refers to a small quantity of the underlined noun? Which sentence describes or classifies the underlined noun?

B. Discuss your answers with the class and read the Meaning and Use Notes to check them.

Meaning and Use Notes

ONLINE
PRACTICE

Introducing Nouns with Indefinite Articles

▶ **1A** Use *a/an* or no article (Ø) to introduce a common noun when it is first mentioned.

First Mentioned

A: What did you do last night?

B: I watched **a movie**. What did you do?

A: I had **Ø friends** over and made **Ø dinner**.

▶ **1B** Usually when a common noun is introduced, it is specific for the speaker, but not specific for the listener. This means that the speaker has an idea or a mental picture of the noun, but the listener does not. Sometimes the noun is not specific for the speaker or the listener.

Specific for the Speaker Only

Jill: I bought **a new coat** yesterday.
(Jill has a specific coat in mind, but the listener doesn't.)

Not Specific for the Speaker or Listener

Joe: I need **new shirts**.
(Joe doesn't have any specific shirts in mind, and the listener doesn't either.)

▶ **1C** When introducing singular count nouns, *a* and *an* often express the quantity "one." When introducing plural count and noncount nouns, some and any are often used to express a small quantity.

Singular Count Nouns	**Plural Count and Noncount Nouns**
Would you like **a cookie**?	Would you like **some cookies**?
I'd like to order **a steak**, please.	I'd like to order **some steaks**, please.
	Do you have **any information** about this medicine?

Classifying and Describing Nouns

▶ **2** Common nouns with *a*, *an*, and Ø are often used in sentences with *be* to classify or describe nouns. *Some* and *any* are not used this way.

My father is **a teacher**.

What are those? They're **vitamins**. x They're some vitamins. (INCORRECT)

C1 Listening for Meaning and Use   ▶ Notes 1A–1C

CD2 T19 Listen to each situation. Is the noun specific or not specific for the speaker? Check (✓) the correct column.

		SPECIFIC	NOT SPECIFIC
1.	orange juice	✓	
2.	apples		✓
3.	a new doctor	✓	✓
4.	a friend	✓	
5.	some soup	✓	
6.	an appointment		✓
7.	a book		✓
8.	cough medicine	✓	

C2 Introducing New Information

▶ Notes 1A–1C

Complete these conversations with a sentence that introduces new information with three indefinite nouns. Use *a/an*, *some*, or Ø.

1. **A:** What did you do last night?

   B: I read a book, watched a movie, and took a bath.

2. **A:** What did you buy at the supermarket?

   B: I bought a bottle of juice and some cookies.

3. **A:** What do you take on a trip?

   B: I take a bag

4. **A:** What do you want for your birthday?

   B: I want to have a cake.

5. **A:** What do you keep in your pockets?

   B: I keep a candy

6. **A:** What can you buy at a hardware store?

   B: _____

C3 Classifying Nouns

▶ Note 2

A. Make a list of all the foods you have eaten in the last two days. Do not list specific quantities. Use *a/an*, *some*, or Ø next to each noun that you list. Then sort the nouns into three categories: Healthy, Unhealthy, or Not Sure.

HEALTHY	UNHEALTHY	NOT SURE
an apple	potato chips	eggs
milk	a candy bar	
cereal		

B. Share your list with a partner. Discuss whether you agree with the way your partner has classified each item. What foods are you not sure about? Why?

A: *Do you think eggs are healthy or unhealthy?*

B: *I think they're healthy.*

D

The Definite Article

Think Critically About Meaning and Use

A. Read the sentences and answer the questions below.

a. Did you hear what <u>the mayor</u> said this morning on <u>the news</u>?

b. I bought a sweater and a shirt but <u>the sweater</u> was too small.

c. Please pass the <u>salt</u>.

1. **ANALYZE** In which sentence does the speaker mention the underlined noun more than once?

2. **ANALYZE** In which sentence are the speaker and the listener from the same geographic area?

3. **ANALYZE** In which sentence can the listener see the underlined noun?

B. Discuss your answers with the class and read the Meaning and Use Notes to check them.

Meaning and Use Notes

ONLINE PRACTICE

Identifying Nouns with the Definite Article
The is used with a common noun when it is specific for both the speaker and the listener because of information they share. Following are some different ways that speakers and listeners share information about a noun.

▶ **1A** The listener can identify the noun if it has already been mentioned in a conversation or text. When it is mentioned again, the speaker uses *the*. Notice that the exact words do not have to be repeated.

First Mentioned	**Mentioned Again**
I ordered <u>a steak</u> and <u>a salad</u> for lunch.	**The steak** was great, but **the salad** was awful.
<u>A kitten</u> was found in a box near my house.	**The poor creature** was cold and hungry.

▶ **1B** The listener can identify the noun if he or she can see or hear it.

Visual Context

Mother: Watch out! Don't shake **the table**. You'll spill **the milk**.

Son: OK. Could you please pass **the rice**?

(Continued on page 266)

▶ 1C	The listener can identify the noun from the situation or from general knowledge.

General Knowledge

I went to <u>an unusual wedding</u>. **The bride** and **groom** wore jogging clothes.
    (The listener knows that a wedding has a bride and a groom.)

▶ 1D	The listener can identify the noun if the listener and speaker share geographic or social information.

Shared Information

A: Do you think **the secretaries** make enough money?

B: Yes. I think they do.
    (The listener assumes that this means the secretaries who work with them.)

▶ 1E	Certain names of places and things that are very familiar to the speaker almost always use *the*. The listener may not know the specific identity of the noun but assumes that it refers to a place that the speaker habitually goes to, an object the speaker habitually uses, and so on.

Familiar Nouns

the bank	the doctor	the library	the office	the radio
the beach	the gym	the mall	the park	the store
the dentist	the hospital	the movies	the post office	the TV

When you go to **the store**, could you buy some milk? And turn off **the TV** before
    you go.

▶ 1F	The listener can identify the noun if the noun is unique (there is only one).

Unique Nouns

I took my guests to **the best restaurant** in town, and they chose **the most expensive**
    item on the menu.

Earth rotates around **the sun** once every 365 days.

Please look at **the top** of this page.

▶ 1G	The listener can identify the noun with the help of modifiers in the noun phrase.

Noun Modifiers

I took my guests to **the best restaurant** in town, and they chose **the most expensive**
    item on the menu.

The book <u>that's on sale</u> is on the counter. (*that's on sale* tells which book)

The <u>red</u> **book** is mine. (*red* tells which book)

D1 Listening for Meaning and Use

▶ Notes 1A–1C, 1F, 1G

CD2 T20 **Listen to each sentence. Would the sentence that follows use a definite or indefinite article? Choose the sentence that is more likely to follow.**

1. a. I bought a blue shirt.
   b. I bought the blue shirt.

2. a. The poor child lost all the money.
   b. A poor child lost all the money.

3. a. Does anyone know a writer?
   b. Does anyone know the writer?

4. a. Did the bride wear a long gown?
   b. Did a bride wear the long gown?

5. a. A steering wheel.
   b. The steering wheel.

6. a. Not anymore. I lent the CD to Joan.
   b. Not anymore. I lent a CD to Joan.

7. a. A doorbell is ringing.
   b. The doorbell is ringing.

8. a. Should I send a new one?
   b. Should I send the new one?

D2 Choosing Definite or Indefinite Articles

▶ Notes 1A–1G

 Work with a partner. Read each situation and decide whether to use *a*, *an*, or *the*. Then discuss the reasons why you chose your answers.

1. If there are no chairs left in this classroom, you'll have to sit on ___the___ floor.
   ₁
   Or maybe you should go next door and ask if you can borrow ___a___ chair from
   ₂
   that classroom.

2. ___The___ apartment that I live in now is too small. I have to start looking for
   ₁
   ___a___ new one. I'd really like to find ___an___ apartment with
   ₂   ₃
   ___a___ garden.
   ₄

3. There's ___an___ interesting exercise in your textbook. Please look at ___the___
   ₁   ₂
   bottom of page 10.

4. Did you read ___the___ magazine that I sent you last week? It had ___an___
   ₁   ₂
   interesting story about ___the___ mayor of Philadelphia.
   ₃

5. Would you answer ___the___ telephone, please? I'm trying to diaper ___the___ baby.
   ₁   ₂

Vocabulary Notes

Another vs. *The Other* ~~versus~~

Another is indefinite like *a/an*. It means "one more" or "a different one."

There are several cookies on a plate. Your friend asks:

Do you want **another** cookie?

The other is definite. It refers to a specific alternative when you are choosing between two things.

There are only two cookies on a plate. Your friend takes one and asks:

Do you want **the other** cookie?

D3 Using *Another* and *The Other*

 Work with a partner. Make up two short conversations for each of these contexts. Use *another* in one conversation and *the other* in the second conversation.

1. at a friend's house

   Conversation 1
   A: There are a few cookies left. Would you like another one?
   B: No thanks. I've already had several.

2. at the supermarket

3. at school

4. at a restaurant

5. at a department store

D4 Making Inferences Based on General Knowledge ▶ Note 1C

Read each sentence and then write a related sentence with a definite noun that you can identify based on the context. Use these nouns:

the author   the mechanic   the bank teller
the driver   the receptionist   the waiter

1. Last summer I took a bus ride through a terrible storm.

   The driver was excellent, and we reached our destination safely.

2. I had lunch at the Pinewood Restaurant yesterday.

3. My car began making a strange noise, so I took it to a garage.

_____

4. I went to deposit some money at the bank this morning.

_____

5. I read a great book during my vacation.

_____

6. I called my doctor's office yesterday afternoon.

_____

Beyond the Sentence

Connecting Information

Like pronouns, articles help make sentences clear and connect ideas in a paragraph or conversation. Indefinite nouns are used to introduce new information. Definite nouns are used to refer to old information, which is more specific.

> We've just bought **a new rabbit**. We brought her home last week, and **she's** doing fine. **My son** is so protective of **the rabbit** that **he** insisted on getting up to check on **her** for the first few nights. But now that **he** is convinced that **the rabbit** can stay alone, **he** doesn't get up to check on **her** anymore. **He** sleeps through the night in the comfort of **his own room**, and the rabbit spends **her nights** in **her little house** in the backyard.

D5 Connecting Information

A. Work with a partner. Number these sentences to make a meaningful paragraph. Pay attention to the articles and pronouns to help you decide on the order.

_____ He cut the wire and jumped from the window into a creek.

_____ No one knows exactly where he found the ladder.

___1___ Another prisoner has escaped from the local prison.

_____ He was able to reach a high window covered with wire.

_____ He swam across the creek, climbed over a wall, stole a car, and drove away.

_____ Sometime during the night, the prisoner climbed up a ladder.

 B. Read the story aloud to see if it sounds right. Be ready to explain your choices.

D6 Talking About Familiar Nouns

▶ Note 1E

Work with a partner. Take turns saying each of these sentences. Add a specific identity for each underlined noun. Do any of the nouns have different identities for you and your partner? Why?

1. I went to <u>the supermarket</u> last night.

   I went to the A & P supermarket near my house last night.

2. I went to <u>the bank</u> before I came to class.

3. I bought <u>the newspaper</u> before I came to class.

4. <u>The mayor</u> is going to speak on television tonight.

5. I didn't feel well yesterday, so I went to <u>the doctor</u>.

D7 Understanding Shared Information

▶ Notes 1A–1D, 1G

A. Work in small groups. Imagine that you overhear the conversations below. Think about each situation and try to figure out what information the speaker and listener(s) share. Use your imagination.

1. Two women are talking. One of them says, "Did you order <u>the flowers</u> yet?"

   The women are sisters. They're sending a gift to their mother. OR

   The women are friends. One of them is getting married soon and they're discussing the wedding.

2. Two young men are talking. One says, "<u>The car</u> costs $2,500." The other says, "I don't know how I'll be able to afford it."

3. A woman approaches a man and says, "I got <u>the money</u>."

4. Three women are talking. One asks, "Did you bring <u>the photographs</u>?"

5. A woman is talking to a man. The woman says, "How could you forget to pay <u>the bill</u>?"

6. Two men are talking. One says, "Oh, by the way, I <u>got the tickets</u>."

B. Choose one of the situations from part A. Make a list of details about the situation. Then write a paragraph about it. Begin with a clear topic sentence.

   Two sisters are talking about a gift that they have planned to send their mother for her birthday. The gift is a large bouquet of her favorite flowers. After the flowers arrive, they are going to take their mother to an elegant restaurant for to celebrate. She doesn't know that all of her friends will be there.

Article Use with Generic Nouns

Think Critically About Meaning and Use

A. Read the sentences and answer the questions below.

1a. Unfortunately, my children have <u>colds</u> at the moment.
1b. <u>Colds</u> cannot be cured by antibiotics.
2a. <u>Garlic</u> can help fight certain diseases.
2b. I put <u>garlic</u> in the soup.
3a. I have <u>a mango</u> in the refrigerator.
3b. <u>A mango</u> is a sweet-tasting fruit.
4a. <u>The typewriter</u> is not used much anymore in most offices.
4b. I put <u>the typewriter</u> away because we never use it.

1. **ANALYZE** Which underlined noun in each pair refers to a whole class or group of nouns?

2. **ANALYZE** Which underlined noun in each pair refers to a specific noun or nouns?

B. Discuss your answers with the class and read the Meaning and Use Notes to check them.

Meaning and Use Notes

ONLINE PRACTICE

Overview of Generic Nouns

▶ 1 We don't always use a noun to refer to a specific object, event, or concept. Sometimes we use the noun to refer to a whole class or group of objects, events, or concepts. This noun is called a generic noun, and statements about a generic noun are called generic statements.

Ø

Flies are insects.

I like **rice**.

A/An

A bird can fly, but **a reptile** can't.

The

The laser has become an important tool in surgery.

(Continued on page 272)

Using No Article (Ø)

▶ 2 Plural count nouns and noncount nouns are the most common type of generic nouns. No articles are used with them. They are often used in generic statements to classify nouns, express likes or dislikes, and give opinions.

Classification	Likes and Dislikes	Opinions
Flies are insects.	I don't like **rice**.	**Carrots** are good for you.

Using *A/An*

▶ 3 Singular count nouns with *a/an* can also be used as generic nouns to represent all members of a class. The nouns are often used in definitions and in sentences expressing general factual information.

Definitions

A locksmith is **a person** who makes and repairs locks and keys.

A penguin is **a black and white bird** that lives in the Antarctic.

Factual Information

A bird can fly.

A child has six to ten colds per year. **An adult** has two colds per year.

Using *The*

▶ 4A The use of generic nouns with *the* is less common than the use of other types of generic nouns. Definite generic nouns express a more formal tone and are used more often in scientific and technical writing. They usually refer to plants, animals, mechanical objects, and other scientific phenomena.

More Formal Writing	Less Formal Writing
The mosquito can spread malaria.	Mosquitoes can spread malaria.
The computer has changed our lives.	Computers have changed our lives.

 Remember that *the* with a plural noun is not used generically. It refers to specific plural nouns.

The computers that we bought last year have helped our business.

▶ 4B Musical instruments are often referred to generically with the definite article.

I used to play **the piano** and **the violin**.

E1 Listening for Meaning and Use

▶ Notes 1–3, 4A

CD2 T21 Listen to each situation. Check (✓) *Generic* if the noun refers to a class of things or *Specific* if the noun refers to a particular thing.

		GENERIC	SPECIFIC
1.	the carrot		✓
2.	almonds		
3.	garlic		
4.	food		
5.	the onion		
6.	a cold		
7.	vitamins		
8.	a headache		

E2 Defining Nouns with *A/An*

▶ Notes 1, 3

Work with a partner. Make up a simple generic statement that defines each noun below. Use singular count nouns with *a/an*. You may need a dictionary.

A spatula is a cooking utensil.

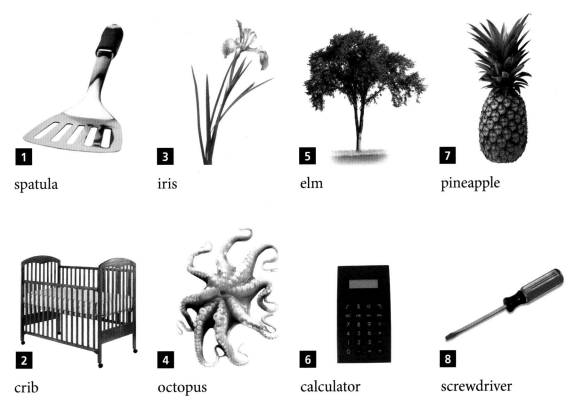

1 spatula

3 iris

5 elm

7 pineapple

2 crib

4 octopus

6 calculator

8 screwdriver

E3 Rephrasing Formal Generic Sentences

▶ Note 4A

A. Rewrite this paragraph as a less formal version. Use plural generic nouns instead of definite generic nouns. Change pronouns and verbs when necessary. Start your paragraph with *Kangaroos are...*

The kangaroo is an Australian animal with very distinctive physical features. It has large back legs that are used for hopping very fast, and it has a very large tail that helps it maintain its balance. The female kangaroo carries her young around in a special pocket of skin on her stomach that is called a pouch.

B. Read these statements. Rewrite one of them as a less formal sentence and use it to introduce a short, informal explanation that you will present to the class.

The computer doesn't always make life easier.
The trumpet is important in orchestras as well as jazz bands.
The human heart is like a machine.
The digital camera has revolutionized popular photogaphy.

Computers don't always make life easier. Sometimes they actually make life more frustrating when they break down. For example, last week at the bank...

Beyond the Sentence

Indefinite Generic Nouns in Discourse

An indefinite generic noun (with *a, an, Ø*) can remain indefinite throughout a paragraph or conversation as long as it continues to refer to a whole class or group of nouns instead of to a specific noun.

An onion is a small white vegetable with a strong smell and a strong taste. Researchers have found that it is actually the strong taste that makes **an onion** good for your blood. Unfortunately, sweet or mild **onions** do not have this effect on your blood. Someday, according to researchers, **an onion** will taste sweet and benefit your health at the same time.

E4 Choosing Between Generic and Specific Nouns

A. In these following sentences, some nouns are used generically with no article, and others are used to refer to a specific thing. Distinguish between these generic and specific uses by writing *a, an, the,* or *Ø*.

1. I don't really like _____Ø_____ desserts, but my neighbor makes _____ dessert that I'm very fond of.
   ₁   ₂

2. _____ cell phone is useful in an emergency. However, in many places, it is
   1
unlawful to use _____ cell phone while driving.
              2

3. It's hard to find _____ inexpensive clothing. _____ clothing in the
                    1   2
stores is so expensive these days.

4. I eat _____ rice at almost every meal. _____ rice that I buy is usually
        1   2
on sale downtown. It's _____ very flavorful kind of rice.
                      3

5. _____ camels are animals with long necks and humps on their back. In
   1
desert areas, people ride on _____ camels and use them for transportation.
                            2

6. He's allergic to _____ cats. When he goes near _____ cat, he starts
                   1   2
to sneeze.

B. **Choose one of these sentences as the introduction to a paragraph. Write a
description that continues to refer to the underlined generic noun.**

I don't usually like <u>fancy restaurants</u>.
<u>A vacation</u> isn't always relaxing.
<u>Teachers</u> have to be patient.
<u>A laptop computer</u> is useful in college.

*I don't usually like fancy restaurants. Sometimes they have good food, but most of
the time the food is drowned in exotic sauces and the portions are very small. The
worst thing about them is that the atmosphere is always very stuffy and pretentious,
and I never feel at home in them. They also have outrageously expensive prices.*

Think Critically About Meaning and Use

A. Read each sentence and the statements that follow. Write *T* if the statement is true or *F* if it is false.

1. I bought a tennis racket last night.

   _T_ **a.** The speaker has a specific tennis racket in mind.

   _F_ **b.** The listener has a specific tennis racket in mind.

2. I looked at an apartment last night, but the kitchen was too small.

   _F_ **a.** The listener has seen the kitchen.

   _T_ **b.** The listener has just heard about this apartment.

3. Please take the other cookie.

   _T_ **a.** The speaker is referring to the last cookie.

   _T_ **b.** Someone already took a cookie.

4. I'd like some cheese, please.

   _T_ **a.** The speaker is referring to a small quantity of cheese.

   _F_ **b.** The listener knows exactly which cheese the speaker wants.

5. Open a window, please.

   _F_ **a.** The speaker wants a particular window to be opened.

   _T_ **b.** There are at least two windows.

6.   **Mother:** Wear the dress to school.

  Daughter: No, not today.

   _T_ **a.** The mother has a specific dress in mind.

   _T_ **b.** The daughter has a specific dress in mind.

7. I saw Maria at the post office yesterday.

     ___T̶ R̶___ **a.** The speaker usually goes to that post office.

     ___F___ **b.** The listener may not know that post office.

8. The snake is frightening that little girl.

     ___T___ **a.** The speaker is referring to a particular snake.

     ___F___ **b.** The sentence is about all snakes.

B. Discuss these questions in small groups.

1. **ANALYZE** Look at sentence 2. What can we assume about the listener if the speaker had said, "I looked at the apartment last night…"

2. **PREDICT** Look at sentence 8. What would the speaker have said if he or she wanted to make a statement about the effect that snakes generally have on the little girl?

Edit

Some of these sentences have errors. Find the errors and correct them.

1. I need *a* new coat. Please help me find one.

2. When you get to my house, you don't have to ring *the* doorbell. Just walk in.

3. We have plenty of sandwiches. Please take the another one.

4. My grandparents were some immigrants. They came to this country in 1920.

5. She graduated with a major in the mathematics and physics.

6. The life is not always easy.

7. Calcium is *a* mineral.

8. Please pass the rice and the salt.

9. *The* Book I bought was on sale.

10. Let's sit in a last row so that we can leave quickly when the play is over.
the

Write

Imagine you work as a writer for a public relations firm that does work for a family health clinic. Write the first page of a pamphlet about healthy eating. Use count, noncount, and generic nouns with definite, indefinite, and no articles, as needed.

1. **BRAINSTORM** Think of all the ways that food contributes to good/poor health. Make a list of healthy/unhealthy foods. Then use these categories to help you organize your ideas into paragraphs:
   - **What is the relationship between food and good health?** What lessons should parents teach their children about eating well and maintaining a healthy weight?
   - **What kinds of foods keep us healthy?** What health benefits do these foods offer? How often should we eat them?
   - **What foods should we avoid?** What are the bad effects of these foods? What advice can you give to parents and children?

2. **WRITE A FIRST DRAFT** Before you write your first draft, read the checklist below and look at the examples of how writers discuss certain foods on pages 256–257 and 274. Write your draft using indefinite and definite articles.

3. **EDIT** Read your work and check it against the checklist below. Circle grammar, spelling, and punctuation errors.

DO I ...	YES
use indefinite articles (*a/an, some/any*) for nonspecific nouns?	☐
use no article (Ø) for nonspecific plural count nouns and noncount nouns?	☐
use the definite article *the* with specific nouns?	☐
use plural count nouns and noncount nouns without articles to make generic statements?	☐

4. **PEER REVIEW** Work with a partner to help you decide how to fix your errors and improve the content. Use the checklist above.

5. **REWRITE YOUR DRAFT** Using the comments from your partner, write a final draft.

FAMILY FOOD FACTS We Are What We Eat

Providing our children with nutritious meals is one of the greatest responsibilities of parenthood. It's also one of the greatest gifts we can give our families...

13

Relative Clauses with Subject Relative Pronouns

Office Outfits That Work

A1 Before You Read

Discuss these questions.

What kind of clothes do you think professional people and their staffs should wear to work: more formal or less formal? Do you think clothing affects job performance?

A2 Read

 CD2 T22 Read this newspaper article to find out what advice an employment expert gives to a male college student and a female executive.

OFFICE OUTFITS THAT WORK
Advice for Dressing Successfully in the Workplace

Q: *I'm a male college student who is starting to job hunt. What advice can you give me about clothes that are suitable for interviews? I'm hoping to*
5 *talk to a number of major software companies, which supposedly have "business casual" dress codes. Does that mean I don't have to wear a suit?*
　　A: Let's start with your second
10 question. "Business casual" means different things at different companies. Generally speaking, it *doesn't* mean dressing in formal business wear, which for men means suits and ties.
15 What it *does* mean is dressing in a relaxed, yet neat and professional-looking style. At some companies this might include cotton pants and knit shirts with collars, while other
20 companies might even allow jeans and T-shirts.
　　But does that mean you should leave your suit and tie in the closet on the day of a big interview? Most
25 managers would say, "Well, it *may* be OK, but it's not worth the risk." Interviewers are more likely to be impressed by job candidates who dress in a neat, professional way. If you're a
30 male college grad who wants to make the best possible impression, you can't go wrong with a classic business suit.

Ideally, you should look for a suit that looks good and feels good. This will help you project the image of a person who is confident and capable. Suit colors like navy blue or gray are always a good choice. Then you can complete the look with a matching tie, a well-ironed, long-sleeved white shirt, and well-shined shoes.

Q: *I'm a fashion-conscious female executive who doesn't have a lot of time to worry about her wardrobe. Can you recommend any books or websites for women like me?*

A: I'm glad you asked! There are several sites for female executives who want to show their stylish side. One of my favorites is a blog called "execu-chic," which is written by a top-level woman consultant. For example, this week's entry recommends classic but trendy low-heeled shoes for the busy female executive who is on her feet all day.

Our column next week will feature advice on pants suits and skirt suits, so I'm sure you'll find it useful.

---

capable: having the right skills and abilities
confident: sure of oneself and one's abilities
executive: top-level manager

fashion-conscious: interested in wearing stylish clothes
supposedly: according to what people say
wardrobe: all of a person's clothing

A3 After You Read

Write *T* for true or *F* for false for each statement. Then change the false statements to true ones.

____F____ **1.** The person who sent in the first question is a college graduate.

The person who wrote the first question is still in college.

_____ **2.** Companies do not always agree on the meaning of "business casual."

_____ **3.** The writer of the column thinks the man should definitely wear a suit to his interviews.

_____ **4.** The woman who submitted the second question is not interested in dressing fashionably.

_____ **5.** The writer of the column also writes a blog called "execu-chic."

_____ **6.** The writer's next column will probably appeal to the woman who submitted the second question.

B FORM

Relative Clauses with Subject Relative Pronouns

Think Critically About Form

A. Look back at the article on page 280 and complete the tasks below.

1. **IDENTIFY** Three examples of relative clauses are underlined. Find nine more examples.

2. **RECOGNIZE** Circle the subject relative pronoun (*who, which,* or *that*) in each relative clause. Circle the noun or noun phrase it refers to.

3. **LABEL** Nonrestrictive relative clauses are set off from the nouns they modify by commas. There are three in the text (including one of the examples). Find them, and label them *NR*.

B. Discuss your answers with the class and read the Form charts to check them.

▶ Restrictive Relative Clauses

ONLINE
PRACTICE

RELATIVE CLAUSES AFTER THE MAIN CLAUSE				
MAIN CLAUSE		RELATIVE CLAUSE		
	NOUN	SUBJECT RELATIVE PRONOUN	VERB	
I know	a woman	**who** **that**	**works**	**at Jones & Roe**.
They have	rules	**which** **that**	**require**	**business suits**.

RELATIVE CLAUSES INSIDE THE MAIN CLAUSE				
MAIN CLAUSE				
RELATIVE CLAUSE				
NOUN	SUBJECT RELATIVE PRONOUN	VERB		
A woman	**who** **that**	**works**	**there**	won't wear a suit.
The rules	**which** **that**	**require**	**suits**	are strictly enforced.

▶ Nonrestrictive Relative Clauses

RELATIVE CLAUSES AFTER THE MAIN CLAUSE				
MAIN CLAUSE		RELATIVE CLAUSE		
	NOUN	SUBJECT RELATIVE PRONOUN	VERB	
I know	Sue Dunn,	**who**	**works**	**at Jones & Roe**.
No one likes	the rules,	**which**	**are**	**strictly enforced**.

RELATIVE CLAUSES INSIDE THE MAIN CLAUSE				
MAIN CLAUSE				
	RELATIVE CLAUSE			
NOUN	SUBJECT RELATIVE PRONOUN	VERB		
Sue Dunn,	**who**	**works**	**at Jones & Roe**,	won't wear a suit.
The rules,	**which**	**are**	**strictly enforced**,	require business suits.

Restrictive and Nonrestrictive Relative Clauses

- Relative clauses (also called adjective clauses) modify nouns (or noun phrases). There are two types of relative clauses: restrictive and nonrestrictive.
- Restrictive relative clauses distinguish one noun from another.

  I know <u>the woman</u> **who works at Jones & Roe**. I don't know <u>the woman</u> **who works at Transco**.

- Nonrestrictive relative clauses give extra information about a noun and are separated from that noun by commas. (In speech, a pause signals the commas.)

  <u>Sue Dunn</u>, **who works at Jones & Roe**, won't wear a suit.

- As with all clauses, relative clauses have a subject and verb. They are dependent clauses. They cannot stand alone as complete sentences. They must be attached to a main clause.
- A relative clause can occur anywhere in a sentence but it must follow the noun it refers to.

  I know <u>a woman</u> **who works at Jones & Roe**.

  <u>A woman</u> **who works at Jones & Roe** won't wear a suit.

Subject Relative Pronouns

- When *who*, *which*, or *that* is the subject of a relative clause, it is a subject relative pronoun.

(Continued on page 284)

- In restrictive clauses, *who* and *that* are used for people. *Which* and *that* are used for things and animals.
- In nonrestrictive clauses, *who* is used for people and *which* is used for things.
- A subject relative pronoun is followed by a verb. The verb agrees with the noun that the subject relative pronoun refers to.

   I know <u>a man</u> **who** <u>works</u> at Jones & Roe.

   I know two <u>men</u> **who** <u>work</u> at Jones & Roe.

- A subject relative pronoun always has the same form, whether or not it refers to a singular noun (a man) or a plural noun (men).
- Sentences with subject relative pronouns can be thought of as a combination of two sentences.

   I know a woman. <u>She</u> works there. = I know a woman **who** works there.

- Do not repeat the noun or pronoun in the relative clause.

   x I know a woman who she works there. (INCORRECT)

B1 Listening for Form

CD2 T23 **Listen to these comments about dress codes. Choose the main clause or relative clause that you hear. (Not every sentence contains a relative clause.)**

1. **(a.)** clothes that express my individuality

   b. clothes express my individuality

2. **a.** the dress code, which is very casual

   b. the dress code is very casual

3. **a.** Ms. Chang, who is the manager

   b. Ms. Chang is the manager

4. **a.** the dress code is still very conservative

   b. the dress code that is still very conservative

5. **a.** Barker Bank has a strict dress code

   b. Barker Bank, which has a strict dress code

6. **a.** clothes were more formal

   b. clothes that were more formal

7. **a.** the men, who don't have to wear ties anymore

   b. the men don't have to wear ties anymore

8. **a.** my boss dresses very casually

   b. my boss, who dresses very casually

B2 Identifying Relative Clauses

Work with a partner. Find the relative clauses in the conversation. Underline them and circle the noun phrases that they modify. Then practice the conversation.

Paul: What should I wear to my job interview, Dad?

Dad: How about your gray suit and the shirt that matches it?

Paul: Do you mean my new blue shirt, which is at the cleaners?

Dad: Oh. Well, what about the shirts that are hanging here on the door?

Paul: Hmm . . . should I wear the white one or the one that has pinstripes?

Dad: Wear the one that feels more comfortable. What time is the interview?

Paul: The boss's secretary, who called to confirm yesterday, said 10:15, although the manager who originally contacted me said 10:30. I'd better be there at 10:15.

Dad: By the way, was the Department of Labor booklet helpful?

Paul: Yes, especially part 3, which had a lot of practical advice.

Dad: Is the position that's open a new one?

Paul: No. I know the person who has it now. She's leaving to work at the Boston branch, which opens after the first of the year.

B3 Building Sentences with Subject Relative Pronouns

Build as many meaningful sentences as possible. Use an item from each column. Punctuate your sentences correctly.

We like the man that works in the bakery.

we like	the man Gary, the new phone cards, cars	that who which	works in the bakery are affordable

We like the man who works in the bakery
We like Gary who works in the bakery
We like the new phone cards which are affordable
We like the cars which are affordable.

B4 Working on Placement of Relative Clauses

A. Rewrite these sentences about dress codes, inserting the restrictive relative clause in parentheses after the appropriate noun.

1. Dress codes can make employees unhappy. (that are too strict)

Dress codes that are too strict can make employees unhappy.

2. Some employers won't hire applicants. (who dress too casually)

Some employers won't hire applicants who dress too casually.

3. Employees believe that clothing is a form of free expression. (who oppose dress codes) Employees believe that clothing is a form

4. Some companies restrict clothing. (that has sports logos on it)

5. A company dress code may not allow women to wear skirts. (that are very short)

B. Rewrite these sentences, inserting the nonrestrictive relative clause in parentheses after the appropriate noun. Remember to add commas.

1. This T-shirt is inappropriate for work. (which has slogans on it)

This T-shirt, which has slogans on it, is inappropriate for work.

2. What do you think about rule number 3? (which restricts very tight clothing) What do you think about rule number 3, which restricts very tight clothing?

3. My nephew Dan often wears very unusual clothing. (who works for a high-tech company) My nephew Dan, who works for a high-tech company, often wears very unusual clothing.

4. My boss is trying to enforce a new dress code. (who has been here only for a year) My boss, who has been here only a year, is trying to enforce a new dress code.

5. Casual dress has become the new standard in many companies. (which is hard to define) Casual dress, which is hard to define, has become the new standard in many companies.

B5 Working on Verb Agreement in Relative Clauses

Work with a partner. Complete each sentence with an appropriate subject relative pronoun and the correct form of the verb in parentheses. (Some items will have two possible answers.) Then practice the conversations with a partner.

1. **A:** Who is the person _____ who sits _____ (sit) next to you in English class?
    ₁

   B: I don't know her name, but she's also in our chemistry class. She's the woman

   _____ who asks _____ (ask) a lot of questions.
    ₂

2. **A:** My notebook, _____ which was _____ (be) on the table before, is missing.
    ₁

   B: There's one over there _____ which looks _____ (look) like your notebook.
    ₂

3. **A:** Sami, ___*who lives*___ (live) across the street, plays with my son. Do you

   know his family?

   B: No. I thought that the people ___*who own*___ (own) that house didn't have

   any children.

4. **A:** I need to see a doctor ___*who treats*___ (treat) skin problems. Do you

   know any?

   B: Yes. Dr. Wu, ___*who has*___ (have) an office near here, is a dermatologist.

5. **A:** Koji and Susan, ___*who finished*___ (finish) the project yesterday, can leave

   early today. Everyone else must stay in class until they finish.

   B: But what about the people ___*who were*___ (be) not in class yesterday?

6. **A:** AC Express, ___*which has*___ (have) an office downtown, can probably ship

   that package overseas. You should call them.

   B: OK. I will. But first I need to finish packing the items ___*which are*___ (be)

   on this list.

B6 Combining Sentences with *Who, That,* or *Which*

Combine each pair of sentences to make a restrictive relative clause using *who, that,* or *which*. There are two possible answers for each item.

1. I picked up the package. It was lying on the front step.

   I picked up the package that/which was lying on the front step.

2. The professor emailed me. He teaches Russian.
   The professor who teaches Russian emailed me.
3. My sister has a cat. It has three kittens.
   My sister has a cat which has there kittens.
4. Did you buy the socks? They were on sale.
   Did you buy the socks that were on sale?
5. The little girl was crying. She hurt her knee.
   The little girl who hurt her knee was crying.
6. They gave us an exam. It lasted an hour.
   They gave us an exam which lasted an hour.
7. I spoke to two women. They saw the accident.
   I spoke to two women who saw the accident.
8. The child went home. He was sick.
   The child who was sick went home.

Identifying Nouns with Restrictive Relative Clauses

 Think Critically About Meaning and Use

A. Read the sentences and answer the questions below.

1a. <u>A man</u> wore a tuxedo today.
1b. <u>A man</u> who works with me wore a tuxedo today.
2a. A dress code is a <u>set of rules</u>.
2b. A dress code is a <u>set of rules</u> that describes the appropriate kind of clothing for work.

1. **ANALYZE** Compare 1a and 1b. Which sentence gives information that identifies the underlined noun?

2. **ANALYZE** Which sentence is a more complete definition, 2a or 2b?

B. Discuss your answers with the class and read the Meaning and Use Notes to check them.

Meaning and Use Notes

ONLINE
PRACTICE

Identifying Nouns

▶ **1A** Restrictive relative clauses identify nouns. They distinguish one person or thing from other people or things. They answer the question *Which one(s)?* Restrictive relative clauses express necessary information. They cannot be omitted without affecting the meaning of the sentence.

With a Relative Clause

A: Are your children in that group over there?

B: Yes, <u>the girl</u> **that's wearing the red sweater** and <u>the boy</u> **who's wearing the gray sweatshirt** are mine.
(The relative clauses clearly identify B's children and distinguish them from the other children.)

Without a Relative Clause

A: Are your children in that group over there?

B: Yes, <u>the girl</u> and <u>the boy</u> are mine.
(B's children have not been clearly identified. The meaning is incomplete.)

▶ **1B**   Restrictive relative clauses are used in definitions.

A locksmith is <u>a person</u> **who makes and repairs locks and keys**.

A penguin is <u>a black and white bird</u> **which lives in the Antarctic**.

▶ **1C**   Restrictive relative clauses are often used to provide information about a noun when it is first mentioned. If the information is new to the listener, the relative clause quickly identifies the noun. If the information is shared with the listener, it reminds the listener of the noun.

New Information

Guess what? <u>A guy</u> **who works with me** bought a house on our street.

Shared Information

Look. There are <u>the dresses</u> **that are on sale**.

Reducing Restrictive Relative Clauses

▶ **2**   Subject relative pronouns + be are often omitted from restrictive relative clauses.

Full Form	**Reduced Form**
Take the food **that/which is on the table**.	Take the food **on the table**.
Look at the man **who/that is wearing a tuxedo**.	Look at the man **wearing a tuxedo**.

C1 Listening for Meaning and Use

▶ Notes 1A, 1C

CD2 T24   **Listen to the questions. Choose the most appropriate answer.**

1. **a.** The woman who is near the window.

   b. The one which is near the window.

2. **a.** The rules are too strict.

   b. The rules that are too strict.

3. **a.** The one that's over there.

   b. The one who's over there.

4. **a.** The man who called yesterday.

   b. The man called yesterday.

5. **a.** The man is working downstairs.

   b. The man who is working downstairs.

6. **a.** The guy who fixes up old cars.

   b. The guy fixes up old cars.

7. **a.** The ones that got wet.

   b. The ones who got wet.

8. **a.** A suit is worn on formal occasions.

   b. A suit that is worn on formal occasions.

C2 Identifying Nouns

▶ Notes 1A, 1C

Work with a partner. In each picture one object belongs to you. Describe it using a restrictive relative clause.

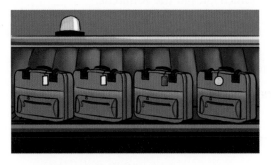

1. You're at the airport, and you're looking for your luggage. There are four suitcases that look like yours.

   My suitcase is the one that has a round luggage tag.

4. You hung up your raincoat on the coat rack at the restaurant. So did two other people.

2. It's dark, and you can't find your car in the parking lot. There are some cars in a row that look like yours.

5. All the students left their backpacks outside the language lab. Several students have backpacks just like yours.

3. You took off your snow boots when you entered the doctor's office. As you're leaving, you notice that there are three other pairs of boots similar to yours.

6. You've lost your keys in a department store. When you go to the lost and found, the clerk shows you three sets of keys.

C3 Identifying and Defining with Subject Relative Pronouns

▶ Notes 1A–1C

Work with a partner. Read each passage and use the information to answer each question with a sentence containing a relative clause.

1. Georgia O'Keeffe was a twentieth-century American artist. She painted well into her eighties. She is famous for painting flowers. The flowers were colorful.

   a. Who was Georgia O'Keeffe?

      Georgia O'Keeffe was a twentieth-century American artist who painted well into her eighties.

   b. What is she famous for?

2. Cancer is a serious condition. It causes tumors to grow in the body. Radiation is a cancer treatment. It can shrink tumors and prevent them from spreading.

   a. What is cancer? *Cancer is a serious condition which can cause tumors to grow in the body.*

   b. What is radiation?

      Radiation is a cancer treatment which can shrink tumors and prevent them from spreading

3. Martin Luther King, Jr., was an African American. He led the civil rights movement in the 1960s. He fought for equal rights through passive resistance. This nonviolent method of protest was previously used by Mahatma Gandhi in the 1940s.

   a. Who was Martin Luther King, Jr.?

   b. What is passive resistance?

4. Phobias are exaggerated fears. These fears can prevent a person from leading a normal life. Some people suffer from agoraphobia. They have a fear of being in open places. Others suffer from claustrophobia. They have a fear of being in closed places.

   a. What is a phobia?

   b. Which people suffer from agoraphobia? Which suffer from claustrophobia?

C4 Defining Words with Relative Clauses

▶ Note 1B

Work with a partner. Describe these different types of doctors by writing sentences with relative clauses. If necessary, use a dictionary.

1. A dermatologist is a doctor who treats skin problems.

2. A neurologist *is a doctor who treats mental disease.*

3. A pediatrician *is a doctor who takes care of baby babies*

4. A dentist *is a doctor who treats teeth problems.*

5. A cardiologist *is a doctor who treats heart problems*

6. A podiatrist *is a doctor who treats feet problems.*

Work with a partner. Look at each picture and answer the question using full and reduced relative clauses. Make up as many answers as possible for each item.

1. Which pair of shoes did you buy?

The shoes that were made in Italy.
The shoes made in Italy.

4. Which man is your father?

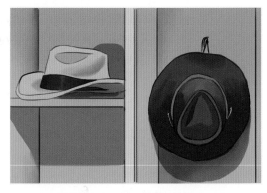

2. Which one is your son?

5. Which hat are you going to wear?

3. Which woman is the office manager?

6. Which iced tea mix do you prefer?

Beyond the Sentence

Combining Sentences with Relative Clauses

A paragraph with many short sentences may seem disconnected and hard to understand. You can use a relative clause to combine sentences that refer to the same noun or noun phrase. Relative clauses help avoid repetition and make the information flow more smoothly.

A Paragraph Without Relative Clauses

This story is about a young woman. She graduated from college with an engineering degree. After college, she worked for a small Internet company. The company sold books. Her friends, on the other hand, worked for well-known companies. These companies paid high salaries. She was frustrated and thought about quitting her job, but she didn't. That decision paid off. That small Internet company was one of the first "dot-coms." It became popular worldwide. Today, she is worth millions of dollars.

A Paragraph with Relative Clauses

This story is about a young woman **who graduated from college with an engineering degree**. After college, she worked for a small Internet company **that sold books**. Her friends, on the other hand, worked for well-known companies **that paid high salaries**. She was frustrated and thought about quitting her job, but she didn't. That decision paid off. That small Internet company was one of the first "dot-coms" **that became popular worldwide**. Today, she is worth millions of dollars.

C6 Connecting Ideas with Relative Clauses

A. Rewrite the following paragraph using relative clauses to make the information flow more smoothly. Make any changes that you think will improve the paragraph.

School dress codes are becoming popular again, although this doesn't necessarily mean that students have to wear uniforms. A school dress code is a set of rules. The rules restrict certain types of clothing. Some dress codes prohibit certain T-shirts. The T-shirts have offensive writing or pictures on them. Other dress codes prohibit certain types of pants or shirts. They prohibit very baggy pants, very tight pants, and very tight shirts. Many others prohibit certain types of skirts and dresses, too. The skirts and dresses are several inches above the knee. Some dress codes go even further. They don't allow sports clothing. This clothing has logos on it.

B. In small groups, compare your rewritten paragraphs. Discuss any differences between your paragraphs. Decide which changes you prefer and why. Combine your paragraphs into one version that you all agree on.

Adding Extra Information with Nonrestrictive Relative Clauses

Think Critically About Meaning and Use

A. Read the sentences and answer the questions below.

a. <u>My brother who lives in Maine loves to fish.</u> My other brother loves to ski.
b. <u>My brother, who lives in Maine, loves to fish.</u> He takes us fishing when we visit.

1. **ANALYZE** Which relative clause gives necessary information that identifies my brother? Which relative clause adds information that is not essential?

2. **ANALYZE** Which underlined sentence implies that the speaker has only one brother?

B. Discuss your answers with the class and read the Meaning and Use Notes to check them.

Meaning and Use Notes

ONLINE
PRACTICE

Adding Extra Information About Nouns

▶ **1A** A nonrestrictive relative clause adds extra information about a noun, but it is not needed to identify the noun. This information is often new to the listener, but it isn't essential; it can be omitted without affecting the meaning of the sentence.

Without a Relative Clause

My son Scott always wears a baseball cap. My son Greg doesn't.

With a Relative Clause

<u>My son Scott</u>, **who is 11**, always wears a baseball cap. <u>My son Greg</u>, **who is 13**, doesn't.
    (The relative clauses give extra information about Scott and Greg but do not change the meaning of the sentences.)

▶ **1B** Nonrestrictive relative clauses can add extra information about proper nouns and other unique nouns. They can also add information about a definite noun that has already been identified.

Proper Noun

<u>Boston</u>, **which is in Massachusetts,** has many colleges and universities.

Noun Already Identified

<u>My antique desk</u> was damaged by the flood. <u>The desk</u>, **which is worth a lot of money**, can probably be repaired.

Unique Noun

My sister, **who is 17**, is in high school.

Contrasting Restrictive and Nonrestrictive Relative Clauses

▶ **2**   Restrictive relative clauses provide essential information in order to distinguish one noun from other similar nouns. Nonrestrictive relative clauses are used when there is only one particular noun or set of nouns. They do not distinguish nouns or provide essential information.

Restrictive Relative Clause

My brother **who lives in Baltimore** calls me every weekend.
(The relative clause distinguishes my brother from a brother who lives elsewhere. It implies that the speaker has more than one brother.)

Nonrestrictive Relative Clause

My brother, **who lives in Baltimore,** calls me every weekend.
(The relative clause is not used to distinguish my brother from anyone else. It implies that the speaker has only one brother.)

Reducing Nonrestrictive Relative Clauses

▶ **3**   Subject relative pronouns + *be* are often omitted from nonrestrictive relative clauses.

Full Form

I spoke to Pedro, **who is the boss**.

Reduced Form

I spoke to Pedro, **the boss**.

D1 Listening for Meaning and Use

▶ Notes 1A, 1B, 2

CD2 T25   **Listen to these situations. Choose the sentence that you hear.**

1. **a.** My sister, who lives in New York, has two children.

    b. My sister who lives in New York has two children.

2. **a.** Have you met her brother, who works at the bank?

    b. Have you met her brother who works at the bank?

3. **a.** Give me the sheet of paper, which has the list of names.

    b. Give me the sheet of paper which has the list of names.

4. **a.** The man, who is talking, is my boss.

    b. The man who is talking is my boss.

5. **a.** She showed me her necklace which had beautiful stones.

    b. She showed me her necklace, which had beautiful stones.

6. **a.** Her grandmother, who lived until 80, was a teacher.

    b. Her grandmother who lived until 80 was a teacher.

D2 Adding Extra Information

▶ Notes 1A, 1B

A. Complete each main clause with a proper noun or other unique noun. Then add more information with a nonrestrictive relative clause at the end of the sentence.

1. I come from _____Queens_____, which _is in New York City._____

2. I once visited ___Los Angles___, which _is in California_____

_____

3. I've never met ___Obama___, who _is the president of America._

_____

4. I'd like to meet ___Jay Chou___, who _is my favorite singer___

_____

B. Complete these sentences by first adding a nonrestrictive relative clause, and then completing the main clause.

1. My next vacation, _which will be in March, is for one week._____

2. My best friend, _who has known me for 18 years, is a nice girl.___

3. My birthday, _which is _____

4. My home, _____

D3 Choosing Restrictive or Nonrestrictive Relative Clauses

▶ Note 2

Work with a partner. Read each situation and related statement. Decide whether the relative clause in each statement is restrictive or nonrestrictive. If the clause is nonrestrictive, add commas to the sentence.

1. Situation: My parents moved to Toronto a few years ago. They used to live in Montreal.

Statement: My parents, who used to live in Montreal, moved to Toronto a few years ago. nonrestrictive

2. Situation: I have two aunts on my mother's side. One of them lives in Rio. The other one lives in São Paulo. One of them invited me to her son's wedding.

Statement: My aunt who lives in Rio invited me to her son's wedding. restrictive

3. Situation: We live in Panama City. It's very warm and humid here.

Statement: We live in Panama City, which is very warm and humid. nonrestrictive

4. **Situation:** My father lives next to a golf course. He loves to play golf.

   Statement: My father, who loves to play golf, lives next to a golf course. *nonrestrictive*

5. **Situation:** My dentist has several dental hygienists. The same one always cleans my teeth. A different one cleans my son's teeth.

   Statement: The dental hygienist who cleans my teeth doesn't clean my son's teeth. *restrictive*

6. **Situation:** One of my sons is in the second grade, one is in the fourth grade, and one is a sophomore in high school.

   Statement: My son who is in the second grade loves math. *restrictive*

7. **Situation:** You've invited your friends Jane and Tina to dinner. Jane and Tina work at the same company. You tell this to Tina.

   Statement: I've invited my friend Jane, who works in the legal division at *nonrestrictive* your company.

8. **Situation:** A newspaper article describes pollution.

   Statement: Pollution, which is still a major problem, was an issue in the last election. *nonrestrictive*

D4 Describing People

 Write two sentences about each person. In the first sentence, identify the person with a restrictive relative clause. In the second sentence, provide further information using a nonrestrictive relative clause. Be ready to tell the class about one of these people.

1. an aunt

   My aunt that lives in San Francisco loves antiques.
   Her daughter, who was just married, has a lot of antiques, too.

2. an uncle

3. a friend

4. a teacher

5. a neighbor

6. a classmate

WRITING Write a "For and Against" Essay

 Think Critically About Meaning and Use

A. Read each sentence and the statements that follow. Write *T* if the statement is true or *F* if it is false.

1. The woman who works for my mother bought a new car.

   _T_   **a.** A woman works for my mother.

   _____   **b.** My mother bought a new car.

2. My brother, who just called my father, lives in Dallas.

   _____   **a.** My brother lives in Dallas.

   _____   **b.** My father called my brother.

3. The man who looked at my car was very old.

   _____   **a.** My car was very old.

   _____   **b.** A man looked at my car.

4. An explosion, which injured 20 people, occurred at about 11:00 last night.

   _____   **a.** An explosion injured 20 people.

   _____   **b.** An explosion occurred at about 11:00.

5. I spoke to my brother, who is very worried about something.

   _____   **a.** I have a brother.

   _____   **b.** I am very worried about something.

6. My son who talked to Mary looks like John.

   _____   **a.** I have more than one son.

   _____   **b.** Mary looks like John.

7. The milk, which is still on the first shelf, is spoiled.

   _____   **a.** The milk is spoiled.

   _____   **b.** There's probably milk on another shelf, too.

8. I took the umbrella, which was in the car.

   _____   **a.** There was only one umbrella.

   _____   **b.** The umbrella was in the car.

B. Discuss these questions in small groups.

1. **EVALUATE** Look at sentence 1. What can we conclude about the number of women on the mother's staff? How does the meaning differ if the sentence had read, "A woman who works for my mother…"

2. **PREDICT** Look at sentence 8. If we change the sentence to read, "I took the umbrella that was in the car," how does it affect your answers to statements a and b?

Edit

Find the errors in these paragraphs and correct them. There may be more than one way to correct an error.

What kind of clothing should people ~~which~~ *who* are going on a job interview wear? Is it ever acceptable to wear jeans to an interview? Should job candidates wear something, that is sporty and comfortable? Or should they wear something what is more professional-looking? These are some of the questions concern many high school and college students which has never been on a job interview before.

Most people agree about the type of clothing is appropriate for interviews nowadays. Many employment websites advise that job applicants should try to dress in clothing is appropriate for a particular job. For example, a man who applying for an entry-level food service or factory job doesn't need to appear for an interview in a three-piece business suit and an expensive silk tie. He should wear sensible, clean, and well-pressed clothing that show a readiness to roll one's sleeves up and get the job done. Someone is applying for a managerial position will obviously need to dress more professionally to make a good first impression. Remember, too, that personal cleanliness is something who can impress an interviewer as much as your clothes. Candidates that shows up for an interview with bad breath or messy hair or fingernails are dirty are not going to make a good impression.

Write

Some people think primary and secondary students in your country should wear school uniforms, while others are strongly against it. Write a "for and against" essay presenting both sides of the issue. Use relative clauses with subject relative pronouns.

1. **BRAINSTORM** Think of all the arguments for and against students wearing school uniforms. Then use these categories to help you organize your ideas into paragraphs.
   - **Introduction:** What is the current situation? Do students wear uniforms? Can they wear what they like? Are there other rules about clothing?
   - **Arguments for:** What are the 2–3 main arguments for wearing school uniforms?
   - **Arguments against:** What are the 2–3 main arguments against wearing uniforms?
   - **Conclusion:** After considering both sides, which side do you support?

2. **WRITE A FIRST DRAFT** Before you write your first draft, read the checklist below and look at the sentences you wrote in C6 on page 293. Write your draft using relative clauses.

3. **EDIT** Read your work and check it against the checklist below. Circle grammar, spelling, and punctuation errors.

DO I ...	YES
organize my ideas into paragraphs?	☐
use relative clauses to connect ideas and combine sentences?	☐
use correct subject relative pronouns and verb forms that agree with the nouns that are modified?	☐
use commas, as needed, to set off nonrestrictive relative clauses?	☐

4. **PEER REVIEW** Work with a partner to help you decide how to fix your errors and improve the content. Use the checklist above.

5. **REWRITE YOUR DRAFT** Using the comments from your partner, write a final draft.

> *I come from a country that has a long tradition of students wearing school uniforms, but now some people are questioning the tradition. On one hand, there are people who want to see the tradition continue. On the other hand, there are people who believe that...*

CHAPTER

14

Relative Clauses with Object Relative Pronouns

The New Face of a Role Model

A1 Before You Read

Discuss these questions.

A role model is a person who is an example for other people to follow. What are some qualities of a role model?

A2 Read

 CD2 T26 Read this magazine article about soccer star Mia Hamm to find out what she thinks about being a role model.

THE NEW FACE OF A ROLE MODEL

In women's soccer, girls finally get the role model they deserve: Mia Hamm

The Women's World Cup, which the media called the biggest female sporting event in history, arrived for the first time in the United States in 1999. Three television
5 networks televised all 32 games, with an estimated one billion viewers. One of the stars was Mia Hamm, who many people call the Michael Jordan of women's soccer.

Though her ballerina mom tried to
10 interest her in dance, it was her father's soccer passion that she followed. Hamm led the University of North Carolina to four championships in the early nineties, won Olympic gold in 1996, won the U.S.
15 Soccer Player of the Year award many times, and broke the international goal-scoring record for males and females.

None of this would have been possible without a law called Title IX, which the
20 U.S. government passed in 1972. This law requires equal funding for girls' school sports. Until 1972, the only role models that female athletes had were female skaters, female gymnasts, and male
25 athletes. Now, more than seven million girls play soccer, and they all want to be like Mia.

Hamm retired from professional soccer in 2004, but she continues to
30 inspire. She has created the Mia Hamm Foundation, which she has dedicated to two causes that are very important to her: encouraging young female athletes and research on bone marrow diseases.
35 (Her brother Garrett died from aplastic anemia.)

Hamm juggles her personal relationships with her busy career. Here are some things that she says about life as

40 sport's newest kind of role model:

Q: Girls today have a wider variety of role models than ever before and you're one of them. What's it like to be a role model?

A: I take it very seriously. I didn't have
45 the role models these girls have. Most of my athletic role models were men.

Q: Will playing team sports help girls as they grow up? How has it helped you?

A: Sports can do so much. It's given me a
50 framework: meeting new people,

confidence, self-esteem, time management, discipline, motivation. I learned all these things, whether I knew I was learning them or not, through sports.

55 **Q:** What's the most important thing your mother taught you?

A: Everyone has goodness. It's just a matter of how it's nurtured. Hopefully, I can do the same thing, nurture my children
60 to grow up with love in their hearts for everyone...

anemia: a disease of the blood
bone marrow: the soft tissue in the center of the bone
foundation: an organization that gives out money for special purposes (e.g., research)

juggle: to do many things at once
the media: television, radio, and newspapers
nurture: to encourage to develop

A3 After You Read

Choose the answer that best completes each sentence.

1. The Women's World Cup _____.

   a. began in the United States

   b. became well known through television

   c. started in 1999

2. Mia Hamm developed her love for soccer because of _____.

   a. her mother

   b. her father

   c. her brother

3. Mia Hamm has won _____ only once.

   a. an Olympic gold medal

   b. a college championship

   c. the Soccer Player of the Year award

4. Hamm broke the international goal-scoring record for _____.

   a. women

   b. men

   c. men and women

5. Title IX is a law that requires equal _____ for girls' and boys' sports.

   a. athletes

   b. stadiums

   c. money

6. Mia Hamm grew up without _____.

   a. an opportunity to dance

   b. a female role model

   c. a busy career

B FORM 1

Relative Clauses with Object Relative Pronouns

Think Critically About Form

A. Look back at the article on page 302 and complete the tasks below.

1. **IDENTIFY** Look at the underlined relative clauses. Circle the object relative pronoun in each clause (*who*, *which*, or *that*) and the noun or noun phrase it modifies.

2. **EVALUATE** Look at the circled relative clauses. These clauses do not have object relative pronouns. Which object relative pronoun is omitted from each clause?

B. Discuss your answers with the class and read the Form charts to check them.

▶ Restrictive Relative Clauses

ONLINE
PRACTICE

RELATIVE CLAUSES AFTER THE MAIN CLAUSE				
MAIN CLAUSE		RELATIVE CLAUSE		
	NOUN	**OBJECT RELATIVE PRONOUN**	**SUBJECT**	**VERB (PHRASE)**
Mia Hamm is	an athlete	**who/whom that/Ø**	**I**	**admire.**
Mia didn't have	the opportunities	**which/that/Ø**	**girls**	**have now.**

RELATIVE CLAUSES INSIDE THE MAIN CLAUSE				
MAIN CLAUSE				
	RELATIVE CLAUSE			
NOUN	**OBJECT RELATIVE PRONOUN**	**SUBJECT**	**VERB (PHRASE)**	
An athlete	**who/whom that/Ø**	**I**	**admire a lot**	is Mia Hamm.
The game	**which/that/Ø**	**the girls**	**won**	was on TV.

▶ Nonrestrictive Relative Clauses

RELATIVE CLAUSES AFTER THE MAIN CLAUSE				
MAIN CLAUSE		RELATIVE CLAUSE		
	NOUN	**OBJECT RELATIVE PRONOUN**	**SUBJECT**	**VERB (PHRASE)**
I met	Mia Hamm,	**who/whom**	**I**	**admire a lot**.
Mia was at	the World Cup,	**which**	**we**	**saw on TV**.

RELATIVE CLAUSES INSIDE THE MAIN CLAUSE				
MAIN CLAUSE				
	RELATIVE CLAUSE			
NOUN	**OBJECT RELATIVE PRONOUN**	**SUBJECT**	**VERB (PHRASE)**	
Mia Hamm,	**who/whom**	**I**	**admire**,	is a soccer player.
The World Cup,	**which**	**we**	**saw on TV**,	was a big media event.

Restrictive and Nonrestrictive Relative Clauses
- Relative clauses (restrictive and nonrestrictive) modify nouns (or noun phrases). They have a subject and a verb and cannot stand alone as complete sentences.
- Relative clauses can be thought of as a combination of two sentences.

    Mia Hamm is an athlete. I admire <u>her</u>. = Mia Hamm is an athlete **who** I admire.

- Restrictive clauses distinguish one noun from another. Nonrestrictive relative clauses add extra information about a noun and are separated by commas.

Object Relative Pronouns
- When *who*, *whom*, *which*, or *that* is the object of a relative clause, it is an object relative pronoun.
- In restrictive clauses, *who*, *whom*, and *that* are used for people. *Which* and *that* are used for things and animals. In nonrestrictive clauses, *who* or *whom* is used for people and *which* is used for things.
- Object relative pronouns are followed by a subject + verb (phrase). The verb agrees with the subject before it. It does not agree with the noun that the clause refers to.

    Mia Hamm is an athlete **who I admire a lot**.

- Object relative pronouns can be omitted from restrictive relative clauses.

    A swimmer **who I know** won a medal. = A swimmer **Ø I know** won a medal.

(Continued on page 306)

- Object relative pronouns are never omitted from nonrestrictive relative clauses.

    x I met Mia Hamm, I admire a lot. (INCORRECT)

- Do not repeat the object noun or pronoun in the relative clause.

    x I met Mia Hamm, who I admire her. (INCORRECT)

B1 Listening for Form

CD2 T27   Listen to these sentences and choose the sentence you hear.

1. a. The team that we played didn't do very well.
   b. The team that played didn't do very well.

2. a. The equipment we broke is expensive to repair.
   b. The equipment which broke is expensive to repair.

3. a. Did you hear about the team that we beat?
   b. Did you hear about the team that beat us?

4. a. We didn't know about the rules that changed.
   b. We didn't know about the rules they changed.

5. a. I didn't meet the player they called.
   b. I didn't meet the player that called.

6. a. The man he called wanted to join the team.
   b. The man who called wanted to join the team.

B2 Examining Relative Clauses with Object Relative Pronouns

Read the paragraphs and look at the underlined relative clauses. Circle the noun or noun phrase that each clause modifies and write *S* over the subject of each relative clause.

Kay Valera used to be a "soccer mom." But now the 40-year-old mom has become a soccer player in a women's league <u>which she joined last spring</u>. One of the things <u>that she has learned</u> is how challenging it is to play a sport that requires players to think, kick, and run at the same time. As she plays, she recalls all the advice <u>that she has given her kids</u>. Everything that looked so easy from the sidelines is now so challenging.

Many kids come to the games to cheer on the moms. They can be very encouraging, but they also love to discuss the mistakes <u>that mom made</u> and the moves <u>that she should have made</u>. They might say, "Don't feel bad, you did your best, but you know that kick <u>that you tried in midfield</u>, well…"

Vocabulary Notes

Object Relative Pronouns

Who and *Whom* In restrictive and nonrestrictive relative clauses, *whom* expresses a much more formal tone than *who*. It is less common than other relative pronouns.

> *Formal Speech:* Let me introduce you to the person **whom I admire most**, my friend and colleague, Stanley Chen.

That and Ø In restrictive relative clauses, *that* is used more often than *who*, *whom*, and *which*. Omitting the object relative pronoun (Ø) is also very common in speech and writing.

> *News Broadcast:* The judge **(that) the president will appoint next week** is a woman.

B3 Using Object Relative Pronouns

Complete the sentences by circling all the words (and Ø) that can form correct sentences.

1. A man { that / who / which / Ø } we { know / knows } sells cars.

2. Marcus, { that / who / which / Ø } we saw on Tuesday, { doesn't / don't } work with us.

3. The bike { that / who / which / Ø } they bought { is / are } missing.

4. Ellen, { that / who / which / Ø } works with me, { is / are } always late for work.

5. The people { that / who / which / Ø } she { visit / visits } live nearby.

6. The teacher { that / who / which / Ø } I like { is / are } not here today.

B4 Combining Sentences Using Relative Clauses

 Work in small groups. Imagine that you are visiting your 45-year-old aunt, who is showing you family photos and souvenirs. Combine the sentences below to describe the underlined noun phrase. Use restrictive or nonrestrictive relative clauses with an object relative pronoun. Practice different alternatives.

1. Let's look at some things. I've been saving them for a long time.

    Let's look at some things that I've been saving for a long time. OR

    Let's look at some things which I've been saving for a long time. OR

    Let's look at some things I've been saving for a long time.

2. Here is a photo of your grandfather. I still miss him so much.

3. Our great grandfather Gus is in this picture. We loved him a lot.

4. The dress is in this box. I wore it to my wedding.

5. I'll never forget the guests. I invited them to my wedding.

6. I remember my high school teacher Miss Pullman. I liked her so much.

7. Here is a poem. I wrote it in her class.

8. This is an award. I received it for my poem.

B5 Asking and Answering Questions with Object Relative Pronouns

 Work with a partner. Take turns asking and answering *what* or *who* questions with restrictive relative clauses, using the words given. Practice different alternatives in your questions and answers.

1. a person/you call every day

    A: Who is a person (that/who) you call every day?

    B: My sister is a person (that/who) I call every day.

2. a game/you liked to play as a child

3. the relative/you look like most

4. the person/you call when you're in trouble

5. a food/you have never tasted

6. a teacher/you will always remember

7. a book/you like to read over and over again

8. a thing/you can't live without

Identifying Nouns and Adding Extra Information

Think Critically About Meaning and Use

A. Read the sentences and complete the tasks below.

1a. The coat that costs $200 is on sale now.
1b. The coat you wanted is on sale now.
2a. Megan Quann, who was only 16, was on the Olympic swimming team.
2b. Megan Quann, who I know, was on the Olympic swimming team.

1. IDENTIFY Underline the relative clause in each sentence. Circle the noun that each clause refers to.

2. EVALUATE In which pair of sentences do the relative clauses help identify the noun? In which pair do they add extra information about the noun?

B. Discuss your answers with the class and read the Meaning and Use Notes to check them.

Meaning and Use Notes

ONLINE PRACTICE

Identifying Nouns

▶ **1A** Restrictive relative clauses with object relative pronouns distinguish one person or thing from other similar people or things. They cannot be omitted without affecting the meaning of the sentence.

With a Relative Clause	**Without a Relative Clause**
Three women tried out. <u>The woman</u> **that I met** made the team. (The relative clause clearly identifies which woman made the team.)	Three women tried out. <u>The woman</u> made the team. (It is unclear which woman made the team. The meaning is incomplete.)

▶ **1B** Restrictive relative clauses are often used to provide information about a noun when it is first mentioned, or to remind the listener about previously mentioned information. The relative clause immediately identifies the noun to the listener.

First Mentioned (New Information)
<u>A man</u> Ø **I know** is a champion swimmer.

Previously Mentioned (Shared Information)
<u>The tennis racket</u> **that we saw yesterday** is now on sale.

(Continued on page 310)

Adding Extra Information

▶ **2A** Nonrestrictive relative clauses with object relative pronouns add extra information about a noun but aren't needed to identify it. They can be omitted without affecting the meaning of the sentence.

With a Relative Clause

The woman's decathlon world record, **which Austra Skujyte set in 2005**, had previously been set in 2004. (The relative clause gives extra information about the record.)

Without a Relative Clause

The woman's decathlon world record had previously been set in 2004. (Without the relative clause, the meaning of the sentence is still complete.)

▶ **2B** Especially at the end of a sentence, nonrestrictive relative clauses with object relative pronouns are a simple way to add extra information to a sentence without starting a new one.

Many young girls now play soccer, **which most high schools didn't offer when I was a student**.

C1 Listening for Meaning and Use ▶ Notes 1A, 1B, 2A, 2B

CD2 T28 Listen to the situations carefully. Then choose the sentence that would most appropriately follow each one.

1. **a.** Really? Do you know her?

   b. Really? How did you meet her?

2. **a.** Why did she quit the girls' team?

   b. What was the name of the girls' team?

3. **a.** She was lucky.

   b. That's too bad.

4. **a.** What sports did they play?

   b. Too bad you didn't know them.

5. **a.** That's not good!

   b. That's surprising!

6. **a.** Was that before the laws were changed?

   b. Why didn't they offer sports in your high school?

C2 Identifying Nouns

▶ Notes 1A, 1B

A. Add a restrictive relative clause with an object relative pronoun to complete the meaning of each sentence.

1. I once had a teacher _who I admired a great deal._

2. My neighbor is a person _who I spoke with yesterday_

3. I know a man _who my friend work with._

4. I'd like a job _which I reach my goal_

5. Someday I'm going to live in a house _which my father bought_

6. I have a friend _who I studied with in high school._

7. I shop in stores _which it has pecial price._

8. My father is someone _who I dream to be like_

B. Choose one of your sentences as the first sentence of a paragraph describing that person, place, or thing. First make a list of five or six characteristics or details that you will include. Then use your list to write a descriptive paragraph with at least two more relative clauses with object relative pronouns.

I once had a teacher who I admired a great deal. He was my role model. He taught history classes that everyone enjoyed…

C3 Adding Extra Information

▶ Notes 2A, 2B

A. Write five simple sentences about specific people, places, or objects related to sports.

1. My brother is the captain of our high school baseball team.

2. A popular women's sport is soccer.

B. Work with a partner. Exchange papers and add extra information to your partner's sentences. Use nonrestrictive relative clauses with object relative pronouns.

1. My brother, who is going to college next year, is the captain of our high school baseball team.

2. A popular women's sport is soccer, which most of the world calls football.

C4 Expressing Your Opinion

▶ Notes 1A, 1B,

Write two sentences that give your opinion about the nouns in parentheses. Begin one sentence with *I like* and the other sentence with *I don't like*. Use restrictive relative clauses with object or subject relative pronouns.

1. (cars) I like cars that go fast.

   I don't like cars (that) you have to fix all the time.

2. (teachers) I like teachers who teach interesting subject.

3. (clothes)

   I don't like clothes which these women wear.

4. (newspapers) I like newspapers which have entertainment news.

5. (friends)

   I don't like friends who tell others my secret.

6. (TV shows)

   I don't like TV shows which are too noisy.

7. (foods)

   I don't like foods which are tasted bad.

8. (music) I like music which my favorite singer sings.

9. (books) I like books which are written by Louis cha.

10. (cell phones)

   I don't like cell phones which are too big.

D FORM 2

Object Relative Pronouns with Prepositions

Think Critically About Form

A. Read the sentences and complete the tasks below.

    a. We saw the movie that everyone is talking about.
    b. We saw the movie about which everyone is talking.

  1. IDENTIFY The relative pronoun in each relative clause is the object of a preposition. Underline each object relative pronoun and circle each preposition.

  2. COMPARE AND CONTRAST Compare a and b. Where does the preposition occur in each relative clause? What other difference do you see?

B. Discuss your answers with the class and read the Form charts to check them.

▶ Relative Clauses Ending in Prepositions

ONLINE PRACTICE

RESTRICTIVE RELATIVE CLAUSES					
MAIN CLAUSE		RELATIVE CLAUSE			
	NOUN	OBJECT RELATIVE PRONOUN	SUBJECT	VERB	PREPOSITION
There's	the coach	who/whom that/Ø	I	spoke	to.
He coaches	the team	which/that/Ø	she	plays	on.

NONRESTRICTIVE RELATIVE CLAUSES					
MAIN CLAUSE		RELATIVE CLAUSE			
	NOUN	OBJECT RELATIVE PRONOUN	SUBJECT	VERB	PREPOSITION
There's	Coach Smith,	who/whom	I	spoke	to.
He coaches	the Liberty team,	which	she	plays	on.

(Continued on page 314)

Relative Clauses Ending in Prepositions

- An object relative pronoun (*who*, *whom*, *that*, or *which*) can be the object of a preposition.

  There's the coach. I spoke <u>to him</u>. = There's the coach **who** I spoke **to**.

- Relative clauses ending in prepositions are usually used in spoken English and less formal written English.

- In restrictive relative clauses that end in prepositions, the object relative pronoun can be omitted.

▶ Relative Clauses Beginning with Prepositions

RESTRICTIVE RELATIVE CLAUSES					
MAIN CLAUSE		RELATIVE CLAUSE			
	NOUN	PREPOSITION	OBJECT RELATIVE PRONOUN	SUBJECT	VERB
There's	<u>the coach</u>	**to**	**whom**	**I**	**spoke**.
He coaches	<u>the team</u>	**on**	**which**	**she**	**plays**.

NONRESTRICTIVE RELATIVE CLAUSES					
MAIN CLAUSE		RELATIVE CLAUSE			
	NOUN	PREPOSITION	OBJECT RELATIVE PRONOUN	SUBJECT	VERB
There's	<u>Coach Smith,</u>	**to**	**whom**	**I**	**spoke**.
He coaches	<u>the Liberty team,</u>	**on**	**which**	**she**	**plays**.

Relative Clauses Beginning with Prepositions

- In very formal English, a preposition can begin a relative clause. The preposition is followed by either *whom* for people or *which* for things. It cannot be followed by *who* or *that*.

- *Whom* and *which* are never omitted after prepositions.

D1 Listening for Form

 CD2 T29 **Listen and choose the sentences you hear.**

1. **a.** Do you know the woman
   he's married to?

   b. Do you know the woman
   to whom he's married?

2. **a.** The man he spoke to helped
   quite a bit.

   b. The man who he spoke to
   helped quite a bit.

3. **a.** Let's look at the book
   I brought in.

   b. Let's look at the book.
   I brought it in.

4. **a.** Did you meet the people
   he works with?

   b. Did you meet the people
   who we work with?

5. **a.** Did you see the doctor
   I was waiting for?

   b. Did you see the doctor?
   I was waiting for her.

D2 Building Relative Clauses Ending in Prepositions

Work in small groups. Add the information that follows each sentence, using a relative clause ending in a preposition.

1. A woman called me last night.
   (My sister works with her.)

   *A woman who my sister works with
   called me last night.* OR

   *A woman that my sister works with
   called me last night.* OR

   *A woman my sister works with
   called me last night.*

   (I always talk to her at the supermarket.)
   (I went to high school with her.)
   (I used to live next door to her.)

2. The movie was great.
   (We went to the movie last night.)
   (You told us about the movie.)
   (I didn't want to go to it.)
   (You reported on it in class.)

3. Do you know the doctor?
   (Young-soo lives across from her.)
   (Eva plays tennis with her.)
   (Luisa works for her.)
   (I was waiting for her.)

4. Have you read the book?
   (The whole class is interested in it.)
   (The teacher looked for it last week.)
   (Julie wrote about it.)
   (I brought in the book.)

5. Today we're going to read the story.
   (You've heard a lot about it.)
   (You listened to a recording of it.)
   (I was working on it.)
   (The lecturer talked about it.)

D3 Working on Relative Clauses Ending in Prepositions

 A. Work in small groups. Read these situations. Use restrictive relative clauses ending in prepositions to distinguish between the people or things.

1. Bill needs to ask one of his neighbors to water his plants while he's away. He works with one of them, but he doesn't work with the other one.

   He decides to ask the person _(who/that) he works with._

2. You know that your friend was born in one small town, but that she grew up in a different small town.

   You ask her the name of the town _____

3. Martha and Luisa are in a store looking for a new desk chair. Martha is sitting on one of them, and Luisa is sitting on another one.

   A salesman recommends the one _____

4. Anna has called her doctor's office twice this week. She spoke to one nurse on Tuesday and another nurse on Wednesday.

   Today she asked for the nurse _____

5. Two movies are playing nearby. Martin has heard about one of them, but he hasn't heard about the other one.

   He decides to see the movie _____

6. Your friend borrowed two CDs from the library. She listened to one of them last night, and she will listen to the other one tomorrow.

   She decided to return the one _____

7. Two players on the soccer team were carded for bad language. The coach talked to one right after the game, but didn't get a chance to talk to the other.

   Today he will talk to the player _____

8. I saw two new ads for teachers in the paper yesterday. I'm more interested in one, but I'm more qualified for the other.

   I think I'll apply for the one _____

B. Now rewrite items 1–4 from part A in very formal English. Use restrictive relative clauses beginning with prepositions.

   1. He decides to ask the person with whom he works.

Reducing Relative Clauses

Think Critically About Meaning and Use

A. Read the sentences and answer the question below.

    a. Give the names of two professors who you have taken courses with.

    b. Give the names of two professors with whom you have taken courses.

    c. Give the names of two professors you have taken courses with.

    ANALYZE Which sentence sounds the most formal?

B. Discuss your answers with the class and read the Meaning and Use Notes to check them.

Meaning and Use Notes

ONLINE
PRACTICE

	Reducing Relative Clauses

▶ 1A In both conversation and writing, object relative pronouns are often omitted from restrictive relative clauses. Remember, a preposition must follow the verb in a reduced relative clause. (It cannot go at the beginning of the clause).

Conversation

The meal **Ø we ate yesterday evening** was delicious. I'm going to write down the name of the restaurant **Ø we went to**. You should try it.

Newspaper Article

The suspect **Ø the police caught this morning** remains in custody.

▶ 1B When relative clauses with prepositions are <u>not</u> reduced, they sometimes sound very formal if the preposition precedes the relative pronoun.

Sounds Formal

Write the name and address of the hotel **in which you are staying**.

Doesn't Sound Formal

Write the name and address of the hotel **which you are staying in**.

(Continued on page 318)

Avoiding Repetition

▶ **2** Object relative pronouns are often omitted when many restrictive relative clauses are used in one context. When two restrictive relative clauses occur next to each other, the first object relative pronoun is often omitted. The second is not.

Interview Question

What is the most important thing ①Ø her mother taught her ②**that she can teach her children**?

Textbook

One issue ①Ø the study mentioned ②**that researchers need to consider further** is the effect of changing climate.

E1 Listening for Meaning and Use ▶ Notes 1A, 1B

 CD2 T30 Listen to each situation and check (✓) whether you think it has a formal or informal tone. Then listen again and think of an appropriate context for each situation.

	FORMAL	INFORMAL	CONTEXT
1.		✓	a conversation between two students
2.			
3.			
4.			
5.			
6.			

E2 Rephrasing Formal Relative Clauses ▶ Notes 1A, 1B

Work with a partner. Take turns changing the formal tone of each sentence to a conversational tone. Use relative clauses ending in prepositions.

Application for Travel Insurance

1. List the names of the family members with whom you will be traveling.

   List the names of the family members who/that/Ø you'll be traveling with.

2. List the city from which you will depart and the city to which you will return.

   List the city from which you will depart from and the city which you will return to.

3. List the name of the tour operator with whom you will be traveling.

List the name of the tour operator whom you will be traveling with.

4. List the hotel in which you will be staying.

List the hotel which you will be staying in.

5. List the code numbers of any extra tours for which you have registered.

List the code numbers of any extra tours which you have registered for.

Job Application

1. Name two colleagues with whom you have worked closely.

Name tow colleagues whom you have worked closely with.

2. Name one supervisor for whom you have worked.

Name one supervisor whom you have worked for.

3. List two different projects on which you have worked.

List two different projects which you have worked on.

4. Name two decisions in which you have played an important role.

Name two decisions which you have played an important role in.

5. Name the job for which you would like to apply.

Name the job which you would like to apply for.

E3 Reducing Relative Clauses Ending in Prepositions ▶ Notes 1A, 1B

Work with a partner. Take turns finding out information about each other. Match a noun from the left box with a verb + preposition from the right box to form reduced relative clauses. Use appropriate tenses.

A: *Name a restaurant you've eaten at recently.*

B: *The Noodle House. It's really good. Now it's your turn. Name a sport...*

NOUN		VERB + PREPOSITION	
a restaurant	a friend	vote for	disagree with
a sport	a CD	eat at	rely on
a politician	a relative	listen to	work on
an assignment	a magazine	participate in	subscribe to

E4 Writing an Email Message

▶ Notes 1A, 1B

Your company has sent you to another country for a long training program. You have been there for a week. Write an email message to your family asking them to send five different items that you left at home. Describe the items carefully using relative clauses. Tell your family why you need them.

From:	Emma
To:	Mom and Dad
Subject:	Things I need

… It's warm here during the day, but it gets cool at night. The jacket I brought is not warm enough. Please send the one that you gave me for my birthday. It's hanging in my closet next to…

Vocabulary Notes

When and *Where* in Relative Clauses

Where and *when* can replace object relative pronouns to introduce relative clauses.

Where is used to express location. It can modify a noun that refers to a place. It can replace *which*, *that*, or Ø and the prepositions *in* or *at*.

That's <u>the building</u> **where** my father lives. = That's <u>the building</u> **in which** my father lives.

= That's <u>the building</u> **that/Ø** my father lives **in**.

When is used to express time. It can replace *that*, Ø, or *during which* to refer to a period of time.

<u>The year</u> **when** I lived in Vancouver was very special. = <u>The year</u> **that/Ø/during which** I lived in Vancouver was very special.

E5 Using *Where, When,* and Object Relative Pronouns

A. Complete the sentences below. Use *where, when, that, which, in which,* or Ø to introduce the relative clauses. More than one answer is possible. Discuss which alternatives you prefer in small groups.

Baseball, _____*which*_____ is the "national pastime" of the United States,
                    1

is also popular in the Dominican Republic. This small country is a place

_____ a large number of famous major-league baseball players
        2

have been born. In fact, one of its small cities, San Pedro de Macoris, is described as the city _____ ₃ more players have been born than anywhere else in the world. According to the record books, from 1960 to the present day, no fewer than 79 major leaguers have come from the tiny Dominican town _____ ₄ people refer to as San Pedro.

Baseball star Robinson Cano is one of San Pedro's most-loved native sons. He says he'll never forget his childhood, _____ ₅ his father José (another San Pedroan who played briefly in the major leagues) taught him how to play the game. In his early teens, Cano spent three years in New Jersey, during _____ ₆ he attended his first New York Yankee baseball game and became convinced that the Yankees were the team _____ ₇ he wanted to play for. The year 2005 was the year _____ ₈ his dream came true. The champion hitter still visits San Pedro in winter, _____ ₉ he enjoys spending his time being a role model and helping as many kids as he can. He is also the head of the Robinson Cano Foundation, _____ ₁₀ he founded to raise money to help Dominican children with heart diseases.

B. Write three sentences each about a place and a time from your past. Use *where* and *when* to introduce a relative clause in each sentence.

The house where I grew up was very small for my big family.
Dinnertime, when all of us tried to eat together, was chaotic.

C. Exchange papers with a partner. Pick two of your partner's sentences to rewrite using object relative pronouns (*who, that, which, Ø*). Make any necessary changes.

The house (that) I grew up in was very small for my big family.
Dinnertime, during which all of us tried to eat together, was chaotic.

WRITING

Write a Report About Women's Sports in Your Country

Think Critically About Meaning and Use

A. Read each sentence and the statements that follow. Write *T* if the statement is true or *F* if it is false.

1. My brother, who I resemble, lives in Jordan.

   _F_   **a.** I live in Jordan.

   _____   **b.** I resemble my brother.

2. The man my sister works with has a sailboat.

   _____   **a.** My sister has a sailboat.

   _____   **b.** My sister works on a sailboat.

3. The team I wanted to win lost in the semifinals.

   _____   **a.** The team lost.

   _____   **b.** I wanted to win.

4. Andrei still loves playing hockey, which he learned when he was five.

   _____   **a.** Andrei is five years old.

   _____   **b.** Andrei plays hockey.

5. I looked at some equipment that my neighbors were selling at a garage sale.

   _____   **a.** I sold some equipment at a garage sale.

   _____   **b.** My neighbors looked at some equipment at a garage sale.

6. Ms. Wang wrote the book I heard about on a radio show.

   _____   **a.** I listened to a radio show.

   _____   **b.** Ms. Wang heard about a book.

7. The professor assigned a book in which the history of baseball is discussed.

   _____   **a.** The professor gave an assignment.

   _____   **b.** The professor discussed the history of baseball.

8. Charlotte, who I once worked for, took over the company.

   _____   **a.** I once worked for Charlotte.

   _____   **b.** Charlotte took over the company.

B. Discuss these questions in small groups.

1. **IDENTIFY** Which three sentences contain reduced relative clauses that end with prepositions?

2. **GENERATE** How could you rewrite these three sentences to make them sound more formal?

Edit

Find the errors in these paragraphs and correct them.

Sisleide Lima do Amor, ~~which~~ *who* soccer fans know as Sissi, was not discouraged as a child by the boys who wouldn't let her play the game with which she loved most. Eventually, she got her way on the streets of Salvador, Brazil, because the soccer ball that the boys wanted to play with it was hers. Still, she often ran home with her ball after she grew frustrated with the negative attitudes that the boys displayed. Sissi had learned to play soccer by practicing with all kinds of objects what she found around the house. These included rolled-up socks, oranges, bottle caps, and the heads of dolls that her parents had given her them. It was her father who finally decided that she needed a soccer ball to keep her from destroying her dolls.

Sissi showed her admiration for Brazil's male soccer heroes by choosing the jersey number who Romario once wore and by shaving her head to resemble the style in which Ronaldo made famous. During the 1999 Women's World Cup, Sissi displayed the type of skill fans will long remember. Left-footed Sissi scored seven goals for her team, including a goal that she kicked in with her weaker right foot. According to Sissi, her seventh goal was the one about which she kept thinking about long after the 1999 Women's World Cup was over. During a 3–3 tie, she kicked the ball into a spot the goalkeeper couldn't reach it, and her team's 4–3 victory put them into the semifinals.

Write

Write a report about the status of women's sports in your native country. Use relative clauses with object and subject relative pronouns where appropriate.

1. **BRAINSTORM** Think about all the things you can say about the status of women's sports in your country. Use these categories and questions to help you organize your ideas into sections:
   - **Current Situation:** What athletic training do girls typically receive in childhood? Are things different for boys and men? What professional sports do women play?
   - **Developing Trends:** What successes or setbacks have women athletes experienced? Have people's attitudes changed? Have female athletes appeared as role models?
   - **The Future:** What does the future of women's sports look like? How do you see things developing over the next 10–20 years?

2. **WRITE A FIRST DRAFT** Before you write your first draft, read the checklist below and look at the examples of sports writing on pages 302–303 and 323. Write your draft using relative clauses.

3. **EDIT** Read your work and check it against the checklist below. Circle grammar, spelling, and punctuation errors.

DO I ...	YES
use headings to help readers see how the information is organized?	☐
use relative clauses to connect ideas and combine sentences?	☐
use correct relative pronouns?	☐
use at least one object relative pronoun with a preposition?	☐
use appropriate verb forms to reflect past, present, and future time?	☐

4. **PEER REVIEW** Work with a partner to help you decide how to fix your errors and improve the content. Use the checklist above.

5. **REWRITE YOUR DRAFT** Using the comments from your partner, write a final draft.

> The Status of Women's Sports in Greece
> OVERVIEW
> Greece is a country that most people identify with the Olympic Games. But did you know that in ancient times, the Olympics were a competition that women did not take part in? ... In fact, women athletes in Greece really weren't taken seriously until 1992. That was the year that track star Voula Patoulidou won an Olympic gold medal. Since then, ...

PART 5
TEST | Modifying Nouns

Choose the correct word or words to complete each sentence.

1. No one is really sure how the huge stones of Stonehenge, _____, were moved to the south of England thousands of years ago.

   a. that is an ancient monument   **c.** an ancient monument

   b. it is an ancient monument   **d.** is an ancient monument

2. I spoke to the man _____ by the door.

   a. he was sitting   c. who sits

   b. who was sitting   d. sat

3. Do you know anything about the new requirements _____?

   a. that announced   **c.** they announced them

   b. that they announced   **d.** that they announced them

4. The woman _____ gave me a very positive letter of recommendation.

   a. whom I worked   **c.** who I worked

   d. that worked with   **d.** with whom I worked

Choose the correct word to complete each sentence. Choose X when an indefinite or definite article is not necessary in the sentence.

5. _____ microscope was invented in the seventeenth century by a Dutch scientist named Anton van Leeuwenhoek.

   a. The   **b.** One   **c.** Some   **d.** X

6. During the spring semester, _____ chemistry will not be offered.

   a. the   **b.** a   **c.** X   **d.** any

7. Her parents were professors at _____ small university.

   a. a   **b.** the   **c.** any   **d.** X

Choose the correct response to complete each conversation.

8. **A:** The woman who called Helen is a famous athlete.

   B: _____

   a. I didn't know Helen was famous.   **c.** What is the woman's name?

   b. Why did Helen call her?   **d.** I didn't know Helen was an athlete.

9. **A:** I bought some rice.

    B: _____

      a. How many?   **c.** Should I cook them?

      b. Where is it?   **d.** How much did they cost?

10. **A:** There were two witnesses, and I spoke to one of them.

    B: _____

      a. What about another one?   **c.** What about the other one?

      b. What about the others?   **d.** What about another?

11. **A:** The book she ordered hasn't arrived.

    B: _____

      a. When did she order it?   **c.** Who ordered the book?

      b. Why hasn't she arrived?   **d.** Where did she put it?

Rewrite each sentence using the reduced relative clause.

12. I bought the shoes that were made in Italy.

_____

13. Look at the man who is wearing a tuxedo.

_____

14. There are the dresses that are on sale.

_____

Match the sentence ending to the correct beginning.

_____ **15.** French is a language   **a.** that she has to iron.   **e.** whom I've never met.

_____ **16.** He sent her an email   **b.** he can finish quickly.   **f.** she hates to eat.

_____ **17.** He's marrying a woman   **c.** which she hopes to attend.   **g.** which his father built.

      d. I've never studied.   **h.** that she never answered.

Complete each sentence with _a_ or _an_.

18. Sheila has _____ unique singing voice, doesn't she?

19. I don't think there's _____ hospital in his town that can perform open-heart surgery.

20. Mr. Porter will be coming back in about _____ hour.

CHAPTER

15

Real Conditionals, Unreal Conditionals, and Wishes

Reflections on Life

A1 Before You Read

Discuss these questions.

Do you ever make wishes? What do you wish for? Discuss your wishes and decide whether it is possible to achieve them.

A2 Read

CD2 T31 **Read these different perspectives on life. Which selection best reflects your outlook on life?**

CHINESE PROVERB

If there is light in the soul,
there will be beauty in the person.

If there is beauty in the person,
there will be harmony in the house.

If there is harmony in the house,
there will be order in the nation.

If there is order in the nation,
there will be peace in the world.

—Anonymous

If I Had My Life to Live Over

I'd dare to make more mistakes next time. I'd relax, I would limber up. I would be sillier than I have been this trip. I would take fewer things seriously. I would
5 take more chances. I would climb more mountains and swim more rivers. I would eat more ice cream and fewer beans. I would perhaps have more actual troubles, but I'd have fewer imaginary ones.
10 You see, I'm one of those people who lives sensibly and sanely hour after hour, day after day. Oh, I've had my moments, and if I had it to do over again, I'd have more of them. In fact, I'd try to have
15 nothing else.
   If I had my life to live over, I would start barefoot earlier in the spring and stay that way later in the fall. I would go to more dances. I would ride more merry-go-
20 rounds. I would pick more daisies.

—Nadine Stair (85-year-old woman)

You have to count on living every single day in a way you believe will make you feel good about your life so if it were over tomorrow, you'd be content with yourself.

—Jane Seymour (actress)

Wishes of an Elderly Man
Wished at a Garden Party,
June 1914

I wish I loved the human race;
I wish I loved its silly face;
I wish I liked the way it walks;
I wish I liked the way it talks,
And when I'm introduced to one
I wish I thought, what jolly fun!

—Sir Walter Alexander Raleigh
(essayist/critic)

harmony: agreement, peaceful cooperation
jolly: cheerful, happy

limber up: to make the body more flexible, to stretch the muscles so that they move easily

A3 After You Read

Match each reading selection on the left with its main idea on the right.

__d__ 1. Chinese proverb

_____ 2. *If I Had My Life to Live Over*

_____ 3. Quotation by Jane Seymour

_____ 4. *Wishes of an Elderly Man*

a. The writer regrets not taking advantage of more of the joys in life.

b. The writer doesn't like people very much.

c. It is important to be satisfied with the kind of life you lead.

d. There is a logical connection between the individual and the rest of the world.

B FORM

Real Conditionals, Unreal Conditionals, and Wishes

Think Critically About Form

A. Look back at the selections on pages 328–329 and complete the tasks below.

1. **IDENTIFY** An example of the simple present in an *if* clause is underlined in selection 1. Find three more examples.

2. **RECOGNIZE** Find two sentences that show the simple past in an *if* clause in selections 2 and 3. What verb form do you find in each main clause?

3. **RECOGNIZE** Look at the sentences that contain *wish* in selection 4. What is the tense of *wish*? What verb form is used in each clause that follows *wish*?

B. Discuss your answers with the class and read the Form charts to check them.

ONLINE PRACTICE

PRESENT AND FUTURE REAL CONDITIONALS		
⌐ **IF CLAUSE** ⌐		⌐ **MAIN CLAUSE** ⌐
IF + SIMPLE PRESENT	*(THEN)*	SIMPLE PRESENT
If I'm on time,	(then)	I **walk** to work.
IF + SIMPLE PRESENT	*(THEN)*	FUTURE
If it's not too late,	(then)	I**'ll walk** to work. I**'m going to walk** to work.
IF + SIMPLE PRESENT	*(THEN)*	MODAL
If I leave on time,	(then)	I **may walk** to work.
IF + SIMPLE PRESENT	*(THEN)*	IMPERATIVE
If you have time,	(then)	**walk** with me.

PRESENT AND FUTURE UNREAL CONDITIONALS		
⌐ **IF CLAUSE** ⌐		⌐ **MAIN CLAUSE** ⌐
IF + SIMPLE PAST	*(THEN)*	*WOULD* + VERB
If I had the time,	(then)	I **would walk** to work. I**'d walk** to work.
IF + SIMPLE PAST	*(THEN)*	*COULD* + VERB
If I left on time,	(then)	I **could walk** to work.
IF + SIMPLE PAST	*(THEN)*	*MIGHT* + VERB
If I left on time,	(then)	I **might walk** to work.

Real and Unreal Conditionals
• Conditional sentences have a dependent *if* clause and a main clause.

- When the *if* clause comes first, it is followed by a comma. *Then* is usually omitted before the main clause, but it is always implied.

  If I'm on time, (then) **I walk** to work.   **If I had** the time, (then) **I'd walk** to work.

- When the main clause is first, there is no comma and *then* is not used. The meaning is the same.

  I walk to work **if I'm** on time.   **I'd walk** to work **if I had** the time.

- In conditional sentences, either clause or both clauses can be negative.

  If I'm not on time, **I take** the bus.   **If I'm not** on time, **I won't walk** to work.

- Questions with conditionals are formed by putting the main clause in question word order.

  If it's not too late, **are you going to walk** to work?

  If you had the time, **would you walk** to work?

Real Conditionals

- In real conditionals, the verb in the *if* clause is in the present, even if it has future meaning.

  If you go tomorrow, **call** me.

- Real conditionals can also be formed with the present continuous in the *if* clause.

  If you're going tomorrow, **call me**.   **If it's raining, I might take** the bus.

Unreal Conditionals

- When an unreal conditional *if* clause contains the verb *be*, use *were* for all subjects.

  If I were on time, **I'd walk** to work.

- Unreal conditionals can also be formed with the past continuous in the *if* clause.

  If I were leaving now, **I might walk** to work.

- See Appendix 14 for contractions with *would*.

WISHES ABOUT THE PRESENT AND FUTURE	
⌐ *WISH* CLAUSE ⌐	⌐ *THAT* CLAUSE ⌐
SIMPLE PRESENT	(*THAT* +) PAST FORM
I wish	(that) I **were** older. (that) I **didn't have** a cold. (that) you **were going** to the wedding. (that) you**'d help** me. (that) you **could come** with me.

(Continued on page 332)

- In sentences with *wish*, the *wish* clause is the main clause. The *that* clause is the dependent clause.
- In *that* clauses with the verb *be*, *were* is used for all subjects.
- *Could* and *would* (the simple past of *can* and *will*) are often used in the *that* clause.
- *That* is often omitted after *wish*, but it is always implied.
- Short answers with *wish* consist of a subject + *wish* clause + subject + *were/did*.

    A: Are you ready yet?   A: Does he have any money?

    B: No, I **wish I were**.   B: No, but I **wish he did**.

B1 Listening for Form

 CD2 T32   Elena and Irina are twin sisters who attend colleges in different cities. Listen to some sentences from their phone conversation. Choose the verb forms that you hear.

1. **a.** could spend
   b. spent

2. **a.** 'd live
   b. lived

3. **a.** will finish
   b. finish

4. **a.** 'll spend
   b. 'd spend

5. **a.** attended
   b. would attend

6. **a.** wouldn't matter
   b. doesn't matter

7. **a.** didn't want
   b. don't want

8. **a.** do you want
   b. would you want

B2 Working on Real and Unreal Conditionals

A. Work in small groups. Start a real conditional sentence chain with *If the teacher cancels class*, and finish it with a result clause. Use the end of the last person's sentence to begin your own sentence.

    A: *If the teacher cancels class, there will be more time to study.*

    B: *If there's more time to study, we'll do better on the exam.*

    C: *If we do better on the exam,…*

B. Now start an unreal conditional chain with *If I had the day off, I'd….* As before, use the end of the last person's sentence to begin your own sentence.

    A: *If I had the day off, I'd go shopping.*

    B: *If I went shopping, I'd spend a lot of money.*

    C: *If I spent a lot of money, I'd feel bad the next day.*

B3 Building Conditional and *Wish* Sentences

Build as many meaningful sentences as possible. Use an item from each column or from two columns only. Punctuate your sentences correctly.

If I were ready, I'd leave.

| if
I wish | I were ready
she is sick
they were driving | I'd leave
call for help
he'll take over
you could come later |

B4 Working on *Wish* Sentences and Unreal Conditionals

A. Work with a partner. Complete these conversations using the appropriate form of the verbs. Add *would* when necessary. Then practice the conversations.

1. **A:** I wish I ___had___ (have) more money to spend.
      ₁

   B: If you _____ (do), you _____ (buy) things you don't need.
      ₂   ₃

2. **A:** I wish this place _____ (be/not) so crowded. If there _____ (be)
      ₁   ₂

   fewer people, we _____ (get) better service.
      ₃

   B: I know. I wish we _____ (can leave), but it's too late to go anywhere else.
      ₄

3. **A:** Do you ever wish you _____ (have) a different job?
      ₁

   B: Yes, quite often. If I _____ (have) a different job, I _____ (have)
      ₂   ₃

   more free time.

4. **A:** Can you help me fix my car?

   B: I wish I _____ (can), but I'm late. If I _____ (have/not) an
      ₁   ₂

   appointment at three, I _____ (stay) to help.
      ₃

B. Write four wishes. Then write a second sentence explaining each one with a related unreal conditional.

I wish it weren't so hot. If it weren't so hot, we could go for a walk.

B5 Completing Real and Unreal Conditionals

A. Complete these sentences with your own ideas. Use an appropriate verb form in the *if* clause or the main clause.

1. If I missed the bus, _I'd have to walk to work._

2. If I'm late for an appointment, _____

3. If I were sick, _____

4. I'm embarrassed if _____

5. I'd quit my job if _____

6. I'll buy a new computer if _____

B. Now write two real and two unreal *if* clauses or main clauses on a separate sheet of paper. Give them to a classmate to complete.

Informally Speaking

Using *Was*

CD2 T33 Look at the cartoon and listen to the conversation. How is each underlined form in the cartoon different from what you hear?

In informal speech, *was* is often used instead of *were* for unreal conditionals and wishes with *I*, *he*, *she*, and *it*.

I need a jacket, but nothing fits me. I wish I <u>were</u> taller.

If it <u>were</u> earlier, we could go to another store. Let's do that tomorrow.

Standard Form	What You Might Hear
If I **weren't** so busy, I'd go out tonight.	"If I wasn't so busy, I'd go out tonight."
I wish I **weren't** so busy.	"I wish I wasn't so busy."

B6 Understanding Informal Speech

CD2 T34 Listen and write the standard form of the words you hear.

1. If _____ I weren't so tired _____, I'd go out for a cup of coffee with you.

2. What would you do if it _____ to take the bus?

3. I wish my boss _____.

4. If he _____, we could leave now.

5. She'd tell you if she _____ at you.

6. Don't you wish he _____ with us?

MEANING AND USE 1

Real Conditionals

Think Critically About Meaning and Use

A. Read the sentences and answer the questions below.

    a. If two hydrogen atoms combine with one oxygen atom, they form a water molecule.

    b. If you help me, I'll help you.

    c. If you finish the test early, turn over your paper.

    d. If you don't hurry, you'll miss the train.

    EVALUATE Which real conditional sentence do you think is a promise? a statement of fact? a warning? an instruction to do something?

B. Discuss your answers with the class and read the Meaning and Use Notes to check them.

Meaning and Use Notes

ONLINE
PRACTICE

Overview of Real Conditionals

▶ **1** In real conditional sentences, the *if* clause and main clause have a cause-and-effect relationship. The *if* clause introduces a possible condition or event (it may or may not happen). The main clause expresses a possible result (what happens or may happen after the *if* clause).

            ⎯⎯⎯ Possible Condition ⎯⎯⎯   Possible Result

    If she **finds** another apartment, she**'ll move**.

        (She may find an apartment. Under those circumstances, she'll move. Otherwise, she won't.)

Expressing Certainty

▶ **2A** Some conditionals are used to express results that the speaker is certain of. These sentences are sometimes called factual conditionals; the speaker thinks the results will occur whenever the condition in the *if* clause is true.

    If you **lose** your credit card, the bank **replaces** it in a day.

        (This is a fact you are certain of.)

(Continued on page 336)

▶ **2B**   When the result clause is in the simple present, real conditionals can express the kinds of routines and habits, facts, or general truths usually found in simple present sentences.

Routines and Habits	**Facts or General Truths**
If **I take** the 8:05 train, **I get** to work at 8:50.	If air **is heated**, it **rises**.
If **I drive**, **I get** to work earlier.	If you **overcook** fish, it **dries out**.

▶ **2C**   Facts or general truths can also be expressed with the *will* future.

Facts or General Truths

If air **is heated**, it **will rise**.

If you **overcook** fish, it **will dry out**.

Expressing Predictions and Promises

▶ **3**   When the result clause is in a future form, real conditionals can express predictions with varying degrees of certainty. In the first person, they can also express promises.

Predictions

If it **rains** tonight, the game **may be canceled**.

If it **rains** tonight, the game **will be canceled**.

Promises

If you **come over** tomorrow, I**'ll help** you.

Expressing Advice, Warnings, and Instructions

▶ **4**   Real conditionals are often used to give advice, warnings, and instructions. The result clause may use the imperative, a modal, or the future.

Advice

If your **throat** hurts, **try** salt water.

If your **throat** hurts, you **should try** salt water.

If you **gargle** with salt water, you**'ll get** immediate relief.

Warnings

If you **don't get** enough sleep, you**'ll get** sick.

Instructions

If the printer **runs out** of paper, **refill** it immediately.

C1 Listening for Meaning and Use

▶ Notes 1, 2A, 2B, 3, 4

 CD2 T35 Listen to these sentences. How is each conditional sentence used? Check (✓) the correct column.

	FACTS OR GENERAL TRUTHS	ADVICE, WARNINGS, INSTRUCTIONS	PROMISES
1.		✓	
2.			
3.			
4.			
5.			
6.			
7.			
8.			

C2 Describing Factual Conditions

▶ Notes 2A–2C

Work with a partner and read this chart about fees at a ski resort. Use factual conditional sentences to describe the different conditions for membership and discounts.

If you're between 7 and 15, it costs $50 to buy a full-season pass.
If you're a member, you get a 15 percent discount on equipment rentals

WINTER SEASON
Membership Prices (per person)

Age	Full-Season Pass	Half-Season Pass
7–15*	$150	$95
16 & up	$200	$125

* Children 6 and under ski free when accompanied by an adult ticket holder.

Members receive the following year-round:
- 15% discount on equipment rentals
- Two free days of skiing: once before December 23, once after March 6 (One guest allowed each time)

On Membership Appreciation Days (dates to be announced):
- 50% discount on lift tickets for members
- Free lift ticket for one guest per member

C3 Making Promises

Work with a partner. Imagine you are a candidate running for mayor.
Make promises using the words and phrases in real conditional sentences.

1. create jobs

   If I am elected mayor, I will create jobs. OR
   If you vote for me, I will create jobs. OR
   If I become mayor, I will create jobs.

2. improve education

3. build new schools

4. reduce crime

5. hire more police

6. expand health care

7. open more hospitals

8. cut taxes

9. employ more women

10. employ more minorities

C4 Rephrasing Advice with Conditional Sentences

Work in small groups. Read these statements of advice and think of different ways to
rephrase them using real conditional sentences. Try to use the future, modals, or the
imperative in your different result clauses.

1. Turn down your thermostat at night. You won't use so much fuel.

   If you turn down your thermostat at night, you won't use so much fuel.
   *If you don't want to use so much fuel, (you should) turn down your thermostat
   at night.*

2. Study hard, and you won't fail the test.

3. Make calls at night, and your telephone bill won't be so high.

4. Don't eat so much. You won't get indigestion.

5. Read a book for a while. You'll fall asleep easily.

6. Call the doctor, and you'll get some good advice.

Vocabulary Notes

If and Unless

Sentences with *unless* in the dependent clause often have the same meaning as sentences with negative *if* clauses.

Unless	**If**
Unless the cab **comes** at three, you won't make it to the airport.	**If** the cab **doesn't come** at three, you won't make it to the airport.
Unless you **finish** your work, we'll lose the account.	**If** you **don't finish** your work, we'll lose the account.

C5 Giving Warnings with *If* and *Unless* Clauses

A. Complete these health warnings. Use *will* or *won't* in the result clause.

1. If you don't eat more vegetables, _you won't have a balanced diet._

2. _____ if you eat too much fat.

3. If you go to bed too late, _____

4. If you don't get enough calcium, _____

5. If you don't exercise, _____

B. Complete these safety warnings by writing negative conditions in the *if* clauses that could lead to the harmful results.

1. You'll get into an accident if _you don't drive more carefully._

2. If _____, you'll slip.

3. You'll damage your eyes if _____

4. If _____, you'll get sick.

5. You'll start a fire if _____

C. Look at the warnings your partner wrote in part B. Rewrite the warnings that can be rephrased using unless instead of *if*.

You'll get into an accident unless you drive more carefully.

D MEANING AND USE 2

Unreal Conditionals

Think Critically About Meaning and Use

A. Read the sentences and answer the questions below.

1a. If my plane is late, I'll miss the meeting. **2a.** If I were you, I'd leave now.
1b. If my plane were late, I'd miss the meeting. **2b.** You should leave now.

1. **ANALYZE** Compare 1a and 1b. Which one expresses something that is more likely to happen? Which one expresses something that is probably imaginary?

2. **DIFFERENTIATE** Compare 2a and 2b. Which sentence sounds more direct? Which one seems more indirect?

B. Discuss your answers with the class and read the Meaning and Use Notes to check them.

Meaning and Use Notes

ONLINE PRACTICE

Unreal Conditionals

▶ **1A** Unreal conditional sentences express imaginary situations. The *if* clause introduces the imaginary condition or event (it is not true at the present time). The main clause expresses the imaginary result (what would or could happen after the *if* clause).

Imaginary Condition ———⟍ ⟋— Imaginary Result ——⟍
If she **found** another apartment, she **would move**.
    (She hasn't found an apartment, so she isn't moving.)

▶ **1B** In the *if* clause, the simple past or past continuous does not indicate past time; it indicates that the situation is unreal. In the result clause, *would, could/would be able to*, or *might* also indicate that the result is unreal.

If I had a problem, **I'd ask** for your help. (I don't have a problem right now, so I don't need help.)

If I had the money, **I could buy** a new car. (Right now I don't have the money, so I can't buy a new car.)

If we **were staying in Moscow**, we**'d be able to visit** them. (We're not staying in Moscow, so we can't visit them.)

▶ **1C**   *Would* in the result clause expresses more certainty than *could* or *might* about the imaginary results. *Could* or *might* indicates one of several possible outcomes.

> If I **had** the money, I **would buy** a new car. (*Would* expresses more certainty about the imaginary outcome.)

> If I **had** the money, I **might buy** a new car. (*Might* expresses one imaginary outcome. There are other possible outcomes.)

Giving Advice and Opinions

▶ **2**   Unreal conditionals beginning with *If I were you* can be used as an indirect way of giving advice. Unreal conditionals sound softer than modals like *should* or *ought to*.

Advice with Unreal Conditionals	**Advice with Modals**
If I **were** you, I**'d** speak to the instructor.	You **should** speak to the instructor.

Asking Permission

▶ **3**   Unreal conditionals with *would you mind, would it bother you*, or *would it be OK* can be used to ask for permission. Notice that a negative response to the first two questions means you are giving permission.

Permission with Unreal Conditionals	**Permission with Modals**
A: **Would you mind if I opened** the window?	A: **May I open** the window?
B: **No,** go right ahead.	B: **Yes,** go right ahead.
A: **Would it bother you if I opened** the window?	
B: **No,** not at all.	
A: **Would it be OK if I opened** the window?	
B: **Yes,** go ahead.	

D1 Listening for Meaning and Use

▶ Notes 1A–1C, 2, 3

CD2 T36   Listen and choose the best response.

1. **a.** Sure, it would be a pleasure.
   b. No, not at all.

2. **a.** I took a taxi.
   b. I'll call you.

3. **a.** I might.
   b. I did.

4. **a.** I'll have dinner with Cleopatra.
   b. I'd choose Pablo Picasso.

5. **a.** I would.
   b. Maybe.

6. **a.** No, go right ahead.
   b. Yes, if no one is using it.

D2 Asking Questions About Unusual Situations

A. Complete these unreal conditionals. Try to think of unusual or interesting situations that people might like to talk about. Then take turns asking and answering the questions with a partner.

1. What would you do if _you found a million dollars?_____

   I'd probably report it to the police and hope to get a reward.

2. What would you say if _____

3. How would you feel if _____

4. Where would you go if _____

5. Who would you invite if _____

6. Who would you ask for help if _____

B. Ask the class one of your questions.

D3 Giving Advice with *If I Were You*

Work in small groups. Give advice with *If I were you, I'd…* or *If I were you, I wouldn't…* Brainstorm different solutions for each problem.

1. There's a big mistake on my electric bill.

   If I were you, I wouldn't ignore it.
   If I were you, I'd call the electric company and explain the situation.

2. My landlord doesn't repair things when I ask him to.

3. I accepted two invitations to go out, and now I don't know what to do.

4. I get a lot of phone calls, but most of them are wrong numbers.

5. My boss isn't very nice to me.

6. I checked my credit card balance online and discovered some charges for expensive items that I know I didn't buy.

7. I want to buy a computer, but I don't know much about them.

8. I'm not doing very well in my English class.

D4 Asking Permission

 Work with a partner. Read each situation and take turns asking for permission in at least two different ways. Use *Would you mind if...*, *Would it bother you if...*, or *Would it be OK if...*, and respond with appropriate positive or negative answers.

1. You're supposed to pick your friend up at eight o'clock, but you'd prefer to pick her up earlier.

   A: Would you mind if I picked you up earlier?
   B: No, not at all.

2. You want to listen to the news while your roommate is studying. You don't want to disturb him.

3. You think it's too hot in the classroom. You want to open the window.

4. Your friend has an interesting book. You want to borrow it.

Beyond the Sentence

Omitting *If* Clauses

When a single condition has many results, the *if* clause is usually stated only once. The imaginary results are expressed in new sentences with *would*.

> **If I were the boss**, I <u>would</u> try to be considerate of my employees' needs to balance work and family. I <u>would</u> give them more time off for family responsibilities. I <u>would</u> even encourage my employees to volunteer in their children's schools during work hours. I <u>would</u>...

D5 Using Conditionals with Many Results

A. If you could be anyone in the world for one day, who would you like to be? Make a list of things you would do if you were that person.

B. Write a paragraph describing what you would do if you were the person you chose in part A. Start your paragraph with *If I were..., I'd...* Continue expressing imaginary results using sentences with *would*. Do not use any more *if* clauses in your paragraph.

   If I were Bill Gates for one day, I'd fly on one of my private jets to a beautiful tropical paradise. I'd spend the day swimming, relaxing, and having fun with my family. I'd have the finest chefs prepare all of my favorite foods, and...

Wishes

Think Critically About Meaning and Use

A. Read the sentences and answer the questions below.

1a. I wish you'd leave work early tomorrow and come to the picnic.
1b. I wish I were wearing a sweater. It's cold.
2a. I wish you would clean up your room more often.
2b. I wish I could help you, but I don't know the answer.

1. **ANALYZE** Look at sentences 1a and 1b. Which sentence is a wish about the present? Which is a wish about the future?

2. **ANALYZE** Look at sentences 2a and 2b. Which expresses a complaint? Which expresses a regret?

B. Discuss your answers with the class and read the Meaning and Use Notes to check them.

Meaning and Use Notes

ONLINE PRACTICE

	Making Wishes

▶ 1   Use *wish* to express a desire for something that does not exist now. It is a desire to change a real situation into an unreal or impossible one. As in unreal conditional sentences, the past form does not indicate past time; it indicates that the situation is unreal. The past form can be simple past, past continuous, *could*, or *would*.

Wishes About the Present

I live in an apartment, but I **wish I lived** in a house.

I **wish I were living** in Chicago.

I **wish I could swim**, but I can't.

Wishes About the Future

I **wish** you **would come** with me tonight.

I **wish** you **were coming** with me tonight.

I **wish you could come** with me tonight.

Expressing Complaints and Regrets

▶ **2A** Sometimes *wish* sentences with *would* express complaints, especially when you want something to change but think it probably won't.

I **wish** it **would stop** raining. We can't go anywhere in this weather.

I **wish** you **wouldn't leave** the car windows open.

▶ **2B** *Wish* sentences often express regret about a current situation.

A: Can you help me this afternoon?

B: No, I'm sorry. I **wish I could**, but I have a doctor's appointment.

Using *If Only*

▶ **3** Sentences with *if only* often have a similar meaning to sentences with *wish*, but they are more emphatic. *If only* sentences focus on the desire to change a negative situation. Unlike other *if* conditionals, an *if only* clause is often used alone without a result clause.

If Only	Wish
If only I **had** a car!	I **wish** I **had** a car.
If only I **felt** better, then I'd go out.	I **wish** I **felt** better. Perhaps I'd go out.
If only it **would stop** raining.	I **wish** it **would stop** raining.

E1 Listening for Meaning and Use ▶ Note 1

CD2 T37 Listen to each situation and check (✓) whether the item exists or doesn't exist.

		EXISTS	DOESN'T EXIST
1.	a cold	✓	
2.	pictures		
3.	free time		
4.	a car		
5.	a safety lock		
6.	a limit		
7.	a credit card		
8.	your guitar		

E2 Making Wishes About the Present

▶ Note 1

Work in small groups. Take turns making up as many wishes as possible for each situation. Explain your wishes with unreal conditional sentences.

1. Your apartment is too small.

   I wish I had more space. If I had more space, I'd get a pet.
   I wish I could move. If I moved, I'd get a much bigger apartment.

2. You're broke. You have no money.

3. Your new teacher is boring.

4. You're very busy.

5. You live in a big city.

6. You drive to work during rush hour.

7. You need more exercise.

8. You're lost in the woods.

E3 Making Wishes About the Future

▶ Notes 1, 3

Work with a partner. Take turns expressing your wishes for the future by using *wish* and *if only* sentences with *would*.

1. You are waiting to receive your grades in the mail. The mail is late.

   I wish the mail would come!
   If only the mail would come!

2. You want your sister to take better care of herself, but you're afraid that she won't.

3. You want your sister to help you choose a present for your parents' wedding anniversary, but she is always busy. You want her to go shopping with you this weekend.

4. You think that your father is working too hard. You want him to take a vacation.

5. The weather is very bad. Your friend dropped by for a few minutes. You want him to stay until the weather improves, but he seems to be in a hurry.

6. Your brother has just announced that he wants to quit school and go back home. You want him to stay in college.

E4 Complaining with *Wish* and *If Only* Sentences ▶ Notes 2A, 3

 Work with a partner. Imagine you are very unhappy with your college roommate for the reasons listed below. Complain about your roommate's bad habits using *wish* and *if only* sentences with *would* or *wouldn't*.

1. makes a lot of noise in the morning

    I wish he wouldn't make so much noise in the morning. OR
    I wish he would be quieter in the morning. OR
    If only he wouldn't make so much noise!

2. uses up all the hot water in the shower

3. uses up the milk and doesn't replace it

4. doesn't talk to my friends when they visit me

5. doesn't clean up the kitchen

6. plays video games for hours

E5 Expressing Regret with *Wish* Sentences ▶ Note 2B

 Work with a partner. Complete these conversations with expressions of regret. Use the simple past and then give a reason with *but*, explaining the real situation. Then practice the conversations, switching roles.

1. **Roommate A:** Could you please help me with this?

    Roommate B: I'm sorry, I can't. I wish _I could, but I have to leave right now._

2. **Customer:** Do you have any more wallets?

    Salesclerk: No, I'm sorry. I wish _____

3. **Student A:** Can you lend me yesterday's notes?

    Student B: Well, I wish _____

4. **Friend A:** Do you have any free time later this afternoon?

    Friend B: No, I wish _____

5. **Child:** Are there any more cookies left?

    Parent: No, I wish _____

6. **Friend A:** Is it warm outside this morning?

    Friend B: No, I wish _____

Think Critically About Meaning and Use

A. Read each situation and the statements that follow. Write *T* if the statement is true or *F* if it is false.

1. We'd leave if it stopped raining.

   _F_   **a.** We left.

   _____   **b.** It's raining.

2. I'd go to the meeting if I weren't so busy.

   _____   **a.** I'm not very busy.

   _____   **b.** I'm going to the meeting.

3. Unless I call, I'll be home at six.

   _____   **a.** I might call.

   _____   **b.** I plan to be home at six.

4. If it weren't on sale, I couldn't afford it.

   _____   **a.** It's on sale.

   _____   **b.** I can't afford it.

5. If the light flashes, the bell rings five seconds later.

   _____   **a.** The bell won't ring until the light flashes.

   _____   **b.** The light flashes before the bell rings.

6. I wish I didn't have to take the exam.

   _____   **a.** I've taken the exam.

   _____   **b.** I don't have a choice.

7. If you lived in that neighborhood, you'd know Joseph Taylor.

   _____   **a.** You know Joseph Taylor.

   _____   **b.** You don't live in that neighborhood.

8. If only you spoke more slowly, then I'd understand you better.

   _____   **a.** You speak slowly.

   _____   **b.** I understand you very well.

B. Discuss these questions in small groups.

1. **GENERATE** Look at sentence 1. Imagine it's two hours later and still raining. What wishes would you make?

2. **SYNTHESIZE** How could you rewrite sentence 6 as an unreal future conditional beginning with "If I had a choice, …"?

Edit

Find the errors in this text and correct them.

would you
What you ~~would~~ do if there were an earthquake in your area? Would you know what to do? Some people are too frightened to find out about safety precautions. They wish they live somewhere else. If you could, won't you rather find out what to do in advance? Here is some advice about what to do before, during, and after an earthquake.

1. If you don't have a box of emergency equipment and supplies, you will need to prepare one in advance.

2. If you would be indoors during an earthquake, you should stay away from windows, bookcases, and shelves.

3. If it were possible, you should turn off the gas, water, and electricity.

4. After the earthquake, don't walk around unless you are not wearing shoes to protect your feet from broken glass.

Don't wait. Don't wish you are prepared. Be prepared!

Write

Imagine you work for a government agency that produces informational material for publication in newspapers and magazines. Write a one-page public service announcement entitled "Home Safety Tips." Use real and unreal conditionals, where appropriate.

1. **BRAINSTORM** Think of all things that people can do to be safe at home (e.g., installing smoke alarms or child-proof electrical outlets). Write down at least 10 useful ideas.

   Think about how you will introduce your topic and organize your tips: Can you think of unreal conditionals or wishes you might use to catch your readers' attention? Do you want to present tips for different rooms or areas or for different concerns (e.g., children's safety, first aid, fire prevention, home security, emergency response)?

2. **WRITE A FIRST DRAFT** Before you write your first draft, read the checklist below and look at the examples in C4 on page 338 and the editing passage on page 349. Write your draft using real and unreal conditionals.

3. **EDIT** Read your work and check it against the checklist below. Circle grammar, spelling, and punctuation errors.

DO I...	YES
use an unreal conditional or wish to attract my readers' attention?	☐
use factual conditionals to express safety tips?	☐
use a mix of real conditionals and imperatives to give advice and instructions?	☐
give at least one warning with an *if* or *unless* clause?	☐
take care to use correct verb forms in real and unreal conditionals?	☐

4. **PEER REVIEW** Work with a partner to help you decide how to fix your errors and improve the content. Use the checklist above.

5. **REWRITE YOUR DRAFT** Using the comments from your partner, write a final draft.

Home Safety Tips

How would you feel if you walked into the bathroom and saw your four-year-old child surrounded by broken glass? Accidents around the home happen, but if you took a few more precautions, many could be avoided...

16

Past Unreal Conditionals and Past Wishes

The Ifs of History

A1 Before You Read

 Discuss these questions.

Think of a decision that you regret. What should you have done differently? Think of a decision that you have never regretted. Why not?

A2 Read

 CD2 T38 **Read this magazine article to find out about some possible alternatives to actual historical events. Do you agree with this writer's ideas?**

The Ifs of History

by Hans Koning

Franklin Delano Roosevelt

The ifs of history are numberless. For everything that has happened we can, of course, line up infinite alternatives. But not much is gained from this, except for the
5 obvious observation that human history is very iffy.

The ifs I am talking about here are last-minute ifs—that is, I am not going to lose myself and my readers by guessing
10 what would have happened if there had been no Bering Strait or English Channel or no Franklin Delano Roosevelt. A last-minute if is: What would have happened if, in February 1933, Giuseppe Zangara's
15 hand had not been pushed aside in Miami and his bullet had killed Franklin Roosevelt rather than the mayor of Chicago?

This example gets right to the point. Most of my ifs are life-or-death ifs. And
20 that raises the well-known dilemma: Are certain individuals of greater importance to the flow of history? I find it hard to accept that the chance life or death of one person could decide the lives and deaths of
25 millions. But I suspect that the truth lies somewhere in between. A few individuals have influenced destiny, but in the long run, history exhibits its own logic.

If that German officer in Hitler's
30 headquarters who moved a briefcase had minded his own business, then the bomb in the briefcase would have killed Hitler.
A different government would have taken over in Berlin and World War II would
35 have ended. The Allies would have occupied Germany ten months sooner. As many as a million prisoners' lives would have been saved.

If Cleopatra hadn't lived, Marc Antony
40 would have kept his mind on the affairs of
state and not been eliminated from the
race for Roman emperor. He would have
continued sharing power with his brother-
in-law Octavian, whom he hated, and he
45 would have worked to oppose Octavian's
unjust use of force. If Marc Antony had
done that, it would have hastened the fall
of the Roman Empire by a hundred years.
Everything thereafter would have happened
50 one hundred years sooner.

If Joseph Ginoux, a café owner in
Arles, had allowed Vincent van Gogh to
pay for his lodging in paintings instead of
evicting him, then Vincent would have had
55 some peace and security. His nervous
breakdown might have happened later and
been less severe. He would have painted for
five, perhaps ten years more. The people of
Arles wouldn't have drawn up their petition

Sculpture of Cleopatra   Vincent van Gogh,
                                Self-Portrait

60 to have him put in an asylum. In a less
hostile and threatening world, his later
work would have reached an unimaginable
perfection. Gauguin and Picasso would
have been influenced differently; twentieth-
65 century painting would have been different.
(And Ginoux's heirs would have been the
richest people in France.)

Adapted from *Harper's Magazine*

---

asylum: a psychiatric hospital
alternative: a different possibility or choice
dilemma: a difficult choice between alternatives
evict: to force a renter out of his or her apartment

hasten: to cause to happen sooner
iffy: full of uncertainty, doubtful
last-minute: at the final moment before an
    important event

A3 After You Read

Check (✓) the events that actually happened or are true, according to the article.

1. __✓__ A man tried to kill Franklin Delano Roosevelt in Miami.

2. ____ Hitler was killed by a bomb in a briefcase.

3. ____ Marc Antony was eliminated from the race for Roman emperor.

4. ____ Van Gogh was evicted from where he was living.

5. ____ Joseph Ginoux received paintings from van Gogh.

B | FORM

Past Unreal Conditionals and Past Wishes

Think Critically About Form

A. Look back at the article on page 352 and complete the tasks below.

   1. **IDENTIFY** A past unreal conditional sentence is underlined. Find three more examples.

   2. **RECOGNIZE** What form is used in each *if* clause? What form is used in each main clause?

B. Discuss your answers with the class and read the Form charts to check them.

▶ Past Unreal Conditionals

ONLINE PRACTICE

PAST UNREAL CONDITIONALS		
⌐————— IF CLAUSE —————⌐	(THEN)	⌐————— MAIN CLAUSE —————⌐
IF + PAST PERFECT	*(THEN)*	*WOULD HAVE* + PAST PARTICIPLE
If I **had known** the answer,	(then)	I **would have passed** the test.
If I'**d known** the answer,	(then)	I'**d have passed** the test.

IF + PAST PERFECT	*(THEN)*	*COULD HAVE* + PAST PARTICIPLE
If I **had known** the answer,	(then)	I **could have passed** the test.

IF + PAST PERFECT	*(THEN)*	*MIGHT HAVE* + PAST PARTICIPLE
If I **had known** the answer,	(then)	I **might have passed** the test.

- The contraction of both *had* and *would* with pronouns is '*d*.
- When the *if* clause comes first, it is followed by a comma. When the main clause is first, there is no comma and *then* is not used.

     If I had known the answer, (then) **I would have passed** the test.

     I would have passed the test **if I had known** the answer.

- Either clause or both clauses can be negative.

     If I hadn't known the answer, **I would have asked** for help.

     If I hadn't known the answer, **I wouldn't have passed** the test.

- Questions are formed by putting the main clause in question word order.

    If you had known the answer, **would you have passed** the test?
- See Appendix 14 for contractions with *had* and *would*.

▶ Past Wishes

PAST WISHES	
⌐ *WISH* CLAUSE ¬	⌐ *THAT* CLAUSE ¬
SIMPLE PRESENT	(*THAT* +) PAST PERFECT
I **wish**	(that) I **had taken** a vacation last year.

SIMPLE PRESENT	(*THAT* +) *COULD HAVE* +PAST PERFECT
I **wish**	(that) you **could have come** to the show.

- *That* is often omitted after *wish*, but it is always implied.
- Notice the use of past perfect or past modal short forms when a *wish* clause follows *but*.

    I didn't take a vacation last year, but **I wish I had**.

    I invited Joe to the party, but **I wish I hadn't**.

    I didn't go to the show, but **I wish I could have**.

B1 Listening for Form

CD2 T39 **Listen to each conversation and choose the response that you hear.**

1. **a.** Not really. If it had been me, I would have interrupted him.

    b. Not really. If it had been me, I wouldn't have interrupted him.

2. **a.** If I had another chance, I'd prepare more for the interview.

    b. If I'd had another chance, I'd have prepared more for the interview.

3. **a.** No, I wouldn't.

    b. No, I wouldn't have.

4. **a.** If I had listened to my roommate, I would have taken it.

    b. If I had listened to my roommate, I wouldn't have taken it.

5. a. Yes, if I'd had my way, we would have moved to Seattle.

  b. Yes, if I had my way, we would move to Seattle.

6. a. I know. I would have called if it had been so late.

  b. I know. I would have called if it hadn't been so late.

B2 Completing Past Conditional Sentences

A. Complete these sentences with *would have, could have,* or *might have* in a past result clause.

1. If I had studied medicine, <u>I would have become a doctor.</u>

   _____

2. If I had known ten years ago what I know now, _____

   _____

3. If I had listened to my parents, _____

   _____

4. If I hadn't ever learned to read, _____

   _____

5. If I had been born in Australia, _____

   _____

6. If I had lived in another century, _____

   _____

7. If I hadn't studied English, _____

   _____

8. If I hadn't come to school today, _____

   _____

 B. On a separate sheet of paper, write three more past *if* clauses. Then trade papers with your partner and complete the sentences.

B3 Working on Past Conditionals

 Work in small groups. Start a past unreal conditional sentence chain with *If I hadn't slept well last night*, and finish it with a result clause. Use the end of the last person's sentence to begin your own sentence.

A: *If I hadn't slept well last night, I'd have been exhausted this morning.*

B: *If I'd been exhausted this morning, I would have stayed home from work.*

C: *If I'd stayed home from work,…*

Informally Speaking

Reduced Forms of Past Conditionals

 CD2 T40 Look at the cartoon and listen to the conversation. How is each underlined form in the cartoon different from what you hear?

The waiter overcharged me for lunch today, but I didn't say anything.

Well, I <u>would have</u> shown him the mistake. I sure <u>wouldn't have</u> paid the extra money.

In informal speech, would have, could have, and might have are often reduced like other past modals (see Chapter 8, page 175). Have may sound like /əv/. If it is reduced even more, it sounds like /ə/. Notice the reduction of the past perfect in the if clauses as well.

Standard Form	What You Might Hear
If **Tim had** driven, he **would have** arrived earlier.	"If /ˈtɪməd/ driven, he /ˈwʊdəv/ arrived earlier." OR "If /ˈtɪməd/ driven, he /ˈwʊdə/ arrived earlier."
If **Tim had** driven, he **could have** arrived earlier.	"If /ˈtɪməd/ driven, he /ˈkʊdəv/ arrived earlier." OR "If /ˈtɪməd/ driven, he /ˈkʊdə/ arrived earlier."
If **Joe had** been there, I **would not have** gone.	"If /ˈdʒoʊəd/ been there, I /ˈwʊdntəv/ gone." OR "If /ˈdʒoʊəd/ been there, I /ˈwʊdntə/ gone."
If **Joe had** been there, I **might not have** gone.	"If /ˈdʒoʊəd/ been there, I /ˈmaɪtnədəv/ gone." OR "If /ˈdʒoʊəd/ been there, I /ˈmaɪtnədə/ gone."

B4 Understanding Informal Speech

 CD2 T41 Listen and write the standard form of the words you hear.

1. <u>Would you have chosen</u> a different career if you hadn't married so young?

2. If I had studied, I _____ much better on the quiz.

3. We _____ so late if the car had been working.

4. If I hadn't been careful, I _____ an accident.

5. I _____ late if I'd missed the bus.

6. If I hadn't scored, we _____ the game.

B5 Working on Past Wishes

A. **Work with a partner. Complete these conversations with the appropriate forms of the verbs in parentheses to form past wishes. Then practice the conversations.**

1. **A:** _____Does he ever wish_____ (he/ever/wish) that he _____had chosen_____ (choose)
   ₁ ₂
   a different career when he graduated?

   B: Yes. Sometimes he _____ (wish) he _____
   ₃ ₄
   (go) to graduate school right after college.

2. **A:** My sister _____ (wish) she _____ (see) the
   ₁ ₂
   apartment upstairs when she was looking for one.

   B: I didn't know she was interested in a two-bedroom apartment.

   I _____ (wish) I _____ (show) it to her.
   ₃ ₄
   Then we could have been neighbors.

3. **A:** _____ (you/ever/wish) you _____ (learn) to
   ₁ ₂
   ski when you were younger?

   B: Yes, I _____ (wish) I _____ (be) braver when
   ₃ ₄
   my school offered lessons.

B. **Complete these sentences with the short form.**

1. I never learned to swim, but I wish _I had._____

2. He didn't graduate this year, but he wishes _____

3. We didn't see that movie, but we wish _____

4. They took the train, but they wish _____

5. She couldn't attend the meeting yesterday, but she wishes _____

Past Unreal Conditionals

Think Critically About Meaning and Use

A. Read the sentences and answer the questions below.

   a. If she had been a better student, she would have graduated on time.

   b. If she were a better student, she would graduate on time.

   1. EVALUATE Which sentence refers to a situation that was not true in the past?

   2. EVALUATE Which sentence refers to a situation that is not true in the present?

B. Discuss your answers with the class and read the Meaning and Use Notes to check them.

Meaning and Use Notes

ONLINE PRACTICE

Past Unreal Conditionals

▶ **1A**   Past unreal conditional sentences express imaginary situations that were actually not true in the past. In the *if* clause, the past perfect indicates the situation was unreal in the past. In the result clause, *would have, could have,* or *might have* also indicate the result was unreal in the past.

     If I **had been** the boss, I **would have fired** him. (I wasn't the boss, so I didn't fire him.)

▶ **1B**   *Could have* or *might have* in the result clause indicates one of several possible imaginary outcomes. *Would have* indicates that the speaker is more certain about the imaginary results.

     If you**'d had** your car, you **could have left** earlier.

     If you**'d had** your car, you **might not have left** so late. (*Could have* and *might have* both express one of several possible imaginary outcomes.)

     If you**'d had** your car, you **wouldn't have left** so late. (*Would have* expresses more certainty about the imaginary outcome.)

(Continued on page 360)

Giving Advice	

▶ 2 Unreal conditionals beginning with *If I had been you* can be used as an indirect way of giving advice. The *if* clause is often omitted. Unreal conditionals sound softer than modals like *should have*.

Advice with Past Unreal Conditionals	**Advice with Modals**
(If I**'d been** you,) I **would have left** early.	You **should have** left early.

Restating Past Unreal Conditionals with But	

▶ 3 Often, a sentence with *would have* is used without an *if* condition. Instead, the main clause is joined to a true (not imaginary) sentence with *but*. The true sentence with *but* implies the unreal past condition.

True Sentence with But	**Past Unreal Conditional**
I would have watched the tennis match, **but I had to study**.	I would have watched the tennis match **if I hadn't had to study**.
I would have left earlier, **but my car didn't start**.	I would have left earlier **if my car had started**.

C1 Listening for Meaning and Use

▶ Notes 1A, 1B

CD2 T42   Listen and choose the best answer to each question.

1. **a.** I don't know.
   b. I didn't know.

2. **a.** Yes, he did.
   b. He could have.

3. **a.** Maybe, but he'd be quite old.
   b. Maybe he hadn't.

4. **a.** It's hard to say.
   b. They certainly were.

5. **a.** Maybe not.
   b. Yes, they did.

6. **a.** It might be.
   b. It might have.

7. **a.** No, it won't.
   b. No, I doubt it.

8. **a.** No one knows.
   b. No one knew.

C2 Giving Indirect Advice

▶ Note 2

Work with a partner. Take turns giving indirect advice to your partner by telling what you would have done. The *if* clauses may be omitted.

1. **A:** I didn't understand last week's homework, but I didn't do anything about it.

   B: *(If I'd been you,) I would have gone to see the instructor.*

2. **A:** My best friend asked to borrow a lot of money. I gave it to him without asking any questions.

   B: _____

3. **A:** A salesperson was rude to me yesterday when I was buying a gift.

   B: _____

4. **A:** My doctor didn't answer all my questions.

   B: _____

5. **A:** My boss didn't offer me the raise that I wanted. I was disappointed.

   B: _____

6. **A:** The airline refused to change my ticket, even though it was an emergency.

   B: _____

C3 Distinguishing Fact and Fiction

▶ Note 3

Work with a partner. List the two facts that each conditional sentence implies. Then paraphrase the conditional sentence using *would have* followed by a true sentence with *but*.

1. If Alexander the Great hadn't died of yellow fever in 532 B.C., he would have attacked Carthage and Rome.

   Facts: 1. *Alexander the Great died of yellow fever in 532 B.C.*

   2. *He didn't attack Carthage and Rome.*

   Paraphrase: *Alexander the Great would have attacked Carthage and Rome, but he died of yellow fever in 532 B.C.*

(Continued on page 362)

2. If Napoleon's armies had had proper nails for horseshoes, they would have conquered Russia.

      Facts: 1. _____

                2. _____

      Paraphrase: _____

                          _____

3. If Apollo 13 hadn't had an explosion during its flight, it would have landed on the moon as planned.

      Facts: 1. _____

                2. _____

      Paraphrase: _____

                          _____

4. If Mozart hadn't died young, he would have finished his famous piece *Requiem*.

      Facts: 1. _____

                2. _____

      Paraphrase: _____

                          _____

5. If an asteroid or meteorite hadn't crashed into Earth, dinosaurs wouldn't have died out 65 million years ago.

      Facts: 1. _____

                2. _____

      Paraphrase: _____

                          _____

C4 Describing the Ifs of History

▶ Notes 1A, 1B

Work in small groups. Think of five historical events that you know something about. Make up two past unreal conditional sentences about each event.

Apollo 13: If an oxygen tank hadn't exploded during the flight into space, the astronauts' lives wouldn't have been in danger. If the explosion hadn't happened, the astronauts would have landed on the moon.

Past Wishes

Think Critically About Meaning and Use

A. Read the sentences and answer the questions below.

1a. I wish the temperature were warmer. I am freezing.
1b. I wish the temperature had been warmer. I was freezing.
2a. If only he didn't have a cold. He really wants to go out.
2b. If only he hadn't had a cold. He really wanted to go out.

1. **ANALYZE** Which sentences are about present situations? Which are about past situations?

2. **ANALYZE** Which pair of sentences seems to express stronger feelings?

B. Discuss your answers with the class and read the Meaning and Use Notes to check them.

Meaning and Use Notes

ONLINE
PRACTICE

Making Wishes About the Past

▶ 1   Past *wish* sentences refer to past situations that did not occur. They express a desire to change something that happened in the past.

I **wish** the weather **had been** nice yesterday. (It rained yesterday.)

I **wish** you **could have seen** the movie. (You didn't see the movie.)

Expressing Regret or Dissatisfaction

▶ 2   When you use a past *wish* sentence, you express regret or dissatisfaction about a past situation.

I **wish** I **had gone** to the meeting. I completely forgot about it. I **wish** someone **had called** to remind me.

Using If Only

▶ 3   *If only* is often used in place of a past wish to express strong regret. *If only* sentences focus on the wish to change a negative outcome.

If only I **hadn't lost** my wallet!   **If only** the war **had ended** sooner!

D1 Listening for Meaning and Use

▶ Notes 1–3

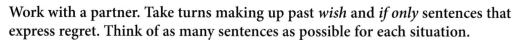 CD2 T43 Listen to each situation and choose the sentence that is true.

1. **a.** I read about World War II.
   b. I saw a movie. *(circled)*

2. **a.** I wasn't home.
   b. I answered the phone.

3. **a.** She wasn't elected.
   b. She represents us now.

4. **a.** You called.
   b. The exam ended.

5. **a.** They got reservations.
   b. They didn't fly home.

6. **a.** There was a tree on the driveway.
   b. I wasn't leaving.

7. **a.** You took a day off last week.
   b. You took today off.

8. **a.** I didn't have a headache.
   b. I didn't stay.

D2 Expressing Regret

▶ Notes 2, 3

Work with a partner. Take turns making up past *wish* and *if only* sentences that express regret. Think of as many sentences as possible for each situation.

1. You refused to lend your brother money. He had to drop out of school for a semester because he couldn't pay his tuition.

   I wish I'd lent him the money.

   If only I'd helped him.

2. You lost your temper today when you were baby-sitting your nephew. He began to cry.

3. You didn't tell your boss how overworked you've been feeling. Now he has changed your schedule, and you can't take a day off.

4. You didn't call the doctor last week when you got sick. Now you've missed a week of classes.

5. You forgot your best friend's birthday. There was a special dinner for your friend and you didn't go.

6. You accepted a job offer on Monday. On Tuesday you got a better offer from another company.

D3 Expressing Regret or Dissatisfaction

▶ Notes 2, 3

 A. Work with a partner. Take turns reacting to the statements by using a past *wish* sentence or *if only* sentence with short forms.

1. **A:** The library was closed yesterday.

   B: _I wish it hadn't been._

2. **A:** Our team didn't win first prize.

   B: _If only we had._

3. **A:** The president raised taxes again.

   B: _____

4. **A:** My TV stopped working.

   B: _____

5. **A:** The train was late.

   B: _____

6. **A:** I didn't invite Peter.

   B: _____

7. **A:** It snowed a lot.

   B: _____

8. **A:** They didn't call back.

   B: _____

 B. With your partner, expand one of the examples above into a longer conversation between two people. (Try to have each person speak three or four times.) Give more details about the situation and try to use at least one more wish sentence, *if only* sentence, or past unreal conditional sentence.

A: The library was closed last night.

B: I know. I wish it hadn't been.

A: I needed to work on my paper. If only I had checked the schedule a few days ago, I would have been able to finish on time.

D4 Explaining Wishes

▶ Note 1

A. Think of two past events in your life that you wish you could have changed. Write a past *wish* sentence about each one. Then write a past *if* sentence to explain your wish.

I wish my family hadn't moved when I was young.
If they hadn't moved, I wouldn't have been so lonely.

B. Now expand one of the events from part A into a paragraph. First, make a list of details that would have been different if your wish had come true. Then use your list to write your paragraph. Use *would have*, *could have*, and *might have*.

I wish my family hadn't moved when I was young. If we hadn't moved, I wouldn't have been so lonely. I wouldn't have had to leave my best friend. Who knows? We might have remained friends forever. We could have…

Think Critically About Meaning and Use

A. Read each sentence and the statements that follow. Write *T* if the statement is true or *F* if it is false.

1. I would have reached you if the phone had been working.

    _F_ **a.** The phone was working.

    _____ **b.** I didn't reach you.

2. I wish I had taken a vacation.

    _____ **a.** I should have taken a vacation.

    _____ **b.** I took a vacation.

3. She wouldn't have taken the medication if she had known about the risks.

    _____ **a.** She knew about the risks.

    _____ **b.** She took the medication.

4. If only I hadn't followed his advice.

    _____ **a.** I didn't follow his advice.

    _____ **b.** I shouldn't have followed his advice.

5. I would have come over, but my car broke down.

    _____ **a.** I couldn't come over because my car broke down.

    _____ **b.** If my car hadn't broken down, I would have come over.

6. If I had been there, I'd have complained to the manager.

    _____ **a.** I complained to the manager.

    _____ **b.** I'd have complained to the manager, but I wasn't there.

7. If we hadn't bought our tickets already, we wouldn't have gone to the show.

    _____ **a.** We had already bought our tickets.

    _____ **b.** We went to the show.

8. If only we'd been told about the delay.

    _____ **a.** No one told us about the delay.

    _____ **b.** I regret that we weren't told about the delay.

B. Discuss these questions in small groups. (Try to come up with three answers, using *would*, *could*, and *might* in each main clause.)

1. **GENERATE** What past unreal conditionals can you think of to explain the wish in sentence 2?

2. **GENERATE** What past unreal conditionals can you think of to explain the if only regrets in sentences 4 and 8?

Edit

Find the errors in these paragraphs and correct them.

Historians love to think about the dramatic "what-ifs" of history. They have even given the name "counterfactual history" to this pursuit. How would history ~~had~~ *have* changed if some key event had been different? What would the consequences been if the weather has been different in a certain battle? What would had happened if a famous person had lived instead of died? These are the sorts of questions that are asked in two recent books that imagine how history might been under different circumstances: *What If?*, edited by R. Cowley and S. Ambrose; and *Virtual History*, edited by N. Ferguson.

Don't just wish you've been alive in a different era. Go back and explore what could have, should have, or might have happened at various times in history. You won't be sorry. You'll wish you'll gone back sooner!

Write

Imagine you are doing a project for a history class. The deadline is in two weeks, but your research isn't going well. Write an email to your instructor expressing regret for the delay and explaining the problems you've had and what you might have done differently. Use past unreal conditionals and at least one past wish or *if only* sentence.

1. **BRAINSTORM** Think about all the problems you've had and what you could have or should have done differently. Then use these categories to help you organize your email into paragraphs:

   - **Opening:** Say why you're writing. Express regret that you will miss the deadline.
   - **Body:** Explain the problems you've encountered. Talk about what you did and how things would have turned out differently if you had done things differently.
   - **Closing:** Make a polite request for an extension. Apologize again, and, if desired, say what you've learned from the experience.

2. **WRITE A FIRST DRAFT** Before you write your first draft, read the checklist below and look at the examples in D2 and D4 on pages 364–365. Write your draft using past unreal conditionals.

3. **EDIT** Read your work and check it against the checklist below. Circle grammar, spelling, and punctuation errors.

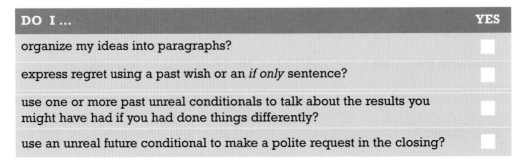

DO I ...	YES
organize my ideas into paragraphs?	☐
express regret using a past wish or an *if only* sentence?	☐
use one or more past unreal conditionals to talk about the results you might have had if you had done things differently?	☐
use an unreal future conditional to make a polite request in the closing?	☐

4. **PEER REVIEW** Work with a partner to help you decide how to fix your errors and improve the content. Use the checklist above.

5. **REWRITE YOUR DRAFT** Using the comments from your partner, write a final draft.

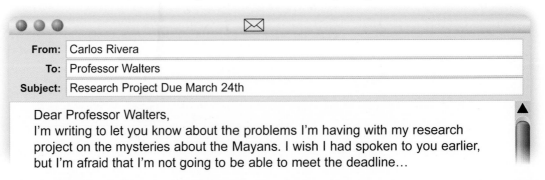

From: Carlos Rivera
To: Professor Walters
Subject: Research Project Due March 24th

Dear Professor Walters,
I'm writing to let you know about the problems I'm having with my research project on the mysteries about the Mayans. I wish I had spoken to you earlier, but I'm afraid that I'm not going to be able to meet the deadline...

Choose the correct word or words to complete each sentence.

1. If they had taken better precautions, _____ they have avoided the problems that they later encountered?

   a. could   **b.** will   **c.** may   **d.** must

2. The candidate said very clearly that he _____ cut funding for education under any circumstances if he were governor.

   a. didn't   **b.** wouldn't   **c.** can't   **d.** won't

3. If alternative sources of energy became widely available, how much more money _____ willing to pay for them?

   a. people are   **b.** people would be   **c.** will people be   **d.** would people be

4. I wish _____ start taking better care of yourself.

   a. he'll   **b.** you'll   **c.** you'd   **d.** you'll be able to

Choose the correct response to complete each conversation.

5. **A:** Did you argue with your brother?
   B: Yes, but _____

   a. I wish I hadn't.   **c.** I wish I did.

   b. I wish I had.   **d.** I wish I wouldn't.

6. **A:** What would you have done if you had missed the flight?
   B: _____

   a. I'd canceled the meeting.   **c.** I must have canceled the meeting.

   b. I'd cancel the meeting.   **d.** I'd have canceled the meeting.

7. **A:** I hope the plane lands early.
   B: _____

   a. When did it land?   **c.** I knew it would.

   b. That'd be nice.   **d.** I'm glad it will.

8. **A:** If only I didn't have to work tomorrow.
   B: _____

   a. Why don't you have to work?   **c.** Why do you have to work?

   b. Why did you have to work?   **d.** Why didn't you have to work?

Complete each conversation using the correct form of the word or words in parentheses. Do not use contractions.

9. **A:** She wanted to be an artist, but her father insisted on her studying medicine.

   B: If I'd been in her position, I _____ (refuse).

10. **A:** Kim's neighbors had another loud party last night. She didn't sleep at all.

   B: If it had been me, _____ (call) the police.

11. **A:** I washed my new sweater, and now it's too small.

   B: If it had been my sweater, _____ (take) it to the dry cleaner's.

Complete the question in each conversation using the correct form of the word or words in parentheses.

12. **A:** If your boss had given you the day off, _____ (you/take) it?

   B: Of course, I would have! But, unfortunately, she'd never do that!

13. **A:** _____ (you/bring) that laptop with you if you had had room in your suitcase?

   B: Definitely not. It's Mike's, and I would have worried about losing it.

14. **A:** Would you have bought the house if _____ (you/know) the economy was going to slow down?

   B: Probably not. We like the house, but it's a real struggle to afford it in this economy.

Match the response to the correct statement below.

_____ 15. I forgot to pay the electric bill.

_____ 16. We won the championship!

_____ 17. You should have apologized.

        a. If only he'd seen the sign.

        b. I wish I had seen the game.

        c. You're right. I wish I had.

        d. I wish you had waited.

        e. If only I'd reminded you.

        f. I wish I'd known her better.

What does each sentence express? Choose the correct answer from the box below.

promise	fact	warning	instruction	prediction	advice

18. If the printer runs out of paper, refill it immediately. _____

19. If you come over tomorrow, I'll help you. _____

20. If two hydrogen atoms combine with one oxygen atom, they form a water molecule.

   _____

PART 7

7

Noun Clauses and Reported Speech

CHAPTER

17

Noun Clauses

Career Currents

A1 Before You Read

Discuss these questions.

What is the best way to find a new job? Would you quit your job before you found a better one? Why or why not?

A2 Read

 CD2 T44 **Read this article from a website to find out some of the benefits of looking for a new job.**

InfoWorld

Career Currents

Even if you're not sure whether you want a new job, it doesn't hurt to look.

Have you ever considered how bad your job has to be before you start looking for a new one?
5 Just how miserable do you have to be? Should you wait until you dread going to work each morning? I recently heard from a reader who was increasingly unhappy with his job and was asking himself these questions.

10 The reader didn't think that his managers treated him with respect. He was beginning to lose his enthusiasm for work. Although he was working toward a master's degree in information systems, he didn't feel that his managers recognized his efforts or his new skills. He wondered whether he should continue at his present job or start to look for a new one.

15 Unlike a lot of questions I receive from readers, this one has an easy answer: He should do both. He should also stop thinking that job hunting and working to improve his current job are opposites. In fact, they're closely related. A traditional job hunt can lead to a new job with a new company. But the steps that you go through to look for a new job can also help you improve your current job.

20   The first step in a job hunt is to find out what opportunities are out there. You learn
      what kinds of skills and experience are required to get those jobs. You also learn how
      much these positions pay. Then you update your résumé and begin selling yourself to
      potential employers in cover letters and interviews.

      You may not know if you would actually end up switching jobs. Nevertheless, having an
25   updated résumé is still a good idea because you now have one if you need it, and
      creating a résumé forces you to think of all that you have accomplished in your current
      job. When you try to match your résumé to the jobs that are available, you will discover
      which areas you need more experience in and which skills you need to improve. You
      will also learn what opportunities are available and what the salaries are. This
30   information could put you in a good position to get a better deal from your current
      employer if you realize that you are not making enough money.

      Try to use what you learn during your job hunt to improve your current position. This
      may mean that you should present your boss with the results of your salary research
      and a list of your accomplishments, and then ask for a raise. Or perhaps you should
35   take some classes or find out if you can work on different types of projects to expand
      your opportunities.

Adapted from *InfoWorld.com*

---

dread: to have feelings of anxiety about something
miserable: extremely unhappy

potential: possible, though not yet actual or real
update: to make something current

A3 After You Read

Check (✓) the advice that is true according to the article.

_✓_ **1.** It's a good idea to find out about other available jobs even if you're not really thinking about quitting.

_____ **2.** Don't update your résumé.

_____ **3.** Quit your job before you look for a new one.

_____ **4.** Find out the salaries of jobs that are similar to yours before you ask for a raise.

_____ **5.** You can sometimes improve your current job by looking for a new job.

Noun Clauses

Think Critically About Form

A. Look back at the article on page 372 and complete the tasks below.

1. **IDENTIFY** There are many noun clauses underlined in the article. Find at least three examples of each of these types:

   a. noun clauses beginning with *wh-* words (e.g., *what*, *how*, *which*)
   b. noun clauses beginning with *if/whether*
   c. noun clauses beginning with *that*

2. **ANALYZE** Circle the subject and verb in one noun clause of each type. Are they in statement word order or question word order?

B. Discuss your answers with the class and read the Form charts to check them.

▶ Noun Clauses

ONLINE PRACTICE

WH- CLAUSES	
MAIN CLAUSE	**WH- CLAUSE**
He wondered	**who I was**. **what she was wearing**. **why I called**.
Can you tell me	**where he is**? **when the train arrives**? **how they do it**?

IF/WHETHER CLAUSES	
MAIN CLAUSE	**IF/WHETHER CLAUSE**
I wonder	**if he left (or not)**.
I don't know	**if he's still here (or not)**.
Can you tell me	**whether he arrived (or not)**? **whether (or not) he arrived**? **if he arrived (or not)**?

THAT CLAUSES	
MAIN CLAUSE	**THAT CLAUSE**
I think	**(that) he called**.
Did they doubt	**(that) he would call**?

Noun Clauses

• There are three different types of noun clauses: *wh-* clauses, *if/whether* clauses, and *that* clauses.

- Noun clauses are dependent clauses that can occur in the same place as a noun or noun phrase in a sentence. All noun clauses have a subject and a verb.

Wh- Clauses

- *Wh-* clauses are sometimes called indirect questions or embedded questions. Although *wh-* clauses begin with *wh-* words, they use statement word order.

  I wonder **where he is**.   x I wonder where is he. (INCORRECT)

- Use a question mark only if the main clause is a question.

  <u>Can you tell me</u> **what happened**?

If/Whether Clauses

- *If/whether* clauses are also sometimes called indirect questions or embedded questions. They also use statement word order.

  Do you know **if you're coming with us**?

  x Do you know if are you coming with us? (INCORRECT)

- *Or not* can be added to the end of *if/whether* clauses if the clauses are not very long.

  I wonder **whether she left <u>or not</u>**.   I wonder **if she left <u>or not</u>**.

- *Or not* can also immediately follow *whether*, but it can't follow *if*.

  I wonder **whether <u>or not</u> she left**.   x I wonder if or not she left. (INCORRECT)

That Clauses

- *That* can usually be omitted.

B1 Listening for Form

CD2 T45   Listen to the sentences. Do you hear a *wh-* clause, an *if/whether* clause, or a *that* clause? Check (✓) the correct column.

	WH- CLAUSE	*IF/WHETHER* CLAUSE	*THAT* CLAUSE
1.	✓		
2.			
3.			
4.			
5.			
6.			
7.			
8.			

B2 Identifying Noun Clauses

Read this information about résumés. Find the *wh-*, *if/whether*, and *that* noun clauses and underline them. Then circle the verb in the main clause related to each noun clause.

Many employment counselors (believe) that your résumé is a kind of personal advertisement. It summarizes what you have accomplished and describes what kind of work you want. Hopefully, it tells why *you* should be hired. A good résumé doesn't always determine whether you will get an interview, but a bad one will certainly eliminate your chances.

Résumés are only one tool that you need to use in your employment search. Many employers don't even use them; employers often decide whether they should hire you based on other information. Nevertheless, most employment counselors believe that it is worthwhile to write a good résumé. It helps you get organized. Most importantly, it helps you figure out what kind of job you really want and whether or not you have the qualifications.

B3 Working on *Wh-* Clauses

 Work with a partner. Complete the noun clauses with the subjects and verbs in parentheses and the correct tense. Then practice the conversations.

1. Person A is looking for Yuki.

   A: Do you know where _____Yuki went_____ (Yuki/go) after lunch?
   ₁

   B: No, and I don't know what time _____she came back_____ (she/come back).
   ₂

2. Person A didn't receive any mail.

   A: I wonder why _____ (the mail/not/come) today.
   ₁

   B: Maybe I'll call the post office and ask what _____ (happen).
   ₂

   Do you know what time _____ (the post office/close)?
   ₃

3. Person A needs information about the chemistry exam.

   A: Do you know when _____ (the chemistry exam/be)?
   ₁

   B: Yes, it's on Thursday, but I'm not sure when _____
   ₂

   (it/start) or how long _____ (it/last).
   ₃

4. Person A is in a department store.

A: I'd like to find out how much _____ (this/cost).
1

B: I'm not sure, but I'll ask the manager as soon as I find out where

_____ (he/be).
2

B4 Working on *If/Whether* Clauses

Work with a partner. Use your own words to complete the *if/whether* clauses. Use appropriate tenses depending on the context. Then practice the conversations.

1. Two friends are on the way home from work.

A: Do you know if the bank _is open now?_ _____
1

B: I'm not sure if _it is or not._ _____ They've recently changed their hours.
2

2. Person A is getting ready to leave for work.

A: I wonder whether _____
1

B: Take your umbrella if you're not sure.

3. Person A is buying groceries.

A: Can you tell me if _____
1

B: I'm not sure if _____ or not. I'll ask the manager.
2

4. Person A is buying tickets for a concert.

A: I was wondering if you could tell me whether _____
1

B: There aren't any seats left on that date. Should I check whether

_____
2

5. Person A needs to put gas in his car.

A: Do you know if _____ near here?
1

B: I'm not certain if _____. Maybe you should ask
2

someone else.

6. Person A is planning a weekend trip.

A: I wonder if _____ this weekend.
1

B: I didn't see the weather forecast, so I don't know whether

_____ or not.
2

B5 Unscrambling Sentences with *That* Clauses

Work with a partner. Unscramble the words to make a statement or a question with a *that* clause. Use every word. The first word of each sentence is underlined for you. *That* has been omitted from some of the sentences.

1. was/that/you/he/angry/notice/<u>did</u>

   Did you notice that he was angry?

2. predict/it/soon/happen/<u>they</u>/will

   _____

3. help/<u>I</u>/some/need/I/that/guess

   _____

4. that/due/remembered/my/is/rent/<u>I</u>/tomorrow

   _____

5. proved/could/<u>he</u>/do/it/he

   _____

B6 Completing Noun Clauses

A. Use the questions in parentheses to complete each main clause. You may have to add *if* or *whether* at the beginning of some noun clauses.

1. I was wondering _what experience you have._

   (What experience do you have?)

2. Could you tell me _____

   (How long did you work there?)

3. I was wondering _____

   (Did you like your job?)

4. Can you tell me _____

   (What is your greatest strength?)

5. Could you explain _____

   (Why are you changing jobs?)

B. Work with a partner. Pretend you are at a job interview. Take turns asking and answering the questions in part A.

Wh- and *If/Whether* Clauses

Think Critically About Meaning and Use

A. Read the sentences and complete the tasks below.

1a. Sally: I can't decide what I need for the trip. Did you get everything on your list?
1b. Pam: I don't know whether I did or not. I lost my list. I wonder if it's in the car.
2a. Excuse me. Is the bus late?
2b. Excuse me. Can you tell me if the bus is late?

1. IDENTIFY Underline the noun clauses in sentences 1a and 1b. Circle the verb that comes before each clause. Which verbs express mental activities?

2. EVALUATE Which question sounds more polite, 2a or 2b?

B. Discuss your answers with the class and read the Meaning and Use Notes to check them.

Meaning and Use Notes

ONLINE
PRACTICE

Noun Clauses After Mental Activity Verbs

▶ **1A** *Wh-* clauses and *if/whether* clauses often follow mental activity verbs. These sentences frequently express uncertainty, curiosity, decisions, and other mental activities.

A: I don't <u>know</u> **how to start my job search**. I can't <u>decide</u> **what kind of job to look for**.

B: I <u>wonder</u> **if she has her cell phone**. You could call her.

▶ **1B** Below are some common mental activity verbs. See Appendix 11 for more verbs commonly followed by noun clauses.

consider	figure out	guess	learn	realize	understand
decide	forget	know	notice	remember	wonder

▶ **1C** *Wh-* and *if/whether* clauses often follow these expressions of uncertainty.

<u>I'm not sure</u> **why she left**.

<u>I'm not certain</u> **if he's coming tonight**.

<u>I have no idea</u> **where he is**.

(Continued on page 380)

Wh- and *If/Whether* Clauses After Other Verbs

▶ **2**   Many other verbs and phrases are commonly followed by *wh-* and *if/whether* clauses.

ask	depend on	hear	rely on	see	tell (someone)
demonstrate	explain	notice	say	show	write

Indirect Questions

▶ **3A**   *Wh-* or *if/whether* clauses often follow certain phrases to express indirect questions. Indirect questions sound more polite than *Wh-* questions or *Yes/No* questions.

Direct Questions	Indirect Questions
When does the train arrive?	Can you (please) tell me **when the train arrives**?
	I was wondering **when the train arrives**.
Has the train arrived yet?	Do you know **if the train has arrived yet**?
	I'd like to find out **if the train has arrived ye**t.

▶ **3B**   Below are some common expressions used to introduce indirect questions.

Do you know…?	Do you remember…?
Can/Could you tell me…?	Do you have any idea…?
Can you remember…?	I'd like to know/find out…
Could you explain…?	I wonder/was wondering…

C1 Listening for Meaning and Use

▶ Notes 1A, 3A, 3B

CD2 T46   **Listen to these situations. Choose the sentence that most appropriately follows what you hear.**

1. a. Yes, it is.
    (b.) Yes, around eight.

2. a. So was I. Let's ask him.
    b. No, I don't.

3. a. Yes, she works.
    b. No, I don't.

4. a. I wonder who.
    b. I wonder why.

5. a. It did.
    b. I did.

6. a. Yes. It's over there.
    b. Yes. I know it.

7. a. In room 2.
    b. Sure. Let me look it up.

8. a. Yes. Be patient.
    b. It certainly is.

C2 Expressing Uncertainty

▶ Notes 1A–1C

Work with a partner. Imagine you are witnesses at the scene of a traffic accident. Take turns asking and answering the police officer's questions. Use a *wh-* clause and a statement of uncertainty: *I can't remember, I'm not sure, I don't know, I'm not certain, I have no idea.*

1. Who was driving the truck?

   I'm not sure who was driving it.

2. What time did the accident occur?

3. What did the truck look like?

4. How many people were in the truck?

5. What was the license plate number on the truck?

6. How fast was the truck going?

7. What color was the truck?

8. What did the driver look like?

Vocabulary Notes

C3 Adding *If/Whether* Clauses to Expressions of Uncertainty

A. Work with a partner. Read each situation and complete the sentences with an *if/whether* clause in the correct tense. Add *or not* to some of your noun clauses.

1. This is the first day of Sheila's new job. She's nervous on her way to work.

   a. She wonders _if she'll like her new job._

   b. She's not sure _____

   c. She has no idea _____

2. Min-woo has seen the house of his dreams. He's going to make an offer to buy it tonight. He's been worrying about it all day.

   a. He wonders _____

   b. He doesn't know _____

   c. He's not sure _____

B. Work on your own. Think of a situation in which you did something for the first time and you were uncertain about it. Make a list of some of the problems you had. Then write a paragraph explaining your uncertainty in detail. Use some statements of uncertainty followed by *if/whether* clauses.

> *Before I moved to France, I had a lot of decisions to make. I wasn't sure whether I should sell my furniture or not. I wondered if it would be cheaper to buy new furniture after I arrived in France. However, I was surprised when I found out how much new furniture costs.*

C4 Asking Indirect Questions with *If/Whether* Clauses

▶ Notes 3A, 3B

Work with a partner. Make each question less direct by using *I was wondering, Can/Could you (please) tell me, Do you know,* or *Do you have any idea* + an *if/whether* clause.

1. Did you have any trouble with the last assignment?

   I was wondering if you had any trouble with the last assignment.

2. Is the library closed during vacation?

3. Is the teacher going to show a film today?

4. Is the assignment due tomorrow?

5. Is the new language lab open yet?

6. Did I miss anything important yesterday?

C5 Asking Indirect Questions with *Wh-* Clauses

▶ Notes 3A, 3B

Work with a partner. Make up a polite question for each situation, using a *wh-* clause. Take turns asking and answering each question.

1. *At the airport*

   a. You're looking for a restroom.

      A: *Excuse me. Can you please tell me where the restroom is?*

      B: *It's downstairs on the left.*

   b. You're looking for the baggage claim.

2. *At a bus stop*

   a. You're asking someone for the time.

   b. You're looking for the bus schedule.

3. *In a department store*

   a. You're asking a salesperson the price of a shirt.

   b. You're asking a salesperson the size of a pair of pants.

4. *In the supermarket*

   a. You're looking for the manager.

   b. You're asking the clerk for the price of broccoli.

5. *On campus*

   a. You're looking for the history department.

   b. You want to pay your tuition bill.

D | MEANING AND USE 2

That Clauses

Think Critically About Meaning and Use

A. Read the sentences and answer the questions below.

1a. I know that he left.
1b. I know that he's leaving.
2a. I remembered that the answer to the question was *ten*.
2b. I remembered that the answer to the question is *ten*.

1. ANALYZE Which pair of sentences has the same meaning?

2. ANALYZE Which pair does not? Why?

B. Discuss your answers with the class and read the Meaning and Use Notes to check them.

Meaning and Use Notes

ONLINE PRACTICE

	***That* Clauses After Mental Activity Verbs**
▶ **1A**	Noun clauses beginning with *that* often follow mental activity verbs to express thoughts and opinions. I <u>remembered</u> **(that) she called yesterday.** I <u>believe</u> **(that) employers should read résumés carefully.**
▶ **1B**	Below are some common mental activity verbs that are followed by *that* clauses. See Appendix 11 for more verbs commonly followed by noun clauses. agree believe doubt feel hope recognize suppose assume bet expect find imagine regret think
▶ **1C**	*That* clauses often follow these expressions: <u>I'm not sure</u> **(that) he can come.** <u>I'm afraid</u> **(that) I can't come.** <u>I'm not certain</u> **(that) he's coming.** <u>It appears</u> **(that) he didn't come.** <u>I had no idea</u> **(that) he was coming.** <u>It seems</u> **(that) he couldn't come.**

Tense Agreement After Mental Activity Verbs

▶ **2A** When the mental activity verb is in the present tense, the verb in the noun clause can be in the present, past, or future. The tense depends on the meaning of the sentence.

Present + Present	**Present + Past**	**Present + Future**
I <u>think</u> **it's OK**.	I <u>believe</u> **she** <u>sent</u> **the letter**.	I <u>assume</u> **they'll come** later.

▶ **2B** When the mental activity verb is in the past, the verb in the noun clause usually takes a past form to express the speaker's past perspective.

Past + Past

I <u>thought</u> **that she** <u>was sleeping</u>.   x I thought that she is sleeping. (INCORRECT)

I <u>assumed</u> **he** <u>was happy</u> **when**   x I assumed he is happy when I called.
    he called.   (INCORRECT)

▶ **2C** When the mental activity verb is in the past, and you want to refer to an earlier past time, use the past perfect in the noun clause.

Earlier Time (Past + Past Perfect)

I <u>knew</u> **that she** <u>had left</u>.

▶ **2D** When the mental activity verb is in the past, and you want to refer to a time that follows the past time, use *was/were going to* or *would* in the noun clause.

Later Time (Past + Past Continuous)	**Later Time (Past + Would)**
I <u>thought</u> **she** <u>was going to come</u> later.	I <u>thought</u> **she** <u>would come</u> later.

Exceptions to Tense Agreement Rules

If a noun clause is a generalization that is true at the present, the present tense can be used in the noun clause instead of the past tense.

Columbus <u>believed</u> **that the world** <u>is</u> round.

If a past mental activity took place quickly, the present, past, or future tense can be used in the noun clause. Spontaneous mental activity verbs include *decide, discover, figure out, forget, find out, learn, notice, prove, realize, recall,* and *remember.*

Last night, I <u>realized</u>
Last night, I <u>decided</u>
      (that) my report <u>is</u> **too long.**
      (that) my report <u>was</u> **too long.**
      (that) my report <u>will be</u> **too long.**

D1 Listening for Meaning and Use

▶ Notes 2A–2D

 CD2 T47 Listen to these situations. Choose the sentence that most appropriately follows.

1. **a.** I hope she's on time.

    b. I hope she was on time.

2. **a.** I think it's Joan. I'll go find out.

    b. I thought it was Joan. I'll go find out.

3. **a.** Why did he leave?

    b. Why doesn't he leave?

4. **a.** How much did you buy?

    b. How much will you buy?

5. **a.** Yes, he was right.

    b. Good for him.

6. **a.** She was.

    b. She is.

D2 Thinking About Tense Agreement with *That* Clauses

▶ Notes 2A–2D

A. Complete the sentences by circling all of the phrases that can form grammatical sentences.

1. I thought it (is snowing/ was going to snow / snowed) in the mountains last night.

2. He doubts that (they'll accept / they accept / they accepted) credit cards.

3. I hoped my plane (won't be / wouldn't be / isn't) late.

4. I left the game early because I assumed our team (will win / had won / wins) the championship.

5. She decided that she (needs / needed / will need) help.

6. He's certain that the show (will start / starts / started) at 8:00.

B. Choose two of the grammatical sentences from part A and write two short dialogues using the sentences in appropriate contexts.

A: We can't ski today.

B: You're kidding. I thought it was going to snow in the mountains last night. I'm so disappointed.

D3 Giving Opinions Using *That* Clauses

▶ Notes 1A, 1B, 2A

A. Work in small groups. Take turns expressing your own opinions about each statement. Use as many mental activity verbs as you can with that clauses.

1. Our community could be doing more to protect the environment.

    I agree that we're not doing enough for the environment. I think...

2. Most people are basically honest.

3. Hybrid cars are a good idea.

4. You can't really change someone.

5. All children should leave home at 18.

6. We learn from our mistakes.

B. On your own, make up two more statements. Read them aloud and ask your group to give opinions using mental activity verbs.

D4 Expressing Opinions About Work

▶ Notes 1A–1C

A. Read these survey results on job satisfaction in the United States. Do people in your country have the same concerns? Discuss your ideas with a partner.

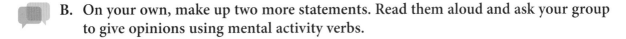

	U.S. Workers find some major problems in the workplace.
	In a survey of 1,000 adults it was found that:

95%	are concerned about spending more time with their family.
92%	don't have enough flexibility in their schedules to take care of family needs.
88%	are concerned about work-related stress.
87%	say they don't get enough sleep.
60%	would take training courses if they were paid for by the employer.
49%	believe on-site child care is important, but only 12% of employers offer this benefit.
46%	work more than 40 hours per week: 18% work more than 50 hours per week.
45%	had to work overtime with little or no advance notice.
44%	think the opportunity to telecommute is important, but only 17% of employers offer telecommuting opportunities.

from U.S. Newswire

B. How do you feel about the workers' concerns in part A? Use the mental activity verbs below and that clauses to organize your ideas. Then discuss with a partner.

I think/believe/agree that…	I don't believe/think that…
I feel/imagine/suppose that…	I doubt that…
It appears/seems that…	I hope/expect that…

I agree that most workers want to spend more time with their families.

Think Critically About Meaning and Use

A. Read each sentence and the statement that follows. Write *T* if the statement is true, *F* if it is false, and *?* if you do not have enough information to decide.

1. I regret that Mary left.

___F___ Mary is going to leave.

2. I think she passed the test.

_____ She passed the test.

3. I'm not sure who rang the bell.

_____ Someone rang the bell.

4. She realized how late it was.

_____ She didn't know if it was late.

5. I wonder whether they left or not.

_____ They didn't leave.

6. She doubts that she will come tonight.

_____ She doesn't think she'll come.

7. He regretted that he left early.

_____ He wasn't sorry that he left early.

8. We assumed they had won.

_____ They won.

B. Discuss these questions in small groups.

1. GENERATE How would you change the statements that follow 1 and 7 to make them true?

2. SYNTHESIZE How would you complete the following sentence so that it means the same as 8:

We supposed _____ (win), but _____ (not/know) for sure.

Edit

Find the errors in these sentences and correct them.

1. I wonder where ~~is~~ *he is* ~~he~~.

2. I asked her if could borrow her pen.

3. I thought that she is sleeping when I called.

4. I can't remember who called?

5. Do you know if are you coming with us?

6. I didn't realize, that she was absent.

7. She thought he will come later.

8. Do you know if or not he's staying?

9. I need John's phone number, but I don't know where the phone book.

10. Frederica didn't understand what was saying the teacher.

Write

Imagine you write for the website of your country's national tourist organization. Write a Frequently Asked Questions (FAQs) page addressing the concerns that a first-time visitor to your country might have. Use mental activity verbs and noun clauses of different types.

1. **BRAINSTORM** Think of all the things a first-time visitor to your country might want to know about. Use some or all of these categories to organize your FAQ page.

   - travel documents and shots
   - best season(s) to travel
   - sights and activities
   - local food to eat
   - accommodation
   - transportation

2. **WRITE A FIRST DRAFT** Before you write your first draft, read the checklist below and look at the way noun clauses and indirect questions are used on pages 374–375 and 380. Write your draft using noun clauses.

3. **EDIT** Read your work and check it against the checklist below. Circle grammar, spelling, and punctuation errors.

DO I ...	YES
add a paragraph at the beginning to introduce the FAQs?	☐
use a range of mental activity and other verbs that are usually followed by noun clauses?	☐
use at least one example of a *wh-* clause, an *if/whether* clause, and a *that* clause?	☐
take care to use statement word order in indirect questions?	☐

4. **PEER REVIEW** Work with a partner to help you decide how to fix your errors and improve the content. Use the checklist above.

5. **REWRITE YOUR DRAFT** Using the comments from your partner, write a final draft.

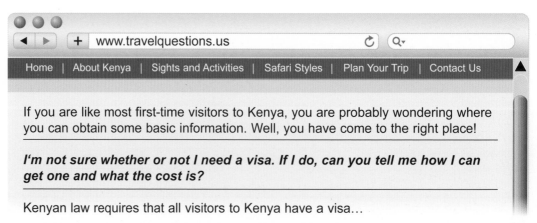

If you are like most first-time visitors to Kenya, you are probably wondering where you can obtain some basic information. Well, you have come to the right place!

I'm not sure whether or not I need a visa. If I do, can you tell me how I can get one and what the cost is?

Kenyan law requires that all visitors to Kenya have a visa...

18

Reported Speech

Doctor-Patient Relationship in Critical Condition

A1 Before You Read

Discuss these questions.

What are some qualities of a good doctor? Have you ever been to a doctor that you didn't like? What were the problems?

A2 Read

⏵ CD2 T48 **Read this magazine article to find out what happens when doctors and patients don't communicate well.**

Doctor-Patient Relationship in Critical Condition

Have you ever walked out of the doctor's office feeling frustrated? Did you understand what the doctor said? Did your doctor understand what you said?

5   Concerns about doctor-patient communication are as important as health problems themselves. Like most other interpersonal relationships, success greatly depends on effective communication

10 between doctors and patients. But what if communication fails?

In a study at the Mayo Clinic, patients were asked to fill out a detailed questionnaire right after they had

15 completed a comprehensive medical examination. The survey asked patients to list their most serious health problems, according to their recent examination. At the same time, their physicians were

20 asked what health problems they had discussed with each patient. More than half of the patients did not know what their doctors considered to be their most important health problems. For example,

25 when physicians reported that cholesterol was a major concern, only 45 percent of those patients reported that they had such problems. Similarly, although doctors said their patients were suffering from obesity,

30 high blood pressure, or certain heart problems, 73 percent of the patients didn't report that they had an obesity problem, 62 percent didn't say they had high blood pressure, and 48 percent never

35 said that there was concern about their heart. The survey concludes that patients often misunderstand their doctors. It also proposes that doctors may be missing the most important concerns of

40 their patients.

The results suggest very clearly that doctors and patients both need to make improvements. First of all, during a discussion, doctors need to make sure to

45 establish eye contact with their patients and frequently ask them if they understand. Doctors should also stop and periodically ask whether there are any questions, and at the end of the visit, they

50 should summarize the discussion in simple terms. Experts suggest that doctors limit their use of medical jargon as much as possible.

Patients also have a lot of work to do.

55 Experts tell patients to plan their visits to the doctor very carefully. They urge making a list of questions, symptoms, and any other concerns, in order of importance, if possible. For example, if

60 there are several issues to discuss, they recommend that patients concentrate on the questions that are most important first. Many doctors complain that too often patients wait until the end of the

65 visit before bringing up important information. In other words, don't mention the wart on your finger before you tell your doctor that you have been experiencing chest pains. And don't be

70 embarrassed about certain issues. Research shows that no matter how embarrassing your problem may be, your doctor has probably dealt with it before.

Perhaps the research confirms

75 something that you have already noticed: the authoritarian doctor and passive patient relationship no longer seems to work. It needs to be replaced by a partnership based more on careful

80 planning, good communication, and shared decision making. In fact, your life may depend on it.

---

authoritarian: demanding that people do exactly what you tell them to do

cholesterol: a substance found in the cells of the body that helps to carry fats

concern: a worry or a matter of importance

critical: very serious or dangerous

jargon: the special language of a profession or trade

obesity: the condition of being very fat

passive: accepting what happens without questioning it

wart: a small, hard, dry growth on the skin caused by a virus

A3 After You Read

Check (✓) the suggestions that would be appropriate for either doctors or patients to follow.

___✓___ **1.** Make sure the discussion is summarized at the end of the visit.

_____ **2.** Learn more medical jargon.

_____ **3.** Plan visits carefully.

_____ **4.** Don't discuss embarrassing issues.

_____ **5.** Don't ask a lot of questions.

_____ **6.** Try to improve your communication skills.

B FORM

Reported Speech

Think Critically About Form

A. Look back at the article on page 392 and complete the tasks below.

1. **IDENTIFY** Examine the underlined examples of reported speech clauses. Each one follows a reporting verb in a main clause. Circle the reporting verb related to each example.

2. **CATEGORIZE** Which underlined reported speech clause is a *wh-* clause? a *that* clause? an *if/whether* clause? an infinitive?

3. **RECOGNIZE** Find other examples of reported speech in the third paragraph (lines 12–40). What reporting verbs are used?

B. Discuss your answers with the class and read the Form charts to check them.

▶ Overview

ONLINE PRACTICE

STATEMENTS
QUOTED SPEECH
"The report is on my desk."

→

REPORTED SPEECH WITH *THAT* CLAUSE
<u>She says</u> **(that) the report is on her desk**.

YES/NO QUESTIONS
QUOTED SPEECH
"Are you staying?"

→

REPORTED SPEECH WITH *IF/WHETHER* CLAUSE
<u>He asked</u> **if I was staying**.

INFORMATION QUESTIONS
QUOTED SPEECH
"Where did you go?"

→

REPORTED SPEECH WITH *WH-* CLAUSE
<u>I asked</u> **where she had gone**.

IMPERATIVES
QUOTED SPEECH
"Press the green button."
"Don't press the red button."

→

REPORTED SPEECH WITH INFINITIVE
<u>He told me</u> **to press the green button**.
<u>He said</u> **not to press the red button**.

▶ Present Tense Reporting

QUOTED SPEECH		REPORTED SPEECH WITH *THAT* CLAUSE	
"It**'s raining**."	⟶		it**'s raining**.
"It**'s going to rain**."	⟶	Joe **says** (that)	it**'s going to rain**.
"It **rained**."	⟶		it **rained**.

▶ Past Tense Reporting

QUOTED SPEECH		REPORTED SPEECH WITH *THAT* CLAUSE	
"I **need** a vacation."	⟶		I **needed** a vacation.
"I**'m working**."	⟶		I **was working**.
"I **left** early."	⟶		I**'d left** early.
"I**'ve finished**."	⟶		I**'d finished**.
"I**'ll see** you later."	⟶		I **would see** you later.
"I**'m going to win**."	⟶		I **was going to win**.
"I **can win**."	⟶	I **said** (that)	I **could win**.
"I **may leave**."	⟶		I **might leave**.
"I **have to try**."	⟶		I **had to try**.
"I **must take** a vacation."	⟶		I **had to take** a vacation.
"I **should stay**."	⟶		I **should stay**.
"I **ought to stay**."	⟶		I **ought to stay**.
"I **could stay**."	⟶		I **could stay**.

Reported Speech
- Reported speech (also called indirect speech) has a reporting verb in the main clause (for example, *say* or *ask*) followed by a noun clause or an infinitive.
- See the Vocabulary Notes on page 402 and Appendix 12 for a list of more reporting verbs.
- Reported speech often differs from quoted speech (also called direct speech) in tense, pronouns, and adverbs.
- Reported speech has no quotation marks or question marks.
- See Appendix 13 for punctuation rules for quoted speech.

(Continued on page 396)

Present Tense Reporting

- If the reporting verb (for example, *say*) is in the present tense, the tense in the *that* clause does not change from the tense of the original quotation.

Past Tense Reporting

- If the reporting verb is in the past tense (for example, *said*), the tense in the *that* clause often changes to a past form.
- The modals *should*, *ought to*, and *could* do not change forms in reported speech.

B1 Listening for Form

CD2 T49   **Listen to these sentences and choose the clause that you hear.**

1. **a.** that he didn't know   5. **a.** what he was doing on Monday night
   b. if he didn't know   **b.** what was he doing on Monday night

2. **a.** if he wanted some books   6. **a.** he can't tell me yet
   b. if he wants some books   **b.** that he couldn't tell me yet

3. **a.** that I'd call him back on Monday   7. **a.** if everything was OK
   b. I'd call him back on Monday   **b.** is everything OK

4. **a.** could I call on Tuesday instead   8. **a.** I shouldn't worry
   b. if I could call on Tuesday instead   **b.** not to worry

B2 Identifying Reported Speech

Underline all the examples of reported speech in these conversations. Circle the reporting verb in each sentence. What other reporting verbs besides *tell*, *ask*, and *say* did you find?

1. **A:** I don't think that the new manager is doing a good job.

   B: Me neither. He told me to come in early yesterday, and he forgot to show up.

   A: You're kidding. Julia said the same thing happened to her on Tuesday. I wonder whether we should complain to Allison. She hired him.

   B: I'm not sure if we should say anything yet. I asked Tom what he thought. He said that we should wait one more week.

2. **A:** Did you hear the news? Channel 7 reported that the superintendent just resigned.

B: I know. I wonder if something happened. Everyone says he was pleased with the way things were going.

A: Yesterday's news mentioned that he hadn't been feeling well lately. Maybe it's something serious and his doctor told him to resign.

3. **A:** Did you speak to the travel agent?

B: Yes. I asked whether I needed to change the flight. He admitted that he'd made a mistake, but he said that he would take care of it. He assured me that everything would work out.

A: Let's hope so. I told you to be careful during the holiday season. They're so busy that they often make mistakes.

Vocabulary Notes

Tell, *Say*, and *Ask*

Tell is used to report statements. It is followed by a noun or pronoun and a *that* clause. This noun or pronoun refers to the original listener.

> He **told me** that he was late.   I **told Julia** I'd be there soon.

Say is also used to report statements. Unlike *tell*, it is not followed by a noun or pronoun.

> He **said** that he was late.   x He said me that he was late. (INCORRECT)

Ask is used to report questions. It can be followed by a noun or pronoun. *Say* and *tell* are not used to report questions.

> She **asked** if it was time to leave.   She **asked him** if it was time to leave.
>
> x She said if it was time to leave. (INCORRECT)

Tell, *say*, and *ask* are used to report imperatives.

> He **told me** to go.   He **said** to go.   He **asked me** to go.

B3 Building Sentences with *Tell*, *Say*, and *Ask*

Build as many meaningful sentences as possible. You may omit the second or third column in some of your sentences. Punctuate your sentences correctly.

He asked them if it was raining.

he asked		if	leave early
I said	them	that	it was raining
she told		to	I had called earlier

B4 Restating Questions with Reported Speech

A. List questions people might ask when they first meet you.

1. _What's your name?_
2. _____
3. _____
4. _____
5. _____
6. _____

B. Use your questions to complete these sentences.

1. People often ask me _what my name is._
2. They also ask me _____
3. They usually want to know _____
4. They sometimes want to know _____
5. Someone typically asks _____
6. Some people even ask _____

B5 Reporting Statements, Questions, and Imperatives

Work with a partner. Read this conversation between a doctor and his patient. Report what each person said, using the verbs *asked*, *said*, and *told*. Change tenses and pronouns where appropriate.

1. **Patient:** How long do I have to stay home from work?

   Doctor: Stay home for a couple of days.

   The patient asked how long she had to stay home from work.

   The doctor said to stay home for a couple of days. OR

   The doctor told her to stay home for a couple of days.

2. **Patient:** Can I have a copy of the test results?

   Doctor: The lab is sending one.

3. **Patient:** How often should I take the medicine?

   Doctor: Don't take it more than three times a day.

4. **Patient:** Do I need to come back?

   Doctor: That won't be necessary unless there's a problem.

5. **Patient:** I need to be better by the weekend.

   Doctor: Why?

6. **Patient:** I'm going out of town for a few days.

   Doctor: You'll be fine. Get lots of sleep.

C MEANING AND USE

Reported Speech

Think Critically About Meaning and Use

A. Read the sentences and answer the questions below.

a. Emily said she has a headache. She needs to rest.
b. Emily said she'd had a headache. It was very painful.
c. Emily said she had a headache. Don't disturb her.

1. ANALYZE In which two sentences does Emily still have a headache?

2. ANALYZE In which sentence is Emily's headache gone?

B. Discuss your answers with the class and read the Meaning and Use Notes to check them.

Meaning and Use Notes

ONLINE PRACTICE

The Reporter's Point of View

▶ **1** Reported speech is used to tell what someone has said or written. It expresses the same meaning as quoted speech, but it expresses the speech from the reporter's point of view rather than from the original speaker's point of view.

Quoted Speech **(Speaker's Point of View)**		**Reported Speech** **(Reporter's Point of View)**
"**I'm having** a great time."	⟶	He said he **was having** a great time.

Tense Changes

▶ **2** The tense in the noun clause may change to a past form if the reporting verb is in the past tense. This tense change usually depends on whether the reporter thinks of the quoted sentences as part of the past.

Quoted Speech		**Past Tense Report**
Alice: **How are** you?	⟶	Alice asked Barbara how she **was**.
Barbara: **I'm** fine.	⟶	Barbara said she **was** fine.

(Continued on page 400)

Keeping the Same Tense

▶ **3A** There are several reasons why the reporter may *not* change the reported speech to a past tense. If the quoted speech just happened, the reporter often keeps the same tense because the time has not changed very much.

Quoted Speech	Immediate Reports (with Tense Unchanged)
"I'm going out for a while."	
A: What did she say? ⟶	She said she**'s going** out for a while. (This sentence was spoken only a few seconds after the first speaker's sentence.)
"Flight 403 **has arrived** at gate 9."	
A: What did the announcement say? ⟶	It said that flight 403 **has arrived** at gate 9. (This sentence was spoken only a few seconds after the announcement.)

▶ **3B** If the reporter wants to show that the quoted speech is a generalization that is always true, the present tense is used.

Quoted Speech	Generalizations (with Tense Unchanged)
"We **don't accept** checks." ⟶	The manager told me that the store **doesn't accept** checks. (The statement is true all the time, not just when the manager spoke.)

▶ **3C** If the event in the quoted speech hasn't happened yet, the future is often used.

Quoted Speech	Future Events (with Tense Unchanged)
"I **am going to appoint** a new judge next week." ⟶	The president announced that she **is going to appoint** a new judge next week. (The event hasn't happened yet.)

Pronoun and Possessive Adjective Changes

▶ **4A** Personal pronouns and possessive adjectives often change to represent the reporter's point of view, instead of the original speaker's point of view.

Quoted Speech	Reported Speech
"**I** need a vacation." ⟶	He said **he** needed a vacation.
"Please take **your** book." ⟶	She told me to take **my** book.
"I like **your** hat." ⟶	I said I liked **his** hat.

▶ **4B**   The words can stay the same when the reporter is repeating his or her own words.

Quoted Speech

"I can't find **my** keys." ⟶ <u>I said</u> I can't find **my** keys.

Reported Speech

Adverb Changes

▶ **5**   Adverbs of time (e.g., *today*, *yesterday*) and place (e.g., *here*, *there*) may change depending on the time of the reported speech and the location of the reporter. They change when the reporter's point of view is different from the speaker's.

Quoted Speech   **Reported Speech**

"I'll call you **tomorrow**." ⟶ He said he would call me **the next day**.

⟶ He said he'd call me **on Monday**.

⟶ He said he'll call me **tomorrow**.

"I'll be **here** until 6:00 P.M." ⟶ He said he'd be **there** until 6:00 P.M.

⟶ He said he'll be **here** until 6:00 P.M.

C1 Listening for Meaning and Use

▶ Notes 1–5

 CD2 T50   Listen to the reported speech. Then choose the quoted speech that most closely expresses the meaning of the reported speech.

1. **a.** "Do you need a prescription?"
   b. "Do I need a prescription? *(circled)*

2. **a.** "She has a headache."
   b. "She had a headache."

3. **a.** "I called when I got the results."
   b. "I'll call when I get the results."

4. **a.** "When did the results come?"
   b. "When will the results come?"

5. **a.** "They had come the next day."
   b. "They'll come tomorrow."

6. **a.** "You missed your last appointment."
   b. "You'd miss your last appointment."

7. **a.** "Your ankle is sprained."
   b. "My ankle is sprained."

8. **a.** "We'd call back that day."
   b. "We'll call back today."

Vocabulary Notes

More Reporting Verbs

Although *say*, *tell*, and *ask* are the most common reporting verbs, there are many others.

Verbs Like *Tell* These verbs are followed by a noun or pronoun and a *that* clause. The noun or pronoun refers to the original listener.

assure	convince	inform	notify	persuade	remind

He **assured me** (that) he had an appointment at three o'clock.

The president **informed the Congress** (that) he was going to form a special committee.

Verbs Like *Say* The following verbs may be used without mentioning the original listener.

admit	complain	indicate	remark	shout
announce	confess	mention	reply	state
comment	explain	point out	report	swear

He **complained** it was too late.   I **explained** that I'd be there soon.

I **admitted** that I'd made a mistake.   She **replied** that she was pleased.

Note that if the original listener is mentioned, *to* is needed.

He **admitted <u>to me</u>** that he was sorry.

See Appendix 12 for a list of more reporting verbs.

C2 Understanding Reported Verbs

Circle the word that best completes the meaning of each sentence.

Kenji left school yesterday. He (said / told) that he couldn't complete the semester.
1

He (informed / explained) me that he had fallen behind in all of his courses. He
2

(assured / confessed) that he hadn't attended two of his courses for over a month. I
3

was shocked. He (reminded / explained) that he'd been looking for a job instead of
4

going to classes. I (told / asked) him if he could go to school part-time instead of
5

quitting. He (replied / persuaded) that it was too late. I (said / advised) him to speak
6   7

to his advisor. He (convinced / promised) that he would, but then he just left town.
8

When I spoke to one of his friends the next day, she (told / asked) me that Kenji
9

had (admitted / told) to her that he had found the work very difficult.
10

C3 Reporting Messages

▶ Notes 1, 2, 4A, 5

Today is Thursday, March 23. Your friend in the hospital has asked you to listen to and report back the messages on his answering machine at home. The messages are from March 20 to 23. Change each message to reported speech using appropriate verb tenses, pronouns, and adverbs.

1. *Monday, March 20*

   a. "This is Nora Green. Please call me back."

   Nora Green called on Monday. She said to call her back. OR
   She asked you to call her back.

   b. "This is Joe's Repair Shop. Call us back. We will be here until 6:00 P.M."

2. *Tuesday, March 21*

   a. "This is Bob. I'll call back later."

   b. "My name is Richard Smith. I'd like to speak to you about an insurance policy. My number is 555-1221."

3. *Wednesday, March 22*

   a. "This is Rosa. I'm just calling to say hello."

   b. "This is Stuart Lee. I've been calling for several days. Is anything wrong? Please call me back soon."

4. *Thursday, March 23*

   a. "This is Eric Martin. Where are you? I have some questions."

   b. "This is Gibson's. We'll be able to deliver the desk you ordered on Monday, March 27."

   c. "This is Tanya. I'm sorry I haven't called. I should have called sooner."

C4 Reporting a News Item

▶ Notes 2, 3A–3C, 4

A. Read this recent news item. Write three or four sentences explaining it, using reported speech. Think about the meaning of the article. Is the situation part of the present or past? How does that affect the tenses used in your report?

A recent news article reported that schools have begun...

Medical Schools Stress Communication

Medical schools have begun to put communication skills into the curriculum. "The time has come," says a spokesman for the Medical Association, "to focus more on doctor-patient communication."

The public seems to agree. According to the latest Smith Public Opinion Poll, "the best doctors talk with their patients. They encourage questions, they explain procedures, and they discuss alternatives. They also know how to listen. Sometimes they even use humor."

As a result, first-year medical students are spending more time speaking and listening in retirement homes, homeless shelters, soup kitchens, and other community agencies. Back in the classroom, they're discussing what kinds of communication skills they need to treat these patients. They're learning how to interact with patients in a variety of situations, instead of just studying diseases.

 B. Compare your sentences with a partner's and discuss any differences you find.

Vocabulary Notes

Reporting Verbs Used for Advising

Base Form in *That* Clauses When the verbs below are followed by a *that* clause, they are often used to tell someone to do something. To express this meaning, the verb in the *that* clause is always in the base form, even if the main clause is in the past.

advise	ask	demand	insist	propose	recommend	suggest

I recommend <u>(that) he stay</u>.   They **suggest** <u>(that) she take a vacation</u>.

I recommended <u>(that) he stay</u>.   They **suggested** <u>(that) she take a vacation</u>.

Should in ***That*** **Clauses with** ***Say/Tell*** With the verbs *say* and *tell*, *should* is often used in a *that* clause to tell someone to do something. Remember that *say* and *tell* can also occur with an infinitive to express the same meaning. However, *say* and *tell* do not occur in the base form pattern of the verbs like *advise* above.

Doctor: Don't eat any spicy foods for a few days.

Patient: The doctor **said/told me that I shouldn't eat** any spicy foods for a few days.

The doctor **said/told me not to eat** any spicy foods for a few days.

C5 Reporting Advice

A. Maria is a 30-year-old elementary school teacher. She is thinking about finding a new career. Her family and friends have given her a lot of different advice. Complete each sentence by reporting each person's advice with an infinitive, a clause with *should*, or a clause with the base form of the verb.

1. Maria's friend told her ___not to quit___
   ___her job until she knows what she___
   ___wants to do.___

   She also recommended that _____
   _____
   _____

Don't quit your job until you know what you want to do.

Go to an employment agency.

2. Her husband suggested _____
   _____
   _____

   He also advised _____
   _____
   _____

Think about getting another degree.

If I were you, I'd find out about different types of graduate programs.

3. Her grandmother proposed _____

_____

_____

She also said _____

_____

_____

> Quit your job and have a baby.

> Try to teach part-time instead of full-time.

4. Her father insisted _____

_____

_____

He also advised _____

_____

_____

> Don't quit. Just take a leave of absence for a year.

> Ask for a raise before you do anything else.

5. Her aunt suggested _____

_____

_____

She also said _____

_____

_____

> Ask to teach a different grade next year.

> Do whatever makes you happy!

B. Work in small groups. First, discuss what parents and other family members used to tell you to do when you were growing up. Use reported speech and try to include different types of reporting verbs such as *suggest, insist, demand, advise,* and so on.

My father always insisted that I be on time.
He said that I shouldn't keep people waiting.

C. Write a paragraph describing one of your examples in more detail.

Punctuality was important to my father. He always insisted that I be on time. He said that I shouldn't keep people waiting. He even suggested that I wake up 15 minutes earlier than necessary in the morning in order to be prepared for anything that might cause delay. Unfortunately, one day...

Think Critically About Meaning and Use

A. Read each sentence and the statements that follow. Write *T* if the statement is true, *F* if it is false, or *?* if you do not have enough information to decide.

1. Charles told me that I got a raise.

   _F_ **a.** Charles got a raise.

   _____ **b.** I got a raise.

2. Sandra told me that Amy had been sick.

   _____ **a.** Amy is sick.

   _____ **b.** Sandra spoke to Amy.

3. Hector asked his sister to pick up his laptop.

   _____ **a.** The laptop belongs to Hector.

   _____ **b.** Hector spoke to his sister.

4. I said I'd see Marie.

   _____ **a.** I saw Marie.

   _____ **b.** When I said that, I hadn't seen Marie yet.

5. She suggested that I go home.

   _____ **a.** I went home.

   _____ **b.** She wanted me to go home.

6. Amelia asked if I was sick.

   _____ **a.** I was sick.

   _____ **b.** Amelia inquired whether I was sick.

7. We told him not to drive.

   _____ **a.** He didn't drive.

   _____ **b.** We said he shouldn't drive.

8. It is recommended that we make a reservation.

   _____ **a.** Reservations are suggested.

   _____ **b.** Reservations are required.

(Continued on page 408)

B. Discuss these questions in small groups.

1. **COMPARE AND CONTRAST** What's the difference in meaning between 4 and the sentence "I said I'd seen her." How would you change each back to quoted speech?

2. **COMPARE AND CONTRAST** What's the difference in meaning between 6 and the sentence "Amelia asked if I'd been sick?" How would you change each back to quoted speech?

Edit

Find the errors in these paragraphs and correct them.

Linguist Deborah Tannen claims men and women have different conversational styles. She argues that the differences can cause miscommunication between the sexes. Here's a typical example of what Professor Tannen means.

A married couple met at the end of the day. They greeted each other, and he asked her how had her day been. She replied that she has a very busy day. She explained him that she had attended several different meetings, and she had seen four clients. She described how she had felt and what had she been thinking. After that, she eagerly turned to her husband and asked how your day had been. He replied that it had been the same as usual. She looked disappointed, but quickly forgot about it until later that evening when they met friends for dinner. During the meal, her husband told the group that something extraordinary had happened to him today. He went on to explain the amusing details. Everyone laughed except his wife. She felt quite frustrated and confused. She didn't understand why he hadn't told her the story earlier in the evening.

According to Tannen, the answer relates to the difference in conversational styles between men and women. She tells that women use conversation to establish closeness in a relationship, but men consider conversation to be more of a public activity. Men use it to establish their status in a group. Do you agree with this distinction? Do you know men or women like this?

Write

Imagine that you have a problem with a company's product or service. You call Customer Service and have a bad experience with a representative. Write an email to the person's supervisor complaining about the problem. Use reported speech, where possible, with a variety of reporting verbs.

1. **BRAINSTORM** Think about all the details of the incident you want to complain about to the supervisor. Use these categories to help you organize your email into paragraphs:
   - **Opening:** Say why you're writing.
   - **Body:** Sum up the problem was and the bad experience with the representative.
   - **Closing:** Restate your dissatisfaction. Suggest actions you think should be taken.

2. **WRITE A FIRST DRAFT** Before you write your first draft, read the checklist below and look at the examples on pages 399–402. Write your draft using reported speech.

3. **EDIT** Read your work and check it against the checklist below. Circle grammar, spelling, and punctuation errors.

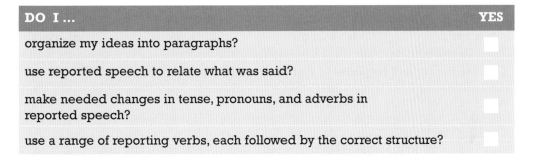

DO I ...	YES
organize my ideas into paragraphs?	☐
use reported speech to relate what was said?	☐
make needed changes in tense, pronouns, and adverbs in reported speech?	☐
use a range of reporting verbs, each followed by the correct structure?	☐

4. **PEER REVIEW** Work with a partner to help you decide how to fix your errors and improve the content. Use the checklist above.

5. **REWRITE YOUR DRAFT** Using the comments from your partner, write a final draft.

From: Edward Krieg

To: Tanya Robeson, Customer Service Supervisor

Subject: Continuing Problems with Unauthorized Charges on My Credit Card Account

Dear Ms. Robeson,
I'm writing to inform you of the continuing problems I've had in removing unauthorized charges from my credit card account.
On April 22nd, I spoke to Ava Brown (ID # 199AF) and reported that my statement contained charges for items I had not bought...

Choose the correct word or words to complete each sentence.

1. Instead of learning specific job skills in college, students learn _____ to solve problems, the greatest skill of all.
   a. what   b. that   c. how   d. if

2. Do you know when _____ ?
   a. the gift being purchased   c. the gift is being purchased
   b. the gift purchased   d. is the gift being purchased

3. It was announced that the university _____ accepted more students into the program.
   a. would   b. had   c. were   d. be

4. Safety experts _____ motorists to make frequent stops during a long trip, especially at night.
   a. advise   b. demand   c. insist   d. recommend

5. They _____ if I wanted a ride home, but I had already made other plans.
   a. said   b. told me   c. told   d. asked

Choose the correct response to complete each conversation.

6. **A:** Do you know what Diane forgot?
   B: _____
   a. She didn't forget them.   c. Yes, she did.
   b. Yes, the keys.   d. No, I didn't.

7. **A:** I'm certain that I didn't tell Mary.
   B: _____
   a. Why didn't you?   c. When did you?
   b. Why did you?   d. Yes, she's sure.

8. **A:** What did Jeff say when he called last week?
   B: _____
   a. That it's raining.   c. That it has been raining.
   b. That it must rain.   d. That it was raining.

9. **A:** Emily said she'd found a job.
   B: _____
   a. I hope she does.   c. I'm glad she did.
   b. I wonder if she will.   d. I know she would

10. A: Why did you leave the game before the end?

    B: I was sure _____

       a. we will win.   **c.** we would win.

       b. we win.   **d.** we won.

11. A: Mr. Burns is going to resign.

    B: _____

       a. I know why.   **c.** I know who.

       b. I know what.   **d.** I know how.

12. A: What did you tell the boss about the report?

    B: _____

       a. He told me it was fine.   **c.** Yes, I was still working on it.

       b. No, I didn't ask him.   **d.** I said it would be on his desk in the morning.

13. A: The professor suggested that we look at a few articles.

    B: Which ones did he _____

       a. recommend?   **c.** promise?

       b. demand?   **d.** inform?

Change each direct question to an indirect question.

14. Did you like your job?

    I was wondering if _____

15. Why are you cleaning the house again?

    Could you explain _____

16. How much is this coat?

    I'd like to know _____

17. What experience do you have?

    I was wondering _____

Rewrite the reported speech as quoted speech. Include quotation marks. Use contractions where possible.

18. She told me not to come back the next day.

    _____

19. The patient asked the doctor how often he should take the medication.

    _____

20. He asked if I was staying.

    _____

Appendices

1 Spelling of Verbs and Nouns Ending in -s and -es

1. For most third-person singular verbs and plural nouns, add -s to the base form.

Verbs	Nouns
swim — swims	lake — lakes

2. If the base form ends with the letters s, z, sh, ch, or x, add -es.

Verbs	Nouns
miss — misses	box — boxes

3. If the base form ends with a consonant + y, change y to i and add -es.
   (Compare vowel + y: obey — obeys; toy — toys.)

Verbs	Nouns
try — tries	baby — babies

4. If the base form ends with a consonant + o, add -s or -es. Some words take -s, -es, or both -s and -es. (Compare vowel + o: radio — radios; zoo — zoos.)

-s	-es	Both -s and -es
auto — autos	do — does	tornado — tornados/tornadoes
photo — photos	echo — echoes	volcano — volcanos/volcanoes
piano — pianos	go — goes	zero — zeros/zeroes
solo — solos	hero — heroes	
	potato — potatoes	
	tomato — tomatoes	

5. If the base form of certain nouns ends in a single f or in fe, change the f or fe to v and add -es.

   calf — calves
   shelf — shelves
   knife — knives

   Exceptions

   belief — beliefs
   chief — chiefs
   roof — roofs
   scarf — scarfs/scarves

2 Pronunciation of Verbs and Nouns Ending in -s and -es

1. If the base form of the verb or noun ends with the sounds /s/, /z/, /ʃ/, /ʒ/, /tʃ/, /dʒ/, or /ks/, then pronounce -es as an extra syllable /ɪz/.

Verbs

slice — slices   watch — watches
lose — loses   judge — judges
wash — washes   relax — relaxes

Nouns

price — prices   inch — inches
size — sizes   language — languages
dish — dishes   tax — taxes
garage — garages

2. If the base form ends with the voiceless sounds /p/, /t/, /k/, /f/, or /θ/, then pronounce -s and -es as /s/.

Verbs

sleep — sleeps   work — works
hit — hits   laugh — laughs

Nouns

grape — grapes   cuff — cuffs
cat — cats   fifth — fifths
book — books

3. If the base form ends with any other consonant or with a vowel sound, then pronounce -s and -es as /z/.

Verbs

learn — learns
go — goes

Nouns

name — names
boy — boys

3 Spelling of Verbs Ending in -ing

1. For most verbs, add -ing to the base form of the verb.

sleep — sleeping   talk — talking

2. If the base form ends in a single e, drop the e and add -ing (exception: be – being).

live — living   write — writing

3. If the base form ends in ie, change ie to y and add -ing.

die — dying   lie — lying

4. If the base form of a one-syllable verb ends with a single vowel + consonant, double the final consonant and add -ing. (Compare two vowels + consonant: eat — eating.)

hit — hitting   stop — stopping

5. If the base form of a verb with two or more syllables ends in a single vowel + consonant, double the final consonant only if the stress is on the final syllable. Do not double the final consonant if the stress is not on the final syllable.

admit — admitting   begin — beginning   develop — developing   listen — listening

6. Do not double the final consonants x, w, and y.

fix — fixing   plow — plowing   obey — obeying

4 Spelling of Verbs Ending in -ed

1. To form the simple past and past participle of most regular verbs, add -ed to the base form.

   brush — brushed   play — played

2. If the base form ends with e, just add -d.

   close — closed   live — lived

3. If the base form ends with a consonant + y, change the y to i and add -ed. (Compare vowel +y: play — played; enjoy — enjoyed.)

   study — studied   dry — dried

4. If the base form of a one-syllable verb ends with a single vowel + consonant, double the final consonant and add -ed.

   plan — planned   shop — shopped

5. If the base form of a verb with two or more syllables ends in a single vowel + consonant, double the final consonant and add -ed only when the stress is on the final syllable. Do not double the final consonant if the stress is not on the final syllable.

   prefér — preferred   énter — entered

6. Do not double the final consonants x, w, and y.

   coax — coaxed   snow — snowed   stay — stayed

5 Pronunciation of Verbs Ending in -ed

1. If the base form of the verb ends with the sounds /t/ or /d/, then pronounce -ed as an extra syllable /ɪd/.

/t/	/d/
start — started	need — needed
wait — waited	decide — decided

2. If the base form ends with the voiceless sounds /f/, /k/, /p/, /s/, /ʃ/, /tʃ/, or /ks/, then pronounce -ed as /t/.

laugh — laughed	jump — jumped	wish — wished	fax — faxed
look — looked	slice — sliced	watch — watched	

3. If the base form ends with the voiced sounds /b/, /g/, /dʒ/, /m/, /n/, /ŋ/, /l/, /r/, /ð/, /v/, /z/, or with a vowel, then pronounce -ed as /d/.

rob — robbed	hum — hummed	call — called	wave — waved
brag — bragged	rain — rained	order — ordered	close — closed
judge — judged	bang — banged	bathe — bathed	play — played

6 Irregular Verbs

Base Form	Simple Past	Past Participle	Base Form	Simple Past	Past Participle
arise	arose	arisen	forget	forgot	forgotten
be	was/were	been	forgive	forgave	forgiven
beat	beat	beaten	freeze	froze	frozen
become	became	become	get	got	gotten
begin	began	begun	give	gave	given
bend	bent	bent	go	went	gone
bet	bet	bet	grind	ground	ground
bind	bound	bound	grow	grew	grown
bite	bit	bitten	hang	hung	hung
bleed	bled	bled	have	had	had
blow	blew	blown	hear	heard	heard
break	broke	broken	hide	hid	hidden
bring	brought	brought	hit	hit	hit
build	built	built	hold	held	held
burst	burst	burst	hurt	hurt	hurt
buy	bought	bought	keep	kept	kept
catch	caught	caught	know	knew	known
choose	chose	chosen	lay (= put)	laid	laid
cling	clung	clung	lead	led	led
come	came	come	leave	left	left
cost	cost	cost	lend	lent	lent
creep	crept	crept	let	let	let
cut	cut	cut	lie (= recline)	lay	lain
deal	dealt	dealt	light	lit	lit
dig	dug	dug	lose	lost	lost
dive	dove/dived	dived	make	made	made
do	did	done	mean	meant	meant
draw	drew	drawn	meet	met	met
drink	drank	drunk	pay	paid	paid
drive	drove	driven	prove	proved	proven/proved
eat	ate	eaten	put	put	put
fall	fell	fallen	quit	quit	quit
feed	fed	fed	read	read	read
feel	felt	felt	ride	rode	ridden
fight	fought	fought	ring	rang	rung
find	found	found	rise	rose	risen
fit	fit	fit	run	ran	run
flee	fled	fled	say	said	said
fly	flew	flown	see	saw	seen
forbid	forbade	forbidden	seek	sought	sought

Base Form	Simple Past	Past Participle	Base Form	Simple Past	Past Participle
sell	sold	sold	sting	stung	stung
send	sent	sent	stink	stank	stunk
set	set	set	strike	struck	struck
sew	sewed	sewn	string	strung	strung
shake	shook	shaken	swear	swore	sworn
shine	shone	shone	sweep	swept	swept
shoot	shot	shot	swim	swam	swum
show	showed	shown	swing	swung	swung
shrink	shrank	shrunk	take	took	taken
shut	shut	shut	teach	taught	taught
sing	sang	sung	tear	tore	torn
sink	sank	sunk	tell	told	told
sit	sat	sat	think	thought	thought
sleep	slept	slept	throw	threw	thrown
slide	slid	slid	understand	understood	understood
speak	spoke	spoken	undertake	undertook	undertaken
speed	sped	sped	upset	upset	upset
spend	spent	spent	wake	woke	woken
spin	spun	spun	wear	wore	worn
split	split	split	weave	wove	woven
spread	spread	spread	weep	wept	wept
spring	sprang	sprung	wet	wet	wet
stand	stood	stood	win	won	won
steal	stole	stolen	wind	wound	wound
stick	stuck	stuck	write	wrote	written

7 Common Intransitive Verbs

These verbs can only be used intransitively. (They cannot be followed by an object.)

ache	emerge	itch	sit
appear	erupt	laugh	sleep
arrive	faint	live	smile
be	fall	look	snow
come	frown	matter	stand
cry	go	occur	stay
depart	grin	rain	talk
die	happen	remain	weep
disappear	hesitate	seem	

8 Gerunds

Verb + Gerund

These verbs may be followed by gerunds, but not by infinitives:

acknowledge	detest	keep (= continue)	recall
admit	discuss	loathe	recollect
anticipate	dislike	mean (= involve)	recommend
appreciate	endure	mention	regret
avoid	enjoy	mind (= object to)	report
can't help	escape	miss	resent
celebrate	excuse	omit	resist
consider	feel like	postpone	resume
defend	finish	practice	risk
defer	go	prevent	suggest
delay	imagine	prohibit	tolerate
deny	involve	quit	understand

Verb with Preposition + Gerund

These verbs or verb phrases with prepositions may be followed by gerunds, but not by infinitives:

adapt to	believe in	depend on
adjust to	blame for	disapprove of
agree (with someone) on	care about	discourage (someone) from
apologize (to someone) for	complain (to someone) about	engage in
approve of	concentrate on	forgive (someone) for
argue (with someone) about	consist of	help (someone) with
ask about	decide on	

Be + Adjective + Preposition + Gerund

Adjectives with prepositions typically occur in be + adjective phrases. These phrases may be followed by gerunds, but not by infinitives:

be accustomed to	be famous for	be proud of
be afraid of	be fond of	be responsible for
be angry (at someone) about	be glad about	be sad about
be ashamed of	be good at	be successful in
be capable of	be happy about	be suitable for
be certain of/about	be incapable of	be tired of
be concerned with	be interested in	be tolerant of
be critical of	be jealous of	be upset about
be discouraged from	be known for	be used to
be enthusiastic about	be nervous about	be useful for
be familiar with	be perfect for	be worried about

9 Infinitives

These verbs may be followed by infinitives, but not by gerunds:

Verb + Infinitive

agree	decide	manage	struggle
aim	decline	plan	swear
appear	demand	pledge	tend
arrange	fail	pretend	volunteer
care	guarantee	refuse	wait
claim	hope	resolve	
consent	intend	seem	

Verb + Object + Infinitive

advise	get	persuade	tell
command	hire	remind	trust
convince	invite	require	urge
force	order	teach	warn

Verb + (Object) + Infinitive

ask	desire	need	promise
beg	expect	offer	want
choose	help	pay	wish
dare	know	prepare	would like

Adjective + Infinitive

afraid	distressed	hesitant	reluctant
alarmed	disturbed	impossible	right
amazed	eager	interested	sad
anxious	easy	likely	scared
astonished	embarrassed	lucky	shocked
careful	excited	necessary	sorry
curious	fascinated	pleased	surprised
delighted	fortunate	possible	unlikely
depressed	frightened	prepared	unnecessary
determined	glad	proud	willing
difficult	happy	ready	wrong
disappointed	hard	relieved	

10 Verb + Infinitive or Gerund

These verbs may be followed by infinitives or gerunds:

attempt	cease	like	propose	stop
begin	continue	love	regret	try
can't bear	forget	neglect	remember	
can't stand	hate	prefer	start	

11 Mental Activity Verbs

These mental activity verbs are followed by noun clauses:

agree	decide	find (out)	learn	recognize
assume	discover	forget	mean	regret
believe	doubt	guess	notice	remember
bet	dream	hear	pretend	suppose
calculate	expect	hope	prove	think
conclude	feel	imagine	realize	understand
consider	figure out	know	recall	wonder

12 Reporting Verbs

Verb + Noun Clause

These reporting verbs are followed by noun clauses:

acknowledge	conclude	instruct (someone)	report
add	confess	maintain	respond
admit	confirm	mention	roar
advise (someone)	convince (someone)	murmur	say
affirm	cry	mutter	scream
agree	declare	note	shout
announce	demand	notify (someone)	shriek
answer	deny	observe	sneer
argue	emphasize	persuade (someone)	stammer
ask	estimate	point out	state
assert	exclaim	promise	suggest
assure (someone)	explain	propose	swear
boast	grumble	protest	tell (someone)
brag	guess	recommend	threaten
caution	imply	remark	
claim	indicate	remind (someone)	
comment	inform (someone)	repeat	
complain	insist	reply	

Verb + Infinitive

These reporting verbs are used with infinitives:

advise (someone) to
ask (someone) to
beg (someone) to
command (someone) to
direct (someone) to

forbid (someone) to
instruct (someone) to
oblige (someone) to
order (someone) to
request (someone) to

tell (someone) to
urge (someone) to
want (someone) to

13 Punctuation Rules for Quoted Speech

1.   If quoted speech comes after the reporting verb:

   - Place a comma after the reporting verb.
   - Place quotation marks at the beginning and end of reported speech. Put them near the top of the letter.
   - Begin quoted speech with a capital letter.
   - Use the correct punctuation (a period, an exclamation mark, or a question mark) and place the punctuation inside the quotation marks.

   Examples
   He said, "We are staying."
   He shouted, "We are staying!"
   He asked me, "Are we staying?"

2.   If quoted speech comes before the reporting verb:

   - Place quotation marks at the beginning and end of reported speech. Put them near the top of the letter.
   - Begin quoted speech with a capital letter.
   - Use a comma if the quoted speech is a statement. Use an exclamation if the quoted speech is an exclamation. Use a question mark if the quoted speech is a question. Place the punctuation inside the quotation marks.
   - Begin the phrase that follows the quoted speech with a lowercase letter.
   - Use a period at the end of the main sentence.

   Examples
   "We are staying," he said.
   "We are staying!" he shouted.
   "Are we staying?" he asked me.

14 Contractions with Verb and Modal Forms

Contractions with *Be*

I am	= I'm
you are	= you're
he is	= he's
she is	= she's
it is	= it's
we are	= we're
you are	= you're
they are	= they're

I am not	= I'm not
you are not	= you're not / you aren't
he is not	= he's not / he isn't
she is not	= she's not / she isn't
it is not	= it's not / it isn't
we are not	= we're not / we aren't
you are not	= you're not / you aren't
they are not	= they're not / they aren't

Contractions with *Be Going To*

I am going to	= I'm going to
you are going to	= you're going to
he is going to	= he's going to
she is going to	= she's going to
it is going to	= it's going to
we are going to	= we're going to
you are going to	= you're going to
they are going to	= they're going to
you are not going to	= you're not going to / you aren't going to

Contractions with *Will*

I will	= I'll
you will	= you'll
he will	= he'll
she will	= she'll
it will	= it'll
we will	= we'll
you will	= you'll
they will	= they'll
will not	= won't

Contractions with *Would*

I would	= I'd
you would	= you'd
he would	= he'd
she would	= she'd
we would	= we'd
you would	= you'd
they would	= they'd
would not	= wouldn't

Contractions with *Was* and *Were*

was not	= wasn't
were not	= weren't

Contractions with *Have*

I have	= I've
you have	= you've
he has	= he's
she has	= she's
it has	= it's
we have	= we've
you have	= you've
they have	= they've
have not	= haven't
has not	= hasn't

Contractions with *Had*

I had	= I'd
you had	= you'd
he had	= he'd
she had	= she'd
it had	= it'd
we had	= we'd
you had	= you'd
they had	= they'd
had not	= hadn't

Contractions with *Do* and *Did*

do not	= don't
does not	= doesn't
did not	= didn't

Contractions with Modals and Phrasal Modals

cannot/can not	= can't
could not	= couldn't
should not	= shouldn't
have got to	= 've got to
has got to	= 's got to

15 Phrasal Verbs

Separable Phrasal Verbs

Many two-word phrasal verbs are separable. This means that a noun object can separate the two words of the phrasal verb or follow the phrasal verb. If the object is a pronoun *(me, you, him, her, it, us, them)*, the pronoun must separate the two words.

Noun Object	**Pronoun Object**
She **turned** the offer **down**.	She **turned** it **down**.
She **turned down** the offer.	x She turned down it. (INCORRECT)

These are some common separable phrasal verbs and their meanings:

Phrasal Verb	**Meaning**
ask (someone) out	invite someone to go out
ask (someone) over	invite someone to come to your house
blow (something) up	inflate, cause something to explode
boot (something) up	start or get a computer ready for use
bring (someone) up	raise a child
bring (something) up	introduce or call attention to a topic
burn (something) down	destroy by fire
call (someone) back	return a phone call to someone
call (something) off	cancel something
call (someone) up	telephone
call (something) up	retrieve from the memory of a computer
check (something) out	borrow a book, tape, video from the library; verify
clean (something) out	clean the inside of something thoroughly
clean (something) up	clean thoroughly and remove anything unwanted
clear (something) up	explain a problem
cross (something) out	draw a line through
cut (something) up	cut into little pieces
do (something) over	do something again
figure (something) out	solve a problem
fill (something) in	write in a blank or a space
fill (something) out	write information on a form
fill (something) up	fill completely with something
find (something) out	discover information
give (something) back	return something
give (something) up	quit something; get rid of something
hand (something) in	submit homework, a test, an application
hand (something) out	distribute something
hang (something) up	put on a clothes hanger; end a telephone call
keep (someone) up	prevent someone from going to sleep
kick (someone) out	force someone to leave
leave (something) out	omit

Phrasal Verb	Meaning
look (something) over	examine carefully
look (something) up	look for information in a book
make (something) up	create or invent something; do work that was missed
make (something) up to (someone)	return a favor to someone
pay (someone) back	return money owned to someone
pick (something) out	choose
pick (something/someone) up	lift something or someone; stop to get something or someone
point (something) out	mention, draw attention to something
put (something) away	put something in its usual place
put (something) back	return something to its original place
put (something) down	stop holding something
put (something) in	install
put (something) off	postpone
put (something) on	get dressed
put (something) out	extinguish a fire, cigarette, or cigar
put (something) over on (someone)	deceive someone
set (something) up	make something ready for use
shut (something) off	turn off a machine
start (something) over	start again
take (something) away	remove
take (a time period) off	have a break from work or school
take (something) off	remove
take (someone) out	accompany to the theater, a restaurant, a movie
take (something) out	remove something from something else
tear (something) down	destroy completely
tear (something) off	detach something
tear (something) up	tear into pieces
think (something) over	reflect upon something before making a decision
think (something) up	invent
throw (something) away	put something in the trash
throw (something) out	put something in the trash
try (something) on	put on clothing to see how it looks
turn (something) down	lower the volume; refuse an offer or invitation
turn (something) in	return; submit homework, a test, an application
turn (something) off	stop a machine or light
turn (something) on	start a machine or light
turn (something) up	increase the volume
use (something) up	use something until no more is left
wake (someone) up	cause someone to stop sleeping
wear (someone) out	cause someone to become exhausted
work (something) out	solve something
write (something) down	write something on a piece of paper

Nonseparable Phrasal Verbs

Some two-word verbs and most three-word verbs are nonseparable. This means that a noun or pronoun object cannot separate the two parts of the phrasal verb.

Noun Object

The teacher **went over** the lesson.

x The teacher went the lesson over. (INCORRECT)

Pronoun Object

The teacher **went over** it.

x The teacher went it over. (INCORRECT)

These are some common nonseparable phrasal verbs and their meanings:

Phrasal Verb	Meaning
blow up	explode
break down	stop functioning properly
break up with (someone)	end a relationship with someone
burn down	be destroyed by fire
call on (someone)	ask someone to answer or speak in class
catch up with (someone/something)	travel fast enough to overtake someone who is ahead
check out of (a hotel)	leave a hotel after paying the bill
clear up	become fair weather
come back	return
come over	visit
come up with (something)	think of a plan or reply
cut down on (something)	reduce
eat out	have a meal in a restaurant
face up to (something)	be brave enough to accept or deal with
fall down	leave a standing position; perform in a disappointing way
get away with (doing something)	not be punished for doing something wrong
get down to (something)	begin to give serious attention to
get off (something)	leave a plane, bus, train
get on (something)	enter a plane, bus, train
get over (something)	recover from an illness or serious life event
get up	arise from a bed or chair
give up	stop trying, lose hope
go back	return
go down	(of computers) stop functioning; (of prices or temperature) become lower; (of ships) sink; (of the sun or moon) set
go off	stop functioning; (of alarms) start functioning; explode or make a loud noise
go on	take place, happen
go out	leave one's house to go to a social event
go out with (someone)	spend time regularly with someone
go over (something)	review
grow up	become an adult

Phrasal Verb	Meaning
hold on	wait on the telephone
keep on (doing something)	continue doing something
keep up with	stay at the same level or position
look out for (something/someone)	be careful of something or someone
move out	stop occupying a residence, especially by removing one's possessions
pack up	prepare all of one's belongings for moving
put up with (something/someone)	tolerate
run out	come to an end, be completely used up
run out of (something)	have no more of something
show up	appear, be seen, arrive at a place
sit down	get into a seated position
stay out	remain out of the house, especially at night
stay up	remain awake, not go to bed
take off	leave (usually by plane)
turn up	appear
wake up	stop sleeping
work out	exercise vigorously

16 Phonetic Symbols

Vowels

i	see /si/	u	too /tu/	oʊ	go /goʊ/
ɪ	sit /sɪt/	ʌ	cup /kʌp/	ər	bird /bərd/
ɛ	ten /tɛn/	ə	about /əˈbaʊt/	ɪr	near /nɪr/
æ	cat /kæt/	eɪ	say /seɪ/	ɛr	hair /hɛr/
ɑ	hot /hɑt/	aɪ	five /faɪv/	ɑr	car /kɑr/
ɔ	saw /sɔ/	ɔɪ	boy /bɔɪ/	ɔr	north /nɔrθ/
ʊ	put /pʊt/	aʊ	now /naʊ/	ʊr	tour /tʊr/

Consonants

p	pen /pɛn/	f	fall /fɔl/	m	man /mæn/
b	bad /bæd/	v	voice /vɔɪs/	n	no /noʊ/
t	tea /ti/	θ	thin /θɪn/	ŋ	sing /sɪŋ/
ţ	butter /ˈbʌţər/	ð	then /ðɛn/	l	leg /lɛg/
d	did /dɪd/	s	so /soʊ/	r	red /rɛd/
k	cat /kæt/	z	zoo /zu/	j	yes /jɛs/
g	got /gɑt/	ʃ	she /ʃi/	w	wet /wɛt/
tʃ	chin /tʃɪn/	ʒ	vision /ˈvɪʒn/		
dʒ	June /dʒun/	h	how /haʊ/		

Glossary of Grammar Terms

ability modal *See* **modal of ability.**

active sentence In active sentences, the agent (the noun that is performing the action) is in subject position and the receiver (the noun that receives or is a result of the action) is in object position. In the following sentence, the subject **Alex** performed the action, and the object **letter** received the action.

Alex mailed the letter.

adjective A word that describes or modifies the meaning of a noun.

the **orange** car   a **strange** noise

adjective clause *See* **relative clause.**

adjective phrase A phrase that functions as an adjective.

These shoes are **too tight**.

adverb A word that describes or modifies the meaning of a verb, another adverb, an adjective, or a sentence. Adverbs answer such questions as *How? When? Where?* or *How often?* They often end in **-ly**.

She ran **quickly**.   She ran **very** quickly.
a **really** hot day   **Maybe** she'll leave.

adverb of frequency An adverb that tells how often a situation occurs. Adverbs of frequency range in meaning from *all of the time* to *none of the time*.

She **always** eats breakfast.
He **never** eats meat.

adverbial phrase A phrase that functions as an adverb.

Amy spoke **very softly**.

affirmative statement A positive sentence that does not have a negative verb.

Linda went to the movies.

agent The noun that is performing the action in a sentence. *See* **active sentence, passive sentence.**

The letter was mailed by **Alex**.

agentless passive A passive sentence that doesn't mention an agent.

The letter was mailed.

agreement The subject and verb of a clause must agree in number. If the subject is singular, the verb form is also singular. If the subject is plural, the verb form is also plural.

He comes home early.
They come home early.

article The words **a**, **an**, and **the** in English. Articles are used to introduce and identify nouns.

a potato   **an** onion   **the** supermarket

auxiliary verb A verb that is used before main verbs (or other auxiliary verbs) in a sentence. Auxiliary verbs are usually used in questions and negative sentences. **Do, have**, and **be** can act as auxiliary verbs. Modals (**may, can, will**, and so on) are also auxiliary verbs.

Do you have the time?
I **have** never been to Italy.
The suitcase **was** taken.   I **may** be late.

base form The form of a verb without any verb endings; the infinitive form without *to*. Also called *simple form*.

sleep   be   stop

clause A group of words that has a subject and a verb. *See also* **dependent clause** and **main clause**.

If I leave,...   The rain stopped.
...when he speaks.   ...that I saw.

common noun A noun that refers to any of a class of people, animals, places, things, or ideas. Common nouns are not capitalized.

man   cat   city   pencil   grammar

communication verb *See* **reporting verb.**

comparative A form of an adjective, adverb, or noun that is used to express differences between two items or situations.

> This book is **heavier than** that one.
> He runs **more quickly than** his brother.
> A CD costs **more money than** a cassette.

complex sentence A sentence that has a main clause and one or more dependent clauses.

> When the bell rang, we were finishing dinner.

conditional sentence A sentence that expresses a real or unreal situation in the *if* clause, and the (real or unreal) expected result in the main clause.

> If I have time, I will travel to Africa.
> If I had time, I would travel to Africa.

contraction The combination of two words into one by omitting certain letters and replacing them with an apostrophe.

> I will = **I'll**   we are = **we're**   are not = **aren't**

count noun A common noun that can be counted. It usually has both a singular and a plural form.

> orange — oranges   woman — women

defining relative clause *See* **restrictive relative clause**.

definite article The word **the** in English. It is used to identify nouns based on assumptions about what information the speaker and listener share about the noun. The definite article is also used for making general statements about a whole class or group of nouns.

> Please give me **the** key.
> **The** scorpion is dangerous.

dependent clause A clause that cannot stand alone as a sentence because it depends on the main clause to complete the meaning of the sentence. Also called *subordinate clause*.

> I'm going home **after he calls**.

determiner A word such as **a, an, the, this, that, these, those, my, some, a few,** and **three**, that is used before a noun to limit its meaning in some way.

> **those** videos

direct speech *See* **quoted speech**.

embedded question *See* **wh- clause**.

future A time that is to come. The future is expressed in English with **will**, **be going to**, the simple present, or the present continuous. These different forms of the future often have different meanings and uses. *See also* **future continuous**.

> I **will** help you later.
> David **is going to** call later.
> The train **leaves** at 6:05 this evening.
> **I'm driving** to Toronto tomorrow.

future continuous A verb form that expresses an activity in progress at a specific time in the future. It is formed with **will** + **be** + main verb + **-ing**.

> **I'll be leaving** for Hawaii at noon tomorrow.

general quantity expression A quantity expression that indicates whether a quantity or an amount is large or small. It does not give an exact amount.

> **a lot of** cookies   **a little** flour

general statement A generalization about a whole class or group of nouns.

> Whales are mammals.
> A daffodil is a flower that grows from a bulb.

generic noun A noun that refers to a whole class or group of nouns.

> I like **rice**.
> **A bird** can fly.
> **The laser** is an important tool.

gerund An **-ing** form of a verb that is used in place of a noun or pronoun to name an activity or a situation.

> **Skiing** is fun.   He doesn't like **being sick**.

identifying relative clause *See* **restrictive relative clause.**

if **clause** A dependent clause that begins with **if** and expresses a real or unreal situation.

> **If I have the time,** I'll paint the kitchen.
> **If I had the time,** I'd paint the kitchen.

if/whether **clause** A noun clause that begins with either **if** or **whether**.

> I don't know **if they're here**.
> I don't know **whether or not they're here**.

imperative A type of sentence, usually without a subject, that tells someone to do something. The verb is in the base form.

Open your books to page 36.
Be ready at eight.

impersonal *you* The use of the pronoun **you** to refer to people in general rather than a particular person or group of people.

Nowadays, **you** can buy anything on the Internet.

indefinite article The words **a** and **an** in English. Indefinite articles introduce a noun as a member of a class of nouns, or make generalizations about a whole class or group of nouns.

Please hand me **a** pencil.
An ocean is **a** large body of water.

independent clause *See* **main clause**.

indirect question *See* **wh- clause**.

indirect speech *See* **reported speech**.

infinitive A verb form that includes **to** + the base form of a verb. An infinitive is used in place of a noun or pronoun to name an activity or situation expressed by a verb.

Do you like **to swim**?

information question A question that begins with a **wh-** word.

Where does she live? Who lives here?

intransitive verb A verb that cannot be followed by an object.

We finally **arrived**.

irregular verb A verb that forms the simple past in a different way than regular verbs.

put — put — put   buy — bought — bought

main clause A clause that can be used by itself as a sentence. Also called *independent clause*.

I'm going home.

main verb A verb that can be used alone in a sentence. A main verb can also occur with an auxiliary verb.

I **ate** lunch at 11:30.
Kate can't **eat** lunch today.

mental activity verb A verb such as **decide, know**, and **understand**, that expresses an opinion, thought, or feeling.

I don't **know** why she left.

modal The auxiliary verbs **can, could, may, might, must, should, will**, and **would**. They modify the meaning of a main verb by expressing ability, authority, formality, politeness, or various degrees of certainty. Also called *modal auxiliary*.

You **should** take something for your headache.
Applicants **must** have a high school diploma.

modal of ability **Can** and **could** are called modals of ability when they express knowledge, skill, opportunity, and capability.

He **can** speak Arabic and English.
Can you play the piano?
Yesterday we **couldn't** leave during the storm.
Seat belts **can** save lives.

modal of possibility **Could, might, may, should, must**, and **will** are called modals of possibility when they express various degrees of certainty ranging from slight possibility to strong certainty.

It **could / might / may / will** rain later.

modal auxiliary *See* **modal**.

modify To add to or change the meaning of a word.

expensive cars (The adjective **expensive** modifies **cars**.)

noncount noun A common noun that cannot be counted. A noncount noun has no plural form and cannot occur with **a, an**, or a number.

information   mathematics   weather

nondefining relative clause *See* **nonrestrictive relative clause**.

nonidentifying relative clause *See* **nonrestrictive relative clause**.

nonrestrictive relative clause A relative clause that adds extra information about the noun that it modifies. This information is not necessary to identify the noun, and it can be omitted. Also called *nondefining* or *nonidentifying relative clause*.

Rick, **who is seven**, plays hockey.

nonseparable Refers to two- or three-word verbs that don't allow a noun or pronoun object to separate the two or three words in the verb phrase. Certain two-word verbs and almost all three-word verbs are nonseparable.

Amy **got off** the bus.
We **cut down on** fat in our diet.

noun A word that typically refers to a person, animal, place, thing, or idea.

Tom   rabbit   store   computer   mathematics

noun clause A dependent clause that can occur in the same place as a noun, pronoun, or noun phrase in a sentence. Noun clauses begin with **wh-** words, **if**, **whether**, or **that**.

I don't know **where he is**.
I wonder **if he's coming**.
I don't know **whether it's true**.
I think **that it's a lie**.

noun phrase A phrase formed by a noun and its modifiers. A noun phrase can substitute for a noun in a sentence.

She drank **milk**.
She drank **chocolate milk**.
She drank **the milk**.

object A noun, pronoun, or noun phrase that follows a transitive verb or a preposition.

Steve threw **the ball**.
She likes **him**.
Go with **her**.

object relative pronoun A relative pronoun that is the object of a relative clause. It comes before the subject noun or pronoun of the relative clause.

the letter **that / which** I wrote
the man **who / whom** I saw

passive sentence Passive sentences emphasize the receiver of an action by changing the usual order of the subject and object in a sentence. The subject (**The letter**) does not perform the action; it receives the action or is the result of an action. The passive is formed with a form of **be** + the past participle of a transitive verb.

The letter was mailed yesterday.

past continuous A verb form that expresses an action or situation in progress at a specific time in the past. The past continuous is formed with **was** or **were** + verb + **-ing**. Also called *past progressive*.

A: What **were** you **doing** last night at eight o'clock?
B: I **was studying**.

past modal A modal that is used to express past certainty, past obligations, and past abilities or opportunities. It is formed with a modal + **have** + past participle of the main verb. Also called *perfect modal*.

He **must have arrived** late.
I **should have called**, but I forgot.
We **could have come**, but no one told us.

past participle A past verb form that may differ from the simple past form of some irregular verbs. It is used to form the present perfect, present perfect continuous, past perfect, past perfect continuous, and the passive.

I have never **seen** that movie.
He's **been** working too much lately.
By noon, we had already **taken** the exam.
She had **been** working since 8:30.
The letter was **sent** on Monday.

past perfect A verb form that expresses a relationship between two past times. The past perfect indicates the earlier event or situation. It is formed with **had** + the past participle of the main verb.

I **had** already **left** when she called.

past perfect continuous A verb form that is like the past perfect, but it emphasizes the duration of the earlier event or situation. It is formed with **had** + **been** + main verb + **-ing**.

When I was offered the position, I **had been looking** for a new job for several months.

past perfect progressive *See* **past perfect continuous**.

past progressive *See* **past continuous**.

past phrasal modal Examples of past phrasal modals are **ought to have**, **have to have**, and **have got to have**.

past unreal conditional sentence A **conditional** sentence that expresses an unreal condition about the past and its imaginary result. It has an **if** clause in the past perfect and a main clause with **would have** + the past participle of the main verb.

> If I had been smarter, I would have complained to the manager.

past *wish* sentence A **wish** sentence that expresses a desire for something that didn't actually happen in the past. It is formed with a **wish** clause + a past perfect clause.

> I wish I had moved to Colorado.

perfect modal *See* **past modal**.

phrasal modal A verb that is not a true modal, but has the same meaning as a modal verb. Examples of phrasal modals are **ought to**, **have to**, and **have got to**.

phrasal verb A two- or three-word verb such as **turn down** or **run out of**. The meaning of a phrasal verb is usually different from the meanings of its individual words.

> She **turned down** the job offer.
> Don't **run out of** gas on the freeway.

phrase A group of words that can form a grammatical unit. A phrase can take the form of a noun phrase, verb phrase, adjective phrase, adverbial phrase, or prepositional phrase. This means it can act as a noun, verb, adjective, adverb, or preposition.

> The **tall man** left.
> Lee **hit the ball**.
> The child was **very quiet**.
> She spoke **too fast**.
> They ran **down the stairs**.

possibility modal *See* **modal of possibility**.

preposition A word such as **at**, **in**, **on**, or **to**, that links nouns, pronouns, and gerunds to other words.

prepositional phrase A phrase that consists of a preposition followed by a noun or noun phrase.

> on Sunday   under the table

present continuous A verb form that indicates that an action is in progress, temporary, or changing. It is formed with **be** + verb + -**ing**. Also called *present progressive*.

> I'm **watering** the garden.
> Ruth **is working** for her uncle.
> He**'s getting** better.

present perfect A verb form that expresses a connection between the past and the present. It indicates indefinite past time, recent past time, or continuing past time. The present perfect is formed with **have** + the past participle of the main verb.

> I**'ve seen** that movie.
> The manager **has** just **resigned**.
> We**'ve been** here for three hours.

present perfect continuous A verb form that focuses on the duration of actions that began in the past and continue into the present or have just ended. It is formed with **have** + **been** + verb + -**ing**.

> They**'ve been waiting** for an hour.
> I**'ve been watering** the garden.

present perfect progressive *See* **present perfect continuous**.

present progressive *See* **present continuous**.

pronoun A word that can replace a noun or noun phrase. **I**, **you**, **he**, **she**, **it**, **mine**, and **yours** are some examples of pronouns.

proper noun A noun that is the name of a particular person, animal, place, thing, or idea. Proper nouns begin with capital letters and are usually not preceded by *the*.

> Peter   Rover   India   Apollo 13   Buddhism

purpose infinitive An infinitive that expresses the reason or purpose for doing something.

> **In order to operate this machine**, press the green button.

quantity expression A word or words that occur before a noun to express a quantity or amount of that noun.

> **a lot of** rain   **few** books   **four** trucks

quoted speech The form of a sentence that uses the exact words of a speaker or writer. Written quoted speech uses quotation marks. Also called *direct speech*.

> **"Where did you go?"** he asked.

real conditional sentence A sentence that expresses a real or possible situation in the **if** clause and the expected result in the main clause. It has an **if** clause in the simple present, and the **will** future in the main clause.

> If I get a raise, I won't look for a new job.

receiver The noun that receives or is the result of an action in a sentence. See **active sentence**, **passive sentence**.

> **The letter** was mailed by Alex.

regular verb A verb that forms the simple past by adding -**ed**, -**d**, or changing **y** to **i** and then adding -**ed** to the simple form.

> hunt — hunted   love — loved   cry — cried

rejoinder A short response used in conversation.

> A: I like sushi.
> B: **Me too**.
> C: **So do I**.

relative clause A clause that modifies a preceding noun. Relative clauses generally begin with **who**, **whom**, **that**, **which**, and **whose**.

> The man **who called** is my cousin.
> We saw the elephant **that was just born**.

relative pronoun A pronoun that begins a relative clause and refers to a noun in the main clause. The words **who**, **whom**, **that**, **which**, and **whose** are relative pronouns.

reported speech A form of a sentence that expresses the meaning of quoted speech or writing from the point of view of the reporter. **Wh-** clauses, **if/whether** clauses, and **that** clauses are used to express reported speech after a reporting verb.

> He explained why he was late.
> He said that he was tired.
> We asked if they could come early.

reporting verb A verb such as **say**, **tell**, **ask**, **explain**, and **complain** that is used to express what has been said or written in both quoted speech and reported speech.

> Tony **complained**, "I'm tired."
> Tony **complained** that he was tired.

restrictive relative clause A relative clause that gives information that helps identify or define the noun that it modifies. In the following sentence, the speaker has more than one aunt. The relative clause **who speaks Russian** identifies which aunt the speaker is talking about. Also called *defining* or *identifying relative clause*.

> My aunt **who speaks Russian** is an interpreter.

separable Refers to certain two-word verbs that allow a noun or pronoun object to separate the two words in the verb phrase.

> She **gave** her job **up**.

short answer An answer to a *Yes/No* question that has *yes* or *no* plus the subject and an auxiliary verb.

> A: Do you speak Chinese?
> B: **Yes, I do. / No, I don't**.

simple past A verb form that expresses actions and situations that were completed at a definite time in the past.

> Carol **ate** lunch.   She **was** hungry.

simple present A verb form that expresses general statements, especially about habitual or repeated activities and permanent situations.

> Every morning I **catch** the 8:00 bus.
> The earth **is** round.

social modals Modal auxiliaries that are used to express politeness, formality, and authority.

> **Would** you please open the window?
> **May** I help you?
> Visitors **must** obey the rules.

stative verb A type of verb that is not usually used in the continuous form because it expresses a condition or state that is not changing. **Know, love, resemble, see**, and **smell** are some examples.

subject A noun, pronoun, or noun phrase that precedes the verb phrase in a sentence. The subject is closely related to the verb as the doer or experiencer of the action or state, or closely related to the noun that is being described in a sentence with *be*.

> **Erica** kicked the ball.
> **He** feels dizzy.
> **The park** is huge.

subject relative pronoun A relative pronoun that is the subject of a relative clause. It comes before the verb in the relative clause.

> the man **who** called

subordinate clause *See* **dependent clause**.

superlative A form of an adjective, adverb, or noun that is used to rank an item or situation first or last in a group of three or more.

> This perfume has **the strongest** scent.
> He speaks **the fastest** of all.
> That machine makes **the most noise** of the three.

that clause A noun clause beginning with **that**.

> I think **that the bus is late**.

three-word verb A phrasal verb such as **break up with**, **cut down on**, and **look out for**. The meaning of a three-word verb is usually different from the individual meanings of the three words.

time clause A dependent clause that begins with a time word such as **while**, **when**, **before**, or **after**. It expresses the relationship in time between two different events in the same sentence.

> **Before Sandy left**, she fixed the copy machine.

transitive verb A verb that is followed by an object.

> I **read** the book.

two-word verb A phrasal verb such as **blow up**, **cross out**, and **hand in**. The meaning of a two-word verb is usually different from the individual meanings of the two words.

unreal conditional sentence A sentence that expresses an unreal situation that is not true at the present time, and its imaginary result. It has an **if** clause in the simple past and a main clause with **would** + main verb.

> If I had the time, I'd walk to work.

used to A special past tense verb. It expresses habitual past situations that no longer exist.

> We **used to** go skiing a lot. Now we go snowboarding.

verb A word that refers to an action or a state.

> Gina **closed** the window.
> Tim **loves** classical music.

verb phrase A phrase that has a main verb and any objects, adverbs, or dependent clauses that complete the meaning of the verb in the sentence.

> Who **called you**?
> He **walked slowly**.
> I **know what his name is**.

voiced Refers to speech sounds that are made by vibrating the vocal cords. Examples of voiced sounds are /b/, /d/, and /g/.

> **b**at   **d**ot   **g**et

voiceless Refers to speech sounds that are made without vibrating the vocal cords. Examples of voiceless sounds are /p/, /t/, and /f/.

> up   it   if

wh- clause A noun clause that begins with a **wh-** word: **who**, **whom**, **what**, **where**, **when**, **why**, **how**, and **which**. Also called *indirect question* or *embedded question*.

> I would like to know **where he is**.
> Could you tell me **how long it takes**?

wh- word Who, **whom**, **what**, **where**, **when**, **why**, **how**, and **which** are **wh-** words. They are used to ask questions and to connect clauses.

wish sentence A sentence that has a **wish** clause in the simple present, and a simple past clause. A **wish** sentence expresses a desire to change a real situation into an unreal or impossible one.

> I wish I had more time.

Yes/No question A question that can be answered with the words **yes** or **no**.

> Can you drive a car?   Does he live here?

Index

This Index is for the full and split editions. Entries for Volume B are in bold.

Grammar Sense

ONLINE PRACTICE

Follow the steps to register for *Grammar Sense Online Practice*.

1. Go to www.grammarsensepractice.com and click on **Register**

2. Read and agree to the terms of use. **I Agree.**

3. Enter the Access Code that came with your Student Book. Your code is written on the inside back cover of your book.

 Enter

4. Enter your personal information (first and last name, email address, and password).

5. Click on the Student Book that you are using for your class.

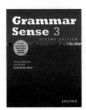

> It is very important to select your book. You are using Grammar Sense 3. Please click the **RED** Grammar Sense 3 cover.

If you don't know which book to select, **STOP**. Continue when you know your book.

6. Enter your class ID to join your class, and click NEXT. Your class ID is on the line below, or your teacher will give it to you on a different piece of paper.

_____ **Next**

You don't need a class ID code. If you do not have a class ID code, click Skip. To enter this code later, choose Join a Class from your Home page.

7. Once you're done, click on Enter Online Practice to begin using *Grammar Sense Online Practice.*

Enter Online Practice

Next time you want to use *Grammar Sense Online Practice*, just go to www.grammarsensepractice.com and log in with your email address and password.